Innovations in XML Applications and Metadata Management:

Advancing Technologies

José Carlos Ramalho
University of Minho, Portugal

Alberto Simões
University of Minho, Portugal

Ricardo Queirós
CRACS & ESEIG/IPP, Porto, Portugal

Information Science
REFERENCE

Managing Director:	Lindsay Johnston
Editorial Director:	Joel Gamon
Book Production Manager:	Jennifer Yoder
Publishing Systems Analyst:	Adrienne Freeland
Development Editor:	Myla Merkel
Assistant Acquisitions Editor:	Kayla Wolfe
Typesetter:	Nicole Sparano
Cover Design:	Nick Newcomer

Published in the United States of America by
Information Science Reference (an imprint of IGI Global)
701 E. Chocolate Avenue
Hershey PA 17033
Tel: 717-533-8845
Fax: 717-533-8661
E-mail: cust@igi-global.com
Web site: http://www.igi-global.com

Library of Congress Cataloging-in-Publication Data

Innovations in XML applications and metadata management: advancing technologies / Jose Carlos Ramalho, Alberto Simoes and Ricardo Queiros, editors.
     pages cm
  Summary: "This book addresses the functionality between XML and its related technologies toward application development based on previous concepts"-- Provided by publisher.
  Includes bibliographical references and index.
  ISBN 978-1-4666-2669-0 (hardcover) -- ISBN (invalid) 978-1-4666-2700-0 (ebook) -- ISBN (invalid) 978-1-4666-2731-4 (print & perpetual access) 1. Metadatabases--Management. 2. XML (Document markup language) I. Ramalho, Jose Carlos, 1967- II. Simoes, Alberto, 1978- III. Queiros, Ricardo, 1975-
  QA76.9D3I5455 2013
  006.7'4--dc23
                                        2012029183

British Cataloguing in Publication Data
A Cataloguing in Publication record for this book is available from the British Library.

All work contributed to this book is new, previously-unpublished material. The views expressed in this book are those of the authors, but not necessarily of the publisher.

This book is dedicated to our respective families.

Editorial Advisory Board

Table of Contents

Section 1
XML Standards and Dialects

Chapter 1
An Example-Based Generator of XSLT Programs 1
José Paulo Leal, University of Porto, Portugal
Ricardo Queirós, CRACS and ESEIG/IPP, Porto, Portugal

Chapter 2
A Secure and Dynamic Mobile Identity Wallet Authorization Architecture Based on a XMPP
Messaging Infrastructure 21
Alexandre B. Augusto, University of Porto, Portugal
Manuel E. Correia, University of Porto, Portugal

Chapter 3
Making Programming Exercises Interoperable with PExIL 38
Ricardo Queirós, CRACS and ESEIG/IPP, Porto, Portugal
José Paulo Leal, University of Porto, Portugal

Chapter 4
GuessXQ: A Query-by-Example Approach for XML Querying 57
Daniela Morais Fonte, University of Minho, Portugal
Daniela da Cruz, University of Minho, Portugal
Pedro Rangel Henriques, University of Minho, Portugal
Alda Lopes Gancarski, Institut Telecom, France

Section 2
Learning Environments

Section 3
Databases and Repositories

Chapter 11

Detailed Table of Contents

Section 1
XML Standards and Dialects

Chapter 1

José Paulo Leal, University of Porto, Portugal

Ricardo Queirós, CRACS and ESEIG/IPP, Porto, Portugal

XSLT is a powerful and widely used language for transforming XML documents. However, its power and complexity can be overwhelming for novice or infrequent users, many of whom simply give up on using this language. On the other hand, many XSLT programs of practical use are simple enough to be automatically inferred from examples of source and target documents. An inferred XSLT program is seldom adequate for production usage but can be used as a skeleton of the final program, or at least as scaffolding in the process of coding it. It should be noted that the authors do not claim that XSLT programs, in general, can be inferred from examples. The aim of Vishnu—the XSLT generator engine described in this chapter—is to produce XSLT programs for processing documents similar to the given examples and with enough readability to be easily understood by a programmer not familiar with the language. The architecture of Vishnu is composed by a graphical editor and a programming engine. In this chapter, the authors focus on the editor as a GWT Web application where the programmer loads and edits document examples and pairs their content using graphical primitives. The programming engine receives the data collected by the editor and produces an XSLT program.

Chapter 2

Alexandre B. Augusto, University of Porto, Portugal

Manuel E. Correia, University of Porto, Portugal

In this chapter, the authors propose and describe an identity management framework that allows users to asynchronously control and effectively share sensitive dynamic data, thus guaranteeing security and privacy in a simple and transparent way. Their approach is realised by a fully secure mobile identity digital wallet, running on mobile devices (Android devices), where users can exercise discretionary control over the access to sensitive dynamic attributes, disclosing their value only to pre-authenticated and authorised users for determined periods of time. For that, the authors rely on an adaptation of the OAuth protocol to authorise and secure the disclosure of personal-private user data by the usage of token exchange and new XML Schemas to establish secure authorisation and disclosure of a set of supported dynamic data types that are being maintained by the personal mobile digital wallet. The communication infrastructure is fully implemented over the XMPP instant messaging protocol and is completely compatible with the public XMPP large messaging infrastructures already deployed on the Internet for real time XML document interchange.

Chapter 3

Ricardo Queirós, CRACS and ESEIG/IPP, Porto, Portugal
José Paulo Leal, University of Porto, Portugal

Several standards have appeared in recent years to formalize the metadata of learning objects, but they are still insufficient to fully describe a specialized domain. In particular, the programming exercise domain requires interdependent resources (e.g. test cases, solution programs, exercise description) usually processed by different services in the programming exercise lifecycle. Moreover, the manual creation of these resources is time-consuming and error-prone, leading to an obstacle to the fast development of programming exercises of good quality. This chapter focuses on the definition of an XML dialect called PExIL (Programming Exercises Interoperability Language). The aim of PExIL is to consolidate all the data required in the programming exercise lifecycle from when it is created to when it is graded, covering also the resolution, the evaluation, and the feedback. The authors introduce the XML Schema used to formalize the relevant data of the programming exercise lifecycle. The validation of this approach is made through the evaluation of the usefulness and expressiveness of the PExIL definition. In the former, the authors present the tools that consume the PExIL definition to automatically generate the specialized resources. In the latter, they use the PExIL definition to capture all the constraints of a set of programming exercises stored in a learning objects repository.

Chapter 4

Daniela Morais Fonte, University of Minho, Portugal
Daniela da Cruz, University of Minho, Portugal
Pedro Rangel Henriques, University of Minho, Portugal
Alda Lopes Gancarski, Institut Telecom, France

XML is a widely used general-purpose annotation formalism for creating custom markup languages. XML annotations give structure to plain documents to interpret their content. To extract information from XML documents XPath and XQuery languages can be used. However, the learning of these dialects requires a considerable effort. In this context, the traditional Query-By-Example methodology (for Relational Databases) can be an important contribution to leverage this learning process, freeing the user from knowing the specific query language details or even the document structure. This chapter describes how to apply the Query-By-Example concept in a Web-application for information retrieval from XML documents, the GuessXQ system. This engine is capable of deducing, from an example, the respective XQuery statement. The example consists of marking the desired components directly on a sample document, picked-up from a collection. After inferring the corresponding query, GuessXQ applies it to the collection to obtain the desired result.

Section 2
Learning Environments

Chapter 5

José Janssen, Open Universiteit, The Netherlands
Adriana J. Berlanga, Open Universiteit, The Netherlands
Rob Koper, Open Universiteit, The Netherlands

Specifications can be considered "hidden" technology: they are deployed in tools and applications without being directly visible. This poses a challenge regarding quality assessment of this type of technology. This chapter describes a framework for quality assessment of learning technology specifications and how it was used to evaluate and improve a case in point: the Learning Path Specification. However, although the importance of raising the quality of a specification is beyond question, this in itself is no guarantee for its (wider) adoption. The final section of this chapter discusses how quality assessment of the Learning Path Specification at best informs us on its chances of gaining adoption, but by no means suffices to establish it. For this discussion, the authors draw on Rogers's work regarding five perceived characteristics of innovations influencing their diffusion: relative advantage, compatibility, complexity, triability, and observability.

Chapter 6

Eugenijus Kurilovas, Vilnius University, Lithuania & Vilnius Gediminas Technical University, Lithuania

This chapter analyzes the quality of XML learning object repositories. Special attention is paid to the models and methods to evaluate the quality of learning repositories. Multiple criteria decision analysis and optimization methods are explored to be applied for evaluating the quality of learning repositories. This chapter also presents the results of several large-scale projects co-funded by EU research programs that have been implemented in the area of learning repositories. Learning repositories' technological quality model (system of criteria) and novel comprehensive model for evaluating the quality of user interfaces of learning repositories are presented in more detail. The general MCEQLS (Multiple Criteria Evaluation of Learning Software) approach is presented in this chapter. It is shown that the MCEQLS approach is suitable for evaluating the quality of learning repositories. The author believes that research results presented in the chapter will be useful for all educational stakeholder groups interested in developing learning repositories.

Chapter 7

Ricardo Queirós, CRACS and ESEIG/IPP, Porto, Portugal
Mário Pinto, ESEIG/IPP, Porto, Portugal

Recent studies of mobile Web trends show the continued explosion of mobile-friend content. However, the wide number and heterogeneity of mobile devices poses several challenges for Web programmers, who want automatic delivery of context and adaptation of the content to mobile devices. Hence, the device detection phase assumes an important role in this process. In this chapter, the authors compare the most used approaches for mobile device detection. Based on this study, they present an architecture for detecting and delivering uniform m-Learning content to students in a Higher School. The authors focus mainly on the XML device capabilities repository and on the REST API Web Service for dealing with device data. In the former, the authors detail the respective capabilities schema and present a new caching approach. In the latter, they present an extension of the current API for dealing with it. Finally, the authors validate their approach by presenting the overall data and statistics collected through the Google Analytics service, in order to better understand the adherence to the mobile Web interface, its evolution over time, and the main weaknesses.

Section 3
Databases and Repositories

Chapter 8

Carlos Aldeias, University of Porto, Portugal
Gabriel David, University of Porto, Portugal
Cristina Ribeiro, University of Porto, Portugal

Data warehouses are used in many application domains, and there is no established method for their preservation. A data warehouse can be implemented in multidimensional structures or in relational databases that represent the dimensional model concepts in the relational model. The focus of this work is on describing the dimensional model of a data warehouse and migrating it to an XML model, in order to achieve a long-term preservation format. This chapter presents the definition of the XML structure that extends the SIARD format used for the description and archive of relational databases, enriching it with a layer of metadata for the data warehouse components. Data Warehouse Extensible Markup Language (DWXML) is the XML language proposed to describe the data warehouse. An application that combines the SIARD format and the DWXML metadata layer supports the XML language and helps to acquire the relevant metadata for the warehouse and to build the archival format.

Chapter 9

Ricardo André Pereira Freitas, Lusiada University, Portugal
José Carlos Ramalho, University of Minho, Portugal

Due to the expansion and growth of information technologies, much of human knowledge is now recorded on digital media. A new problem in the digital universe has arisen: Digital Preservation. This chapter addresses the problems of Digital Preservation and focuses on the conceptual model within a specific class of digital objects: Relational Databases. Previously, a neutral format was adopted to pursue the goal of platform independence and to achieve a standard format in the digital preservation of relational databases, both data and structure (logical model). The authors address the preservation of relational databases by focusing on the conceptual model of the database, considering the database semantics as an important preservation "property." For the representation of this higher layer of abstraction present in databases, they use an ontology-based approach. At this higher abstraction level exists inherent Knowledge associated to the database semantics that the authors tentatively represent using "Web Ontology Language" (OWL). From the initial prototype, they develop a framework (supported by case studies) and establish a mapping algorithm for the conversion between databases and OWL. The ontology approach is adopted to formalize the knowledge associated to the conceptual model of the database and also a methodology to create an abstract representation of it. The system is based on the functional axes (ingestion, administration, dissemination, and preservation) of the OAIS reference model.

Chapter 10

    João Rocha da Silva, University of Porto, Portugal

    Cristina Ribeiro, University of Porto, Portugal

    João Correia Lopes, University of Porto, Portugal

This chapter consists of a solution for the management of research data at a higher education and research institution. The chapter is based on a small-scale data audit study, which included contacts with researchers and yielded some preliminary requirements and use cases. These requirements led to the design of a data curation workflow involving the researcher, the curator, and a data repository. The authors describe the features of the data repository prototype, which is an extension to the widely used DSpace repository platform and introduced a set of features mentioned by the majority of the interviewed researchers as relevant for a data repository. The data repository platform contributes to the curation workflow at the university, with XML technology at its core—data is stored using XML documents, which can be systematically processed and queried unlike its original-format counterpart. This system is capable of indexing, querying, and retrieving, in whole or in part, datasets represented in tabular form. There is also the possibility of using elements from domain-specific XML schemas for the cataloguing process, improving the interoperability and quality of the deposited data.

Chapter 11

    Flavio Xavier Ferreira, University of Minho, Portugal

    Pedro Rangel Henriques, University of Minho, Portugal

    Alda Lopes Gancarski, Institut Telecom, France

This chapter presents an ongoing work in the context of the Portuguese Emigration Museum about information access in XML collections associated with semantic information. The museum asset is made up of documents of more than 8 kinds, ranging from passport records to photos/cards and building-drawings. In this chapter, the authors discuss the approach used to create the exhibition rooms of the virtual Web-based museum. Each room consists of the information contained in those single or interrelated resources. The information exhibited in each room is described by an ontology, written in OWL. The authors also discuss the approach used to take advantage of a combination of structural and semantic information to efficiently retrieve documents from the MEC collection. Both approaches can be automatised to allow a very systematic way to deal with the huge and rich museum assets.

Foreword

In 1967, William W. Tunnicliffe articulated the idea of separating the formatting of a document from its content. Based on this generic coding, Charles Goldfarb, Edward Mosher, and Raymond Lorie developed the Generalized Markup Language (GML). Goldfarb used their surnames to make up the term GML. GML markups (tags) can be used to define the structure of documents (e.g., headers, chapters) without further specifying how particular elements of this structure are to be presented. In 1986, the Standard Generalized Markup Language became an ISO standard. However, its complexity has prevented its widespread application.

In the late 1990s, an SGML subset referred to as the Extensible Markup Language (XML) appeared and soon became a W3C standard in 1999. XML is simpler to parse and process than full SGML and has been widely adopted since then as a format to exchange data. Despite its name, XML is not a language with a given vocabulary but rather a set of syntax rules that can be applied to create languages. Such languages are called applications of XML. Since its standardization, a plethora of XML applications have been developed by industry and academia alike. Today, the Extensible Markup Language is ubiquitous in computing and an indispensable building block in countless software systems.

There are numerous explanations tendered for the success of XML. Certainly, XML's basic simplicity allowed for its rapid acceptance. The original XML specification can be printed on only 30 pages compared to the more than 150-pages SGML specification from which it was derived. Second, when SGML came out, in-memory implementations were prohibitively expensive while alternative stream processing approaches proved to be significantly less useful. Since then, the luxury of using XML has become affordable with the number of available DRAM bits per dollar doubling every two years from 10^5 in 1986 to 10^7 bits per dollar in 1999. Eventually, XML documents are both intelligible for humans and machine readable, which makes it relatively easy to do something with data you get in XML. In particular, one common XML parser can be used to extract the relevant information items of XML documents for all conceivable kinds of XML applications.

A variety of other fundamental applications and supporting technologies build on XML. XML Schema Definition (XSD) is a schema definition language to constrain the content model of an XML instance document to a specific hierarchical element structure and particular element data types. Several other W3C standards such as the Resource Description Framework (RDF)—a general method for the formal description of logical statements about resources—and the Web Ontology Language (OWL)—a knowledge representation language for authoring ontologies—are based on XML and XSD. Custom applications and application specific tools can in turn be built upon these standards.

This book presents in three sections a multifaceted insight into compelling XML applications and conclusive technologies. Section 1 introduces new XML applications and presents approaches to ease the use of existing XML-based standards. Section 2 is concerned with analyzing and ensuring the quality of XML-based learning objects and repositories. Section 3 covers the spectrum from XML to databases and ontologies.

In Section 1, two chapters focus on improving the ease of use of XML by facilitating the generation-by-example of XSLT programs and XQuery expressions. In addition, the PExIL XML application provides for comprehensive descriptions of programming language exercises. Finally, an approach is presented to facilitate the privacy-aware sharing of personal data on the Web by means of an instant messaging protocol.

In Section 2, multi-criteria analysis and optimization methods for the evaluation and the improvement of learning repositories are explored. In addition, a framework is presented for quality assessments of the specifications of learning objects and repositories. Moreover, techniques for the detection of mobile devices are compared followed by the introduction of an architectural model for the delivery of XML-based mobile-learning content.

In Section 3, two chapters focus on database preservation using XML-based technologies. First, the SIARD standard for Software Independent Archival of Relational Databases is extended to include metadata specific to data warehouses. Second, the Web Ontology Language is used to describe conceptual models of relational databases in order to facilitate archival storage. Furthermore, a complete workflow for digital curation based on XML documents is presented. A combination of XML's contextual modeling and ontologies is described in the context of information access for the website of the Portuguese Emigration Museum.

The chapters in this book are extended versions of selected papers of the Ninth XATA Workshop (2011), which was held at the Escola Superior de Estudos Industriais e de Gestão at the Instituto Politécnico do Porto in Portugal. I had the privilege to serve as a member of the editorial advisory board and can warmly recommend this volume as an inspiring compilation of recent approaches in the area of XML and related technologies. At the same time, I suggest that interested readers may consider attending or submitting to the recently established Symposium on Languages, Applications, and Technologies (SLATE), which continues with a dedicated track to cover the topics of the former XATA workshop series.

Computing was not ready when SGML came out. Today we are ready for XML. Enjoy!

Alexander Paar
University of Pretoria, South Africa

Alexander Paar *is a Software Developer, Project Manager, and Computer Scientist. He studied Computer Science at the Clausthal University of Technology, the University of California, Irvine, and the University of Karlsruhe (TH). He earned a Computer Science Doctorate from the University of Karlsruhe (TH) in 2009, then was a post-doctoral research fellow at the University of Pretoria. He contributed to international research projects from conception to completion and has a proven record as a speaker at international computer science workshops and conferences. He served as a program committee member and reviewed submissions for various computer science workshops, conferences, and journals. Alexander authored the Zhi# programming language—the first object-oriented programming language with inherent support for ontologies. He was in second place in the 2001 IEEE CSIDC and won silver and bronze medals for coaching teams for the ACM ICPC. He is a member of ACM, IEEE CS, and Gesellschaft für Informatik.*

Preface

This book is a result of choosing the best papers from a conference held in Vila do Conde, Portugal, in June 2011, named XATA (XML, Applications, and Associated Technologies) together with some other original work.

XATA was a conference on XML, covering a wide range of topics, from the low-level details of the language and all its related standards, up to its usage in Digital Libraries or e-Learning. The 2011 edition of XATA was the last in a series of nine editions, giving place to a new project, named SLATE: Symposium on Languages, Applications, and Technologies, which covers not just XML and related technologies, but all other markup languages, as well as programming languages and human (natural) languages. The first edition of this event took place on the 21st and 22nd of June, 2012.

XML has been in the last years the de facto language for interoperability between systems, serializing data structures, construct e-learning materials and repositories, and in a lot other areas of application. In this book, we cover a broad range of subjects related to these aspects. We think this book is interesting mainly because of the wide range of covered topics, and the different aspects and applications of XML than by each one of the articles by itself. It can be seen as a compendium of how XML is being used in the world, widening the reader's knowledge on XML, its applications, and its associated technologies.

The XML, as we know it today, appeared in 1998, with the first World Wide Web Consortium (W3C) Recommendation. It was the result of making the Standard Generalized Markup Language (SGML) more strict, making it easier to parse, and less ambiguous. This recommendation has evolved during the last years, with the second version of this recommendation in 2000, the third in 2003, the fourth in 2006, and currently, the fifth, that has been stable since 2008. The bases behind the XML philosophy did not change during these years. Just a few enhancements were defined, like the support for namespaces, and the specification on how parsers should report and deal with errors.

Although the XML recommendation has been stable during these years, a lot has been defined and specified related to the XML technologies. Some examples include the XML Path language, which defines a syntax to specify nodes and views in an XML document (second recommendation from 2011), the XML Query language, a powerful query language for XML documents and databases (first W3C recommendation from 2011), the Extensible Stylesheet Language (XSL) for expressing stylesheets (whose version 1.1 recommendation is from 2006), and the XSL Transformations (XSLT), a language to transform XML documents into other XML documents (whose second recommendation is from 2007).

These are just a few examples. Even the way to define the structure or grammar of XML documents has evolved. The first approach, derived from the SGML world, was the use of Document Type Definitions (DTD) that is still widely used, but new approaches have appeared, not just to define the grammar but also the semantics, like the XML Schema Definition (XSD version 1.1 was defined in 2012), the Relax-NG (an ISO standard developed within OASIS group [Advancing Open Standards for the Information Society]).

Note that most of these languages (like XQuery, XSL, XSLT, XSD) are themselves XML dialects. In the dialects world, there is a lot of work as well, ranging from the attempts to transform the HyperText Markup Language (HTML) into an XML dialect (with XHTML), to the specifications on how to define vector graphics with SVG (Scalar Vector Graphics format), to define the structure and the presentation of mathematical formulae with MathML (Math Markup Language), to define music scores with MusicXML, to define how multimedia events are synchronized with SMIL (Synchronized Multimedia Integration Language), and the more recent approaches to encode ontologies into XML defining Resource Definition Framework (RDF), Web Ontology Language (OWL), or even TopicMaps and SKOS (Simple Knowledge Organization System).

The usage of XML to serialize computational objects and foster the interoperability between systems has been growing in an exponential way. XML has been using the text composition, with two relevant standards, DocBook and the Text Encoding Initiative (TEI), in the e-Learning field, with IEEE Learning Object Metadata (LOM) and IMS Question and Test Interoperability (IMS QTI), in the computer assisted translation, with the Translation Memory Interchange format (TMX) and the Term Base Interchange format (TBX), in the health institutions with half a dozen standards from Clinical Data Interchange Standards Consortium, in the e-Publishing industry with the ePub format, etc. Even the major companies like Microsoft switched their proprietary formats for counterpart XML versions.

Nevertheless, XATA and this book are not devoted to the definition of new standards, or just their use, but it, instead, points out problems or challenges on their use and extension and answers or identifies solution paths to these problems. In fact, this book is divided in three main sections, and only the first one is directly related to the usage and definition of standards.

SECTION 1: XML STANDARDS AND DIALECTS

The first section of the book includes four chapters. Two of them present systems that allow the edition of XML dialects such as XSLT and XQuery without the need to understand its syntax and with enough clarity to be easily understood by people who are not familiar with the XML languages. Both cases are based on examples, fostering the learning of these XML dialects.

XML is also used to describe Programming Exercises using an XML Interoperable Language called PExIL. This language covers the entire lifecycle of a programming exercise from its creation to its evaluation. In this lifecycle, several e-learning systems intervene, such as automatic evaluators, repositories of learning objects, and learning management systems.

Finally, an XML language, specifically the Extensible Messaging and Presence Protocol (XMPP) language, is used as the basis for an identity management framework that allows users to control asynchronous and dynamic sharing sensitive data, ensuring the security and privacy in a simple and transparent way.

SECTION 2: LEARNING ENVIRONMENTS

This second section of the book focuses on the assessment of the quality of learning environments and standards. The first chapter describes a framework for quality assessment of learning technology specifications and how it was used to evaluate and improve a case in point: the Learning Path Specification.

The following chapter analyses the quality of XML learning object repositories, more precisely, on the models and methods to evaluate the quality of learning repositories. Multiple criteria decision analysis and optimization methods are explored to be applied for evaluating the quality of learning repositories.

Finally, a chapter on mobile learning is presented where the authors compare the most used approaches for mobile device detection. Based on this study, an architecture for detecting and delivering uniform m-Learning content to students in a high school is presented. This system is based on an XML device capabilities repository and on a REST API Web service for dealing with device data.

SECTION 3: DATABASES AND REPOSITORIES

The final section is dedicated to databases and repositories. The first two chapters focus on relational databases. The former presents the definition of the XML structure, which extends the Software Independent Archiving of Relational Databases (SIARD) format used for the description and archive of relational databases, enriching it with a layer of metadata for the data warehouse components. Data Warehouse Extensible Markup Language (DWXML) is the XML language proposed to describe the data warehouse. The latter addresses the problematic Digital Preservation and focuses on the conceptual model within a specific class of digital objects: Relational Databases. The preservation of relational databases focuses on the conceptual model of the database, considering the database semantics as an important preservation "property." For the representation of this higher layer of abstraction present in databases, the authors use an ontology-based approach.

The third chapter focuses on the management of research data in a higher education and research institution. The work is based on a small-scale data audit study, which included contacts with researchers and yielded some preliminary requirements and use cases. These requirements led to the design of a data curation workflow involving the researcher, the curator and a data repository based on a DSpace repository.

The last chapter of the book relates an ongoing work, in the context of the Portuguese Emigration Museum, about information access in XML collections associated with semantic information. The museum asset is made up of documents of more than eight kinds, ranging from passport records to photos/cards or building-drawings. The authors discuss the approach used to create the exhibition rooms of the virtual Web-based museum. Each room consists of a view over the information contained in those single or interrelated resources. The information exhibited in each room is described by an ontology written in Web Ontology Language (OWL).

In the end, we think this book encompasses a set of interesting chapters from different XML application areas, that can help researchers and professionals to read and learn from previous experiences. However, this book would not be a reality if it was not for the work and dedication from our editorial advisory board, who reviewed and commented on each of the chapters here published, and for the work and interest by the authors who took the time to expand their chapters and include the editorial advisory board comments into them.

Acknowledgment

To all the members of the Editorial Advisory Board, to the reviewers, and to the authors whose names are published in this book, we feel very much grateful. We would like to express our thanks to the publishing team at IGI Global for their expert support and guidance.

José Carlos Ramalho
University of Minho, Portugal

Alberto Simões
University of Minho, Portugal

Ricardo Queirós
CRACS & ESEIG/IPP, Porto, Portugal

Section 1
XML Standards and Dialects

Chapter 1
An Example–Based Generator of XSLT Programs

José Paulo Leal
University of Porto, Portugal

Ricardo Queirós
CRACS and ESEIG/IPP, Porto, Portugal

ABSTRACT

XSLT is a powerful and widely used language for transforming XML documents. However, its power and complexity can be overwhelming for novice or infrequent users, many of whom simply give up on using this language. On the other hand, many XSLT programs of practical use are simple enough to be automatically inferred from examples of source and target documents. An inferred XSLT program is seldom adequate for production usage but can be used as a skeleton of the final program, or at least as scaffolding in the process of coding it. It should be noted that the authors do not claim that XSLT programs, in general, can be inferred from examples. The aim of Vishnu—the XSLT generator engine described in this chapter—is to produce XSLT programs for processing documents similar to the given examples and with enough readability to be easily understood by a programmer not familiar with the language. The architecture of Vishnu is composed by a graphical editor and a programming engine. In this chapter, the authors focus on the editor as a GWT Web application where the programmer loads and edits document examples and pairs their content using graphical primitives. The programming engine receives the data collected by the editor and produces an XSLT program.

DOI: 10.4018/978-1-4666-2669-0.ch001

INTRODUCTION

Generating a XSLT program from a pair of source and target XML documents is straightforward. A transformation with a single template containing the target document solves this requirement, but is valid only for the actual example. Using the information from the source document, we can abstract this transformation. The simplest way is to assume that common strings in both documents correspond to values that must be copied between them. If we explicitly identify these correspondences, we can have more control over which strings are copied and to which positions. However, a transformation created in this fashion is still too specific to the examples and cannot process a similar source document with a slightly different structure. For instance, if the source document type accepts a repeated element and the example has repetitions of the element then the generated program would accept exactly repetitions of that element.

Although too specific, a simple XSLT program can be used as the starting point for generating a sequence of programs that are more general and are better structured, ending in a program with a quality similar to one coded by a human programmer. To refine an XSLT program we can use second order XSLT transformations, i.e. XSLT transformations having XSLT transformations both as source and target documents. In this approach, the role of an XSLT generation engine is to receive source and target examples, and an optional mapping between the strings of the two documents, generate an initial program and control the refinement process towards the final XSLT program.

The aim of this chapter is the presentation of Vishnu—an XSLT engine for generating readable XSLT programs from examples of source and target documents. Readability is an essential feature of the generated programs so that they can be easily understood by a programmer not familiar with the language. The architecture of Vishnu is composed by a graphical editor and a programming engine. The former acts as a client where the programmer loads and edits document examples and pair their content using graphical primitives. The latter receives the data collected by the editor and produces an XSLT program.

There are several use cases for an XSLT generation engine with these features. The Vishnu generator was designed to interact with a component that provides text-editing functions for the end-user or programmer. A client of Vishnu can be a plug-in of an Integrated Development Environment (IDE) such as Eclipse or NetBeans. In this case, the IDE provides several XML tools (highlighting, validation, XSLT execution) and the plug-in is responsible for binding the content of text buffers and editing positions with the engine and retrieving the generated XSLT program. Vishnu can also be used as the back-end of a Web environment for XSLT programming. In this case, the Web front-end is responsible for editing operations and invokes engine functions for setting the example documents and mappings, and retrieving the generated program. The generator can also be used as a command line tool as part of a pipeline for generating and consuming XSLT programs. In this last case, the generator processes example documents in the local file system, making mostly use of default mappings.

This approach visual XSLT programming has obvious limitations. Only a subset of all possible XSLT transformations is programmable by pairing texts on a source and target documents. For instance, second order transformations or recursive templates are out of its scope. Use cases for Vishnu are formatting XML documents in XHTML and conversion among similar formats. For instance, creating an XHTML view of an RSS feed and converting metadata among several XML formats are among the possible uses of Vishnu. Moreover, we do not expect the automated features of Vishnu to produce the final version of an XSLT program. We view its final result as a skeleton of a transformation that can be further refined using other tools already available in Eclipse.

The rest of the chapter is organized as follows. Section 2 presents work related to XSLT editing and generation. In the following section, we present the inner structure of the XSLT generator that is composed of three main components: the context, the generator, and the refiner. In the refiner component, we highlight the two types of refinements: simplifications and abstractions. Then, we evaluate the Vishnu XSLT generation engine from three complementary and interrelated approaches, focusing on the consistency of generation and refinement process, the coverage of the existing rules, and the adequacy of the Vishnu API to XSLT editing environments. Finally, we conclude with a summary of the main contributions of this work and a perspective of future research.

RELATED WORK

The first step to start editing XSLT files is choosing the editor that most suits one's programming environment. There are several environments for programming in XSLT. Usually these tools are integrated in XML IDE's or in general purpose IDE's such as Eclipse. In the former, we can highlight StyleVision and Stylus Studio. StyleVision[1] is a commercial visual stylesheet designer for transforming XML. It allows drag and dropping XML data elements within a WYSIWYG interface. An XSLT stylesheet is automatically generated and can be previewed using the FOP built-in browser. Stylus Studio's[2] is another commercial XML IDE that includes a WYSIWYG XSLT designer. The edition process is guided by simple drag-and-drop operations without requiring prior knowledge of XSLT.

There are also several plug-ins for Eclipse for editing XSLT and the Tiger XSLT Mapper[3] is the most prominent. It is a simple development environment that supports automatic mappings between XML structures and can be edited using the drag-and-drop visual interface. While the mappings and XML structures are modified, the XSLT template is automatically generated and modified.

Other examples of Eclipse plug-ins address the XSLT edition[4, 5, 6] and the XSLT execution[7, 8].

There are other tools analogue to Vishnu that are not integrated into Eclipse, as the dexter-xsl[9] which is intended to be used from the command line, the VXT (Pietriga, 2001) a visual programming language for the specification of XML transformations in an interactive environment and FOA[10] an XSL-FO graphical authoring tool to create XSL-FO stylesheets. It includes a tree visualization scheme to represent the source XML document and the target FO tree structure. FOA generates an XSLT stylesheet that transforms XML content into an XSL-FO document.

Despite the existence of several environments for programming in XSLT, usually integrated into IDE's, they do not use visual editing for programming. Moreover, as far as we know, none of the graphical XSLT programming environment generates programs from examples.

Hori (2004) and Ono (2002) use an example-based annotation tool which relies on a target document editor. The main concepts of their approach are depicted in Figure 1. An annotator can edit a target document (e.g., an HTML page) by using the capabilities of a WYSIWYG authoring tool (1). The editing actions are recorded into an operation history (2). When the editing is finished, the annotation generator creates transformational annotation for the document customization (3), which can be further used by XSLT processor to replicate the transformation from the initial document to the customized document.

Spinks presents an annotation-based page-clipping engine providing a way of performing Web resources adaptation (Spinks, 2001). At content delivery time, the page-clipping engine modifies the original document based on: (1) the page-clipping annotations previously generated in a WYSIWYG authoring tool and (2) the user-agent HTTP header of the client device. The page-clipping annotation language uses the keep and remove elements in the annotation descriptions to indicate whether the content being processed should be preserved or removed.

Figure 1. History-based document transformation

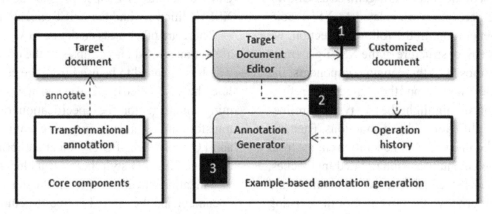

As a simple example, an HTML page and its clipped results are shown in Figure 2. In this example, the header and the first paragraph are preserved. The table element is modified by deleting the third column and the second row. In addition, the whole of the second paragraph is removed. All the structural changes in HTML documents can be easily done by using a WYSIWYG HTML editor. The XML excerpt in Algorithm 1 shows an annotation document that realizes the page clipping.

The description element defines a unit of an annotation statement in the annotation language. The target attribute is an XPath expression identifying the node on which the annotation will be applied, and the take-effect attribute indicates whether the annotation is applied before or after the target node. The following code shows a simple example of an HTML page clipping.

THE VISHNU ENGINE

The Vishnu engine (Leal, 2010) concentrates all the tasks related with the automatic generation of an XSLT program from examples using second order transformations. Nevertheless, it was designed to interact with a client. A client of the Vishnu engine concentrates all the tasks related with user

Figure 2. Simple example of an HTML page clipping

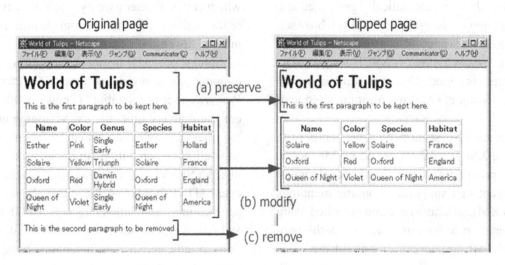

Algorithm 1. Annotation document that realizes the page clipping

```xml
<?xml version='1.0' ?>
<annot version="2.0">
      <!-- (a) Set the default clipping state to 'keep' -->
      <description take-effect="before"
            target="/HTML[1]/BODY[1]/*[1]">
            <keep/>
      </description>
      <!-- (b) Remove a column and a row of the first -->
      <!-- table, and change a cellpadding -->
      <!-- attribute value -->
      <description take-effect="before"
            target="/HTML[1]/BODY[1]/TABLE[1]">
            <keep/>
            <table>
                  <column index="3" clipping="remove"/>
                  <column index="*" clipping="keep"/>
                  <row index="2" clipping="remove"/>
                  <row index="*" clipping="keep"/>
            </table>
            <insertattribute name="cellpadding" value="4"/>
      </description>
      <!-- (c) Set the clipping state to 'remove' -->
      <description take-effect="before"
            target="/HTML[1]/BODY[1]/P[2]">
            <remove/>
      </description>
      <!-- (d) Set the clipping state back to 'keep' -->
      <description take-effect="after"
            target="/HTML[1]/BODY[1]/P[2]">
            <keep/>
      </description>
</annot>
```

interaction where the programmer loads and edits document examples and pairs their content using graphical primitives.

The communication between these two components is regulated by the Vishnu API. Hence, the architecture of the Vishnu application is composed by a Graphical Editor and a Programming Engine as depicted in Figure 3.

The former acts as a client where the programmer loads and edits document examples and pair their content using graphical primitives. The design and implementation of a client for the Vishnu engine is presented in the next section to validate the adequacy of the Vishnu API to XSLT editing environments.

Figure 3. The architecture of Vishnu

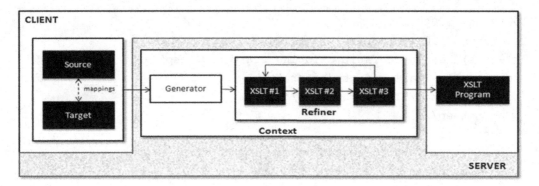

The latter receives the data collected by the editor and produces an XSLT program. The engine relies on the Vishnu API that includes methods for setting the source and target documents as streams of characters, setting a mapping between the strings of these documents using editing locations (offsets), and retrieving the resulting XSLT program. The Vishnu API includes also functions for supporting graphical interaction in the editor and for configuring the generation process. The functions for selecting strings in the XML documents (text and attribute nodes) from editing locations are example functions for supporting graphical interaction. The Vishnu facade class implements this API and hides the inner structure of the XSLT generator that is composed of three main components: the context, the generator, and the refiner.

Context

The central piece of the engine is the generation context. The context holds the source and target documents and the mapping between the two. The mapping can be set manually through a GUI client or inferred. When in automatic pairing mode Vishnu tries to identify pairs based on:

- Text matches (text or attribute nodes);
- Text aggregation.

In the first mode strings occurring on text and attribute type nodes on the source document are searched on the text and attribute nodes of the target document, and only exact matches are considered. In this mode, a single occurrence of a string in the source document may be paired with several occurrences in the target document, as depicted in Figure 4.

In the second mode, Vishnu tries to aggregate strings in the source document to create a string in the target document. In Figure 5, we illustrate with a simple case where 3 strings occurring in attributes and text nodes can be concatenated into a part of the text node on the target document. In

Figure 4. Automatic mapping: exact match between single texts

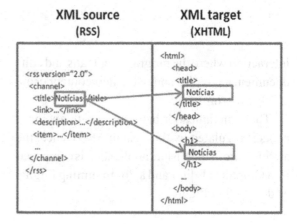

Figure 5. Automatic mapping: subset of aggregation of texts

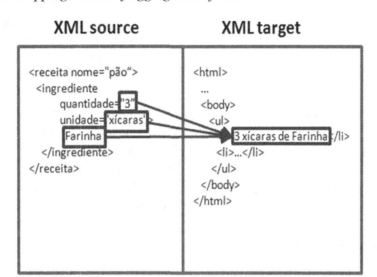

this mode several strings on the source document can be paired with strings on the target document.

After automatic pairing, the inferred correspondences are presented in the GUI with lines connecting the two XML documents. The user can then manually reconstruct the pairing of string between both documents.

The result of pairing the examples is a document including the actual documents and a list of pairs of XPath expressions relating them. This document is formally defined by an XML schema depicted diagrammatically in Figure 6.

The pairing XML language has an element vishnu as the root element with three top elements: source—a copy of the source document; target—a copy of the target document; pairings: list of pairing relating the two documents. Each correspondence is defined by a pairing element with two attributes for selecting textual occurrences in

both documents: source and target. The source attribute includes a valid XPath expression selecting the text to map in the source document. The target attribute includes a valid XPath expression selecting the text of the target document.

As said before the context holds the source and target documents and the mapping between the two and is responsible for converting between the external textual representation provided by the client and the internal XML representation required by the Vishnu. In particular, this component is responsible for converting document position into XPath expressions and vice-versa.

The conversion is managed by the PathLocator class. This class converts text locations (offsets) into *IdPaths* expressions and vice-versa. An *IdPath* is an absolute XPath expression which selects either single texts or attribute nodes in an

Figure 6. The mapping XML language

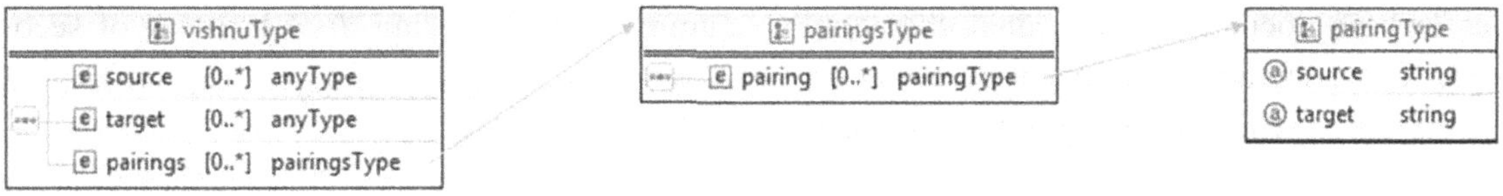

Algoritm 2. General form of an IDPath

```
/n¹[p¹]/.../n^n[p^n]/text()[p^{n+1}]
/n¹[p¹]/.../n^n[p^n]/@attr
```

XML document. The general form of an *IDPath* is shown in Algorithm 2.

It should be noted that locating nodes using their editing positions and the reverse (locating an editing position of a node) are not operations supported by XML processing APIs. The implementation of these operations by the PathLocator class is not trivial. The current version is not yet supporting indexes on references to text nodes. With this limitation, we were not able yet to apply Vishnu no mixed content scenarios. However, upgrading the PathLocator to supported sibling text nodes is a comparatively easy task that we expect to complete in the next version of Vishnu.

The Context component is also responsible for the generation of the mapping between the source and the target documents. It maintains an XML map file identifying the correspondences between both. These identifications can be inferred automatically or manually set through the Editor. Algorithm 3 (based on Figure 3) shows an example of a source, target, and a list of pairs of XPath expressions relating them merged in a file called vishnu.xml. This file will serve as input for the Generator component to produce a XSLT program.

Generation

The purpose of the generator is to produce an initial XSLT program from the source and target, using a string mapping. If no mapping is provided by the client then it uses a default mapping inferred by the context component, linking text or attribute nodes in both documents with equal character strings. The generator component receives as input the paring file and, using a second order

transformation, produces a specific XSLT program. In Algorithm 4, the output of this second order stylesheet based on the example included in the previous subsection. The following code shows an example of the output of the second order stylesheet.

The initial XSLT program has a single template containing an abstraction of the target document. To abstract the target document the target positions in the mapping are replaced with xsl:value-of instructions referring corresponding source positions in the mapping.

Algorithm 4 illustrates the verbosity of the initial template with XPath expressions are very long and difficult to read, with indexes in every path branch. Actually, the expressions are even more complex that those presented here since all elements must be prefixed when namespaces are used. For the sake of clarity namespace prefixes in XPath expressions where omitted in this example. The initial template has also plenty of redundancy. This XSLT transformation generates an XHTML ordered list element (<ol>) with the exact number of item elements (<li>) need to reflect the given example. Thus, the part of the document marked with ellipsis corresponds almost to a repetition of the of the first XHTM item element, with changes only on the index of the RSS item element referred by XPath expressions.

As explained previously, with this level of abstraction the initial transformation is only able to process a document with the exact same structure of the source document provided as input. To be of any practical use this program is submitted to a refinement process.

Refinement

The refinement process produces a sequence of XSLT programs ρ_n starting with the initial program ρ_0 by applying $R = \{r_i\}$ set of second order XSLT transformations called refinements.

Algorithm 3. Source, target, and list of pairs of XPath expressions

```
<vishnu xmlns="http://www.dcc.fc.up.pt/vishnu">
<!-Source document -->
<source>
<rss version="2.0" xmlns="http://backend.userland.com/rss2"/>
    <channel>
      <title>Notícias</title>
      <link>... </link>
      <description>…</description>
      <item>
      ...
      </item>
      </channel>
</rss>
</source>
<!-target document -->
<target>
<html xmlns="http://www.w3.org/1999/xhtml">
 <head><title>Notícias</title></head>
 <body><h1>Notícias</h1>...</body>
</html>
</target>
<!-pairing document-->
<pairings>
      <pairing
source = "/rss[1]/channel[1]/title[1]/text()"
target = "/html[1]/head[1]/title[1]/text()"/>
      <pairing
source = "/rss[1]/channel[1]/title[1]/text()"
target = "/html[1]/body[1]/h1[1]/text()"/>
</pairings>
</vishnu>
```

Refinements can be divided in two categories: simplifications and generalizations.

Let S_0 and T_0 be respectively the example source and target documents. All refinements r_i have the following invariant:

$\rho_n(S_0) = T_0 \Rightarrow r_i(\rho_n)(S_0) = T_0$ that is, if a program maps the example source document to the example target document then the refined program has the same property. A simplification refinement is even more restrictive and any document S that is converted by program S_0 is equally converted by its refinement,

$i.e. \forall S, T \rho_n(S) = T \Rightarrow r_i(\rho_n)(S) = T$.

Simplifications are "safe" refinements but fail to introduce the level of abstraction needed for a transformation to be effective, hence this stronger requirement is relaxed for abstractions.

Algorithm 4. Output of second order stylesheet

```
<xsl:template match="/">
 <html>
   <head>
     <title>
       <xsl:value-of select="/vishnu/source/rss[1]/channel[1]/title[1]/text()"/>
       </title>
     </head>
     <body>
       <h1>
         <xsl:value-of select="/vishnu/source/rss[1]/channel[1]/title[1]/
text()"/>
       </h1>
       <ol>
         <li>
           <a>
             <xsl:attribute name="href">
                 <xsl:value-of
select="/rss[1]/channel[1]/item[1]/link[1]/text()"/>
               </xsl:attribute>
               <xsl:value-of
select="/rss[1]/ channel[1]/item[1]/title[1]/text()"/>
           </a> -
           <i>
             <xsl:value-of
select="/rss[1]/channel[1]/item[1]/description[1]/text()"/>
           </i>
         </li>
         ...
       </ol>
     </body>
   </html>
</xsl:template>
```

An example of a generalization is the refinement that unfolds a single template into a collection of smaller templates. Candidates to top elements in the new template are elements whose XPath expressions in xsl:value-of share a common and non-trivial prefix that can be used match of the new template. As it introduces new templates with relative expressions in the match attribute this refinement is not a simplification. The new template may match with nodes with the same tag occurring in different points in a different source document structure. To minimize the chance of unwanted matches this refinement associates a mode to the new template that is used also by the xsl:apply-template instruction that invokes it. An example of a simplification is the refinement that removes redundant modes from xsl:template and xsl:apply-template instructions. This refinement selects templates with non-empty modes that cannot be matched by other templates. That mode is removed both from the selected template and all xsl:apply-template referring it. The current Vishnu implementation includes over 10 refinements.

The Vishnu engine supports different refinement strategies to control the application of the refinement setR. A refinement strategy indicates the next refinement to use is informed if the suggested refinement has changed the XSLT program and decides when the refinement process is complete. There are several refinement strategies that can be set using the Vishnu API. The most effective strategies implemented so far apply the refinements in a predefined order, repeating the application of refinement while it is effective.

As an illustration, we present the final output of the refinement process based on the example included in the previous subsection in Algorithm 5. The following code shows the final output of the refinement process.

The control of the refinement process is implemented in Java, rather than in XSLT. This separation encourages the modularity and reusability of the refinement transformations which would be harder to achieve if the whole refinement process was encoded in a single XSLT. With this approach is easy to introduce new refinements or to temporarily switch them off. It is easier to change a single and simple XSLT file than to change the code and recompile the application. There are two types of refinements—simplifications and abstractions—that are detailed on following sub-subsections, after which are presented implementation details these second order transformations.

Simplifications are refinements that preserve the semantics of the program while changing its syntax. Preserving the semantics means that, for all documents S and T, if a program P transforms document S in document T then the program P', resulting from a simplification refinement, will also transform S to T.

Simplifications can be used for different purposes. They can be used to improve the readability of XPath expressions or to extract global variables. The following paragraphs illustrate this concept with concrete simplifications and examples of the refinements they introduce.

- **Context:** Extracts the common prefix of all the XPath expressions from value-of elements in the same template and append it as a suffix of the match attribute on the template element (see Table 1);
- **Melt:** Two or more templates with the same containers are merged into one in which the match attribute is an expression that combines the terms of th original attributes match using the operator (|) that computes two or more node-sets (see Table 2);
- **Extract:** Strings inside the templates are assigned to global variables (see Table 3);
- **Join:** Different variables within the same scope and the same content are replaced by a single variable (see Table 4);
- **Braces:** Attribute values defined by XSL elements are replaced by braces with XPath expressions (see Table 5);
- **Mode:** Removes modes that do not contribute to differentiate templates from template definitions and related apply-templates (see Table 6);
- **Orphan:** Remove template with just a single xsl:apply-templates (orphan) with the same mode (must be applied after removing unneeded modes) (see Table 7);

Abstractions are refinements that change both the syntax and the semantics of the program, although retaining the intended semantics of the example documents. This means that, for the documents S and T given as example, if a program P transforms document S in document T then the program P', resulting from a abstraction refinement, will also transform S to T.

Algorithm 5. Final output of the refinement process

```
<xsl:stylesheet version="1.0" ...>
<xsl:template match="rss2:channel">
 <xhtml:html>
<xsl:apply-templates mode="xhtml:head" select="rss2:title"/>
 <xhtml:body>
   <xsl:apply-templates mode="xhtml:h1" select="rss2:title"/>
   <xhtml:ol>
     <xsl:apply-templates select="rss2:item"/>
   </xhtml:ol>
 </xhtml:body>
 </xhtml:html>
</xsl:template>
<xsl:template match="rss2:item">
<xhtml:li>
 <xhtml:a href="{rss2:link}">
   <xsl:value-of select="rss2:title"/>
 </xhtml:a> -
 <xsl:apply-templates select="rss2:description"/>
</xhtml:li>
</xsl:template>

<xsl:template match="rss2:description">
<xhtml:i><xsl:value-of select="."/></xhtml:i>
</xsl:template>
<xsl:template match="rss2:title" mode="xhtml:h1">
 <xhtml:h1><xsl:value-of select="."/></xhtml:h1>
</xsl:template>
<xsl:template match="rss2:title" mode="xhtml:head">
 <xhtml:head>
<xhtml:title><xsl:value-of select="."/></xhtml:title>
 </xhtml:head>
</xsl:template>
</xsl:stylesheet>
```

Table 1. Applying the context refinement

Source XSLT	Result XSLT
<xsl:template match="a"> ... ...<xsl:value-of select="b/c"/> ...<xsl:value-of select="b/d"/> </xsl:template>	<xsl:template match="a/b"> ... ...<xsl:value-of select="c"/> ...<xsl:value-of select="d"/> </xsl:template>

Table 2. Applying the melt refinement

Source XSLT	Result XSLT
<xsl:template match="a"> ... </xsl:template> <xsl:template match="b"> ... </xsl:template>	<xsl:template match="a | b"> ... </xsl:template>

Table 3. Applying the extract refinement

Source XSLT	Result XSLT
<xsl:template ...> xpto </xsl:template>	<xsl:variable name="x" select="'xpto'"/> ... <xsl:template ...> <xsl:value-of select="$x"> </xsl:template>

Table 4. Applying the join refinement

Source XSLT	Result XSLT
<xsl:variable name="x1" select="'xpto'"/> <xsl:variable name="x2" select="'xpto'"/> ... <xsl:value-of select="$x1"/> ... <xsl:value-of select="$x2"/>	<xsl:variable name="x1" select="'xpto'"/> ... <xsl:value-of select="$x1"/> ... <xsl:value-of select="$x1"/>

Table 5. Applying the braces refinement

Source XSLT	Result XSLT
<a> <xsl:attribute name="href" select="item/url"/>... </a>	<a href="{item/url}">...</a>

Table 6. Applying the mode refinement

Source XSLT	Result XSLT
<xsl:template mode="m"> ... </xsl:template> <xsl:apply-templates mode="m"/>	<xsl:template> ... </xsl:template> ... <xsl:apply-templates/>

Table 7. Applying the orphan refinement

Source XSLT	Result XSLT
<xsl:template mode="m"> <xsl:apply-templates mode="m"> </xsl:template>	

Abstractions can be used for different purposes. For instance, they can be used to generalize templates and to restructure large templates in several smaller ones. The following paragraphs illustrate this concept with concrete abstractions and examples of the refinements they introduce:

- **Generalize:** Two or more templates with the same container and a match attribute differing only in the "index" are merged into one and is removed the last predicate of the attribute match. The original transformation accepts only document with a precise number of elements of a certain kind and the abstracted transformation accepts an undetermined number of elements of that kind (see Table 8);

- **Structure:** Fragments templates that contain Xpath expressions with a common prefix. The extracted template will match with elements outside the scope of the original template (see Table 9);

Implementation Details

The refinements implemented in Vishnu are XSL 1.0 transformations. Selecting the version of XSL, both as a target language and for implementation of refinements was a major design decision in Vishnu. After careful consideration, it was decided to use version 1.0 as a target language as this is more disseminated and easier for novice XSLT programmers. Using version 1.0 as target would difficult the use of version 2.0 for refinements. We would have to use two XSLT processors in the generation process, one for refining transformations, and another for testing them. Since this would be an extra burden, we preferred to use consistently a single language version in Vishnu, and selected version 1.0.

The main reason considering XSLT 2.0 was the use of features that otherwise would have to rely on extensions. Fortunately, most of the features needed are available in standard extensions. Thus, we used the Xalan XSLT processor with extensions for string handling, function definition and basic elements and functions. Algorithm 6

Table 8. Applying the generalize refinement

Source XSLT	Result XSLT
<xsl:template match="a[1]"> ... </xsl:template> *<xsl:template match="a[2]"> ... </xsl:template>* *<xsl:template match="a[3]"> ... </xsl:template*	*<xsl:template match="a"> ... </xsl:template>*

Table 9. Applying the structure refinement

Source XSLT	Result XSLT
<xsl:template match="a"> <X> <xsl:value-of select="b/x"> <xsl:value-of select="b/y"> </X> <xsl:value-of select="c"> </xsl:template>	<xsl:template match="a"> <xsl:apply-templates select="b"/> ... <xsl:value-of select="c"> </xsl:template> <xsl:template match="b"> <X> <xsl:value-of select="x"> <xsl:value-of select="y"> </X> </xsl:template>

shows an example of a refinement: the Orphan simplification.

A core feature in Vishnu is comparing two XML fragments. As result of the transformation process two XML fragments may result in different serializations but still be equivalent. To compare XML fragments Vishnu used the package XML Unit version 1.3. This package was developed for implementing by Tim Bacon and Stefan Bodewig to support unit testing in XML development. It provides a diff method to compare XML fragments and can be configured to ignore white space and differences between text and CDATA sections. This package was exposed as an extension function to refinements.

The common features we assembled in a XSLT library that is imported by most refinements. This library provides functions for XPath handling, such as finding common prefixes, and for recursively copying XML fragments while performing certain transformation, such as removing XPath prefixes. It also provides access to the extension functions mentioned previously.

Algorithm 6 presented an example of a particular refinement, the Orphan simplification introduced in sub-subsection 3.5.1 and with an example of its application in Table 5. The root element of this second order transformation reveals all the extensions to XSLT 1.0 used. Among the top elements, there is the import declaration for

Algorithm 6. Orphan simplification

```
<!DOCTYPE xsl:stylesheet [
<!ENTITY xsl "http://www.w3.org/1999/XSL/Transform">
]>
<xsl:stylesheet version="1.0"
      xmlns:func="http://exslt.org/functions"
      xmlns:vishnu="http://www.dcc.fc.up.pt/vishnu"
      xmlns:exslt="http://exslt.org/common"
   xmlns:str="http://exslt.org/strings"
   xmlns:xsl="&xsl;">
  <xsl:import href="../common.xsl" />
  <xsl:output indent="yes" />
  <xsl:template match="xsl:template">
    <xsl:if test="not(
        count(xsl:apply-templates) = 1 and
        (
          (not(@mode) and not(xsl:apply-templates/@mode))
or
          @mode = xsl:apply-templates/@mode
        )                         and count(*) = 1 and
        normalize-space(text())=''
    )">
        <xsl:copy-of select="."/>
  </xsl:if>
  </xsl:template>
</xsl:stylesheet>
```

the common library described above. This single template in this second order transformation removes templates that contain a single apply-template in the same mode of the template, have no other elements besides the apply-templates, and have no content in text nodes but white space.

As can be seen in Algorithm 6, refinements return the original transformation when they cannot be effectively used. Thus, the control of the refinement process is straightforward. The refinement process stops when no change is introduced to the transformation.

VALIDATION

The Vishnu engine was validated in three complementary and interrelated approaches, focusing the:

- Consistency of the generation and refinement process;
- Coverage of the existing rules;
- Adequacy of the Vishnu API to XSLT editing environments.

Consistency and Coverage

By default, Vishnu validates the consistency of the generation and refinement process by checking that each intermediate transformation converts the example source document into the examples target document. After each refinement step, the rewrite engine applies the current version of the transformation to the source example and compares the result with the target document. If this invariant is not satisfied then the refinement process is aborted, and an error is reported to the client. This behaviour is the default in Vishnu. However, it can be switched off by the client to improve the efficiency of generator.

To validate the coverage of the existing rules different scenarios were created. Each scenario includes source and target document and a mapping, as well as the expected program.

The manipulation of a scenario in Vishnu is made by the Scenario class. This class provides a set of methods for testing the Vishnu engine. Typical uses involve a set of scenarios where for each scenario the generated output of the engine is matched with the resources enclosed on the scenario itself. The current scenarios include the conversion of: (1) RSS documents to HTML; (2) Mathematical expressions in MathML to presentation MathML; and (3) Meta-data in LOM (Learning Object Metadata) to RDF. The Figure 7 shows the inner workflow used for testing the RSS to HTML scenario. A mixed-content scenario has not been added since the context component is not yet supporting indexes in text nodes.

Adequacy

Vishnu was conceived as an interactive tool integrated in Eclipse. Nevertheless, it was designed as two autonomous components: the editor and the engine. The editor is an Eclipse plug-in and concentrates all the tasks related with user interaction and integration with other Eclipse tools. The engine concentrates all the tasks related with the automatic creation of an XSLT program from examples using second order transformations. The communication between these two components is regulated by the Vishnu API.

By separating concerns in these two components we enable the non-interactive use of Vishnu. The engine has a command line interface to create XSLT programs from example files. Using Vishnu in this mode is as simple as executing the following command line.

```
$ java vishnu.jar source.xml target.
xml > program.xsl
```

The Vishnu engine can also be invoked from other Java programs through the Vishnu API. This API may be used to create new user interfaces for Vishnu. For instance, a Web interface based on the Google Web Toolkit (GWT) or a Swing-

Figure 7. The RSS to HTML scenario

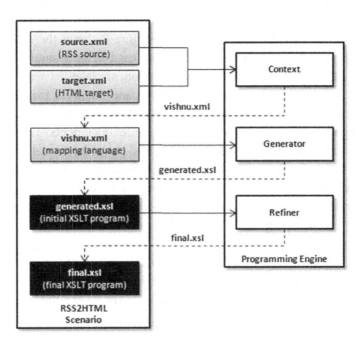

based desktop interface. In general Vishnu may used by any application needing to create XSL transformations from examples. Java programs using the API must instantiate the engine using the static method Engine.getEngine() and use the following methods exposed by the Vishnu API:

```
void setSource(Document source)
    Set source document example for
the intended transformation
Document getSource()
    Get given  source document exam-
ple for the intended transformation
void setTarget(Document target)
    Set  target document example for
the intended transformation
Document getTarget()
    Get given example of target doc-
ument for the intended transformation
void resetPairings()
    Reset all previously defined
pairings
void addPairing(String exprSource,
```

```
String exprTarget)
    Add a pair of XPath location re-
spectively on the source and target
documents
List<Pair> getPairings()
    Returns the list of pairings
void inferPairings()
    Infer pairings from the given
source and target documents
Document program()
    Produce a XSLT program from the
examples and their pairings
Set<String> getFeatureNames()
    Return a list of names of fea-
tures controlling the refinement
process
public boolean getFeature(String
name)
    Get the given feature status
public void setFeature(String name,
boolean value)
    Set the given feature status
```

To validate the adequacy of the Vishnu API we developed a simple Web environment for XSLT programming based on the Google Web Toolkit (GWT), an open source framework for the rapid development of AJAX applications in Java. When the application is deployed, the GWT cross-compiler translates Java classes of the GUI to JavaScript files and guarantees cross-browser portability. The specialized controls are provided by SmartGWT, a GWT API's for SmartClient, a Rich Internet Application (RIA) system.

The graphical interface of the front-end is composed by two panels: Mapping and Program. In the Mapping panel, the "programmer" uses graphical tools to map strings in two XML documents corresponding to a source and a target documents for the intended XSLT transformation.

In the Program panel, the user obtains the resulting XSLT and can continue editing it.

Figure 8 shows the RSS-to-HTML scenario being used on the Vishnu client GUI with its main components labelled with numerals. The Mapping panel includes two side-by-side windows for editing, respectively: (1) the source and (2) the target documents. These documents may be created either from scratch or based in scenarios predefined in the Engine. Regardless of the choice the correspondences between both can be set (3) manually through the Editor or inferred by the Engine.

When setting correspondences manually the programmer is able to pair contents on these windows by selecting and highlighting with color texts where the origin is on the source document and the destination is on the target

Figure 8. Vishnu client front-end

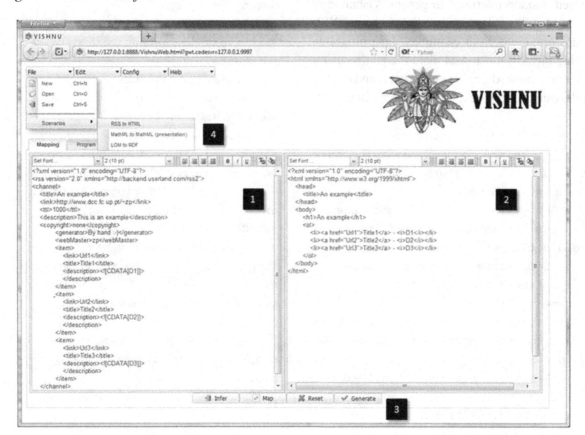

window. Origin and destination must be character data, either text nodes or attribute values.

When automatic correspondence is used Vishnu identifies pairs based on: text matches (text or attribute nodes) or text aggregation. In the first mode strings occurring on text and attribute type nodes on the source document are searched on the text and attribute nodes of the target document, and only exact matches are considered. In the second mode, Vishnu aggregates strings in the source document to create a string in the target document. After automatic pairing, the inferred correspondences are presented in the GUI with colors mapping the two XML documents. The user can then manually reconstruct the pairing of string between both documents.

In complement to creating the source and target documents from scratch, the user can fill in automatically the two rich text editors by using scenarios (4). Each scenario includes source and target document and a mapping, as well as the expected program.

CONCLUSION

In this chapter, we present Vishnu—an XSLT generator engine that aims to produce XSLT programs for processing documents similar to the given examples and with enough readability to be easily understood by a programmer not familiar with the language. At this stage, the generator has already been tested with different scenarios. It still lacks support for transformations with mixed content elements due to current limitations in its XPath locator module. Fixing this limitation is our immediate plans. The project that lead to the development of Vishnu may follow different paths: the engine can be used in other XSLT programming environments; the API of the engine can extended with new functions; and the refinement process can be extended with new refinements. First of all, the Vishnu API was validated with a Web

environment but the appropriate place to apply it would be an IDE with support for XML. Eclipse is particularly suited for this purpose because it is not a XML IDE but rather an IDE for programming in general with tools for handling XML, including XSLT programming. Secondly, the Vishnu engine was designed as a tool for generating simple XSLT programs from examples and can be extended for other uses. The refinement process was designed to improve the quality of a naïve XSLT program automatically generated from examples but can be used to improve any XSLT program. In fact, an interesting side effect of this research is the definition of sort of "canonical XSLT" in terms of second order XSLT transformations. In practical terms we plan to expand the Vishnu API to enable the use of the refinement process on a given XSLT program, rather than only on those generated from examples. This feature may be used in the XSLT programming environment to refractor any XSLT programs, including the generated program after it was edited by the programmer. Finally, Vishnu is an expandable system in the sense that refinements and refinement strategies can be easily integrated. We expect to create new refinements both to improve the quality of automatically generated XSLT programs and to introduce new forms of automatically refactoring existing XSLT programs.

REFERENCES

Hori, M., Ono, K., Abe, M., & Koyanagi, T. (2004). Generating transformational annotation for web document adaptation: Tool support and empirical evaluation. *Journal of Web Semantics*, *2*(1), 1–18. doi:10.1016/j.websem.2004.08.001

Leal, J. P., & Queirós, R. (2010). *Visual programming of XSLT from examples*. Paper presented at 8ª Conferência - XML: Aplicações e Tecnologias Associadas. Vila do Conde, Portugal.

Ono, K., et al. (2002). XSLT stylesheet generation by example with WYSIWYG editing. In *Proceedings of the Symposium on Applications on the Internet (SAINT 2002)*, (pp. 150-159). SAINT.

Pietriga, E., Vion-Dury, J., & Quint, V. (2001). VXT: A visual approach to XML transformations. In *Proceedings of the 2001 ACM Symposium on Document Engineering*. ACM Press.

Spinks, R., Topol, B., Seekamp, C., & Ims, S. (2001). Document clipping with annotation. *IBM DeveloperWorks*. Retrieved from http://www.ibm.com/developerworks/ibm/library/ibmclip/

KEY TERMS AND DEFINITIONS

Application Programming Interface (API): A specification intended to be used as an interface by software components to communicate with each other.

Extensible Markup Language (XML): A markup language that defines a set of rules for encoding documents in a format that is both human-readable and machine-readable.

Extensible Stylesheet Language Transformations (XSLT): A declarative, XML-based language used for the transformation of XML documents.

Formatting Objects Processor (FOP): A Java application that converts XSL Formatting Objects (XSL-FO) files to PDF or other printable formats.

Integrated Development Environment (IDE): A software application that provides comprehensive facilities to computer programmers for software development.

Programming by Example (PbE): An end-user development technique for teaching a computer new behaviour by demonstrating actions on concrete examples.

Refactoring: A technique for restructuring an existing body of code, altering its internal structure without changing its external behaviour.

ENDNOTES

[1] Altova StyleVision – http://www.altova.com/stylevision.html
[2] Stylus Studio – http://www.stylusstudio.com/
[3] Tiger XSLT Mapper – http://www.axizon.com/
[4] XSL Tools – http://marketplace.eclipse.org/content/xsl-tools
[5] oXygen – http://www.oxygenxml.com/eclipse_plugin.html
[6] XMLSpy Eclipse Editor – http://www.altova.com/xmlspy/eclipse-xml-editor.html
[7] OrangevoltXSLT – http://eclipsexslt.sourceforge.net/
[8] X-Assist – http://sourceforge.net/projects/x-assist/
[9] Dexter-xsl – http://code.google.com/p/dexter-xsl/
[10] Formatting Objects Authoring tool – http://foa.sourceforge.net

Chapter 2
A Secure and Dynamic Mobile Identity Wallet Authorization Architecture Based on a XMPP Messaging Infrastructure

Alexandre B. Augusto
University of Porto, Portugal

Manuel E. Correia
University of Porto, Portugal

ABSTRACT

In this chapter, the authors propose and describe an identity management framework that allows users to asynchronously control and effectively share sensitive dynamic data, thus guaranteeing security and privacy in a simple and transparent way. Their approach is realised by a fully secure mobile identity digital wallet, running on mobile devices (Android devices), where users can exercise discretionary control over the access to sensitive dynamic attributes, disclosing their value only to pre-authenticated and authorised users for determined periods of time. For that, the authors rely on an adaptation of the OAuth protocol to authorise and secure the disclosure of personal-private user data by the usage of token exchange and new XML Schemas to establish secure authorisation and disclosure of a set of supported dynamic data types that are being maintained by the personal mobile digital wallet. The communication infrastructure is fully implemented over the XMPP instant messaging protocol and is completely compatible with the public XMPP large messaging infrastructures already deployed on the Internet for real time XML document interchange.

DOI: 10.4018/978-1-4666-2669-0.ch002

INTRODUCTION

The massive aggregation of personal identity attributes is currently one of the most important structural and strategic endeavors currently being carried out all over the Internet. Global Internet companies like *Microsoft, Google,* and *Facebook* are ever more competing over personal user data due to its high strategic commercial value on the market (Gollmann, 2010), making user digital identity a strategic asset that is going to help to redefine what kind of new innovative services are going to be developed and how they are going to be deployed all over the cloud in an interoperable way. This is well illustrated by the current fierce competition being fought by *Google* and *Facebook* about digital identity and their associated authentication, authorization, and data exchange protocols like OpenID (Recordon & Reed, 2006) and OAuth (Hammer-Lahav, 2010).

Currently, identity attributes are normally composed by static values held in the identity management system running in the cloud, which can be a bad idea according to Meiko Jensen (Jensen, Schwenk, Gruschka, & Iacono, 2009). What we intend to do with the work described in this chapter is to expand the universe of managed static identity attributes with dynamic identity attributes that by their very nature are more intimately associated with their owner and therefore can only reside, not in the cloud, but in mobile personal smart devices that follow their owner everywhere and can therefore keep those values up to date on real time. One good example of a dynamic attribute is the GPS coordinates (Lahlou, 2008) of a person that owns a mobile device with GPS.

What we are proposing is to expand the set of current static attributes being managed and held by Internet identity management systems (Tracy, 2008) with a new set of highly dynamic changing attributes. These new identity attributes can be instantiated in classical Identity management systems as symbolic link names that can act as pointers to their real location in the Internet allowing the Relying Party (RP) to locate the digital attribute storage wallets where those dynamic attributes are being maintained and protected.

In this highly dynamic identity infrastructure we are currently developing (Open Federated Environment for the Leveraging of Identity and Authorisation – OFELIA), every time a RP wants to consult the real time value of a certain dynamic attribute it has first to locate the attribute storage wallet where it resides and then ask its owner for permission to access its updated value for a certain period of time, the attribute owner then has the discretionary power to allow or deny that request and provide the RP an OAuth authorisation token, that the RP will present it as proof of previous authorization, every time RP wants to monitor the dynamic attribute during the previously authorised period of time. The attribute owner maintains revocation rights by being able to revoke access at any given moment, thus shifting the balance of power once again to the user, the legitimate owner of the values being monitored and used by cloud services. This is a necessary paradigm shift idea. Highly sensitive dynamic attributes like GPS positioning have high commercial value and therefore access to their updated values should be always put at their owner discretion.

This way privacy is greatly improved by the tools being developed by OFELIA and at the same time users are put into an improved position for bargaining for better services from giant Internet user profiling companies like *Google* and *Facebook* that are constantly taking advantages of users profiles.

It is important to realise that dynamic identity attributes constitute a whole new concept of digital identity because their values are constantly being updated due data owner interactions, the RP has to constantly be able to monitor it as requested. This is easily illustrated by the GPS location scenario, where users usually are in constant movement and their locations are constantly being changed, so only with a dynamic identity attributes the RP can obtain the real near current time position of an individual and not the last time the user or application remembered to update it.

Our major motivation for OFELIA is to create a communication infrastructure based on public XMPP infrastructures, network services, applications, and API libraries to allow sensitive information (Song & Bruza, 2003) such as a GPS position or medical information like a person heartbeat to be exchanged in a secure, reliable, and owner controlled way. Keeping this kind of real time sensitive attributes secure and private between the requester and the data owner is a challenge, especially if the framework makes heavy use of a public XMPP messaging infrastructure like the one currently being operated by *Google*.

We use Android smart mobile phones as our identity digital wallets (Anderson, 2011). Java is native to the Android operating systems so this allows us to have rapidly built a running prototype for user controlled GPS positioning by taking advantage of the numerous libraries, development systems and applications servers which already run on Android. We have used a Java OAuth library (Java OAuth Library, 2011) to handle the authorisation process to data, a XMPP messaging server (der Kinderen, 2011) to exchange messages between the requester and the data owner and new OFELIA XML Schemas to validate the authentication, authorisation, and identity messages exchanged between RP and the Digital Identity wallet on the mobile device (Roussos, Peterson, & Patel, 2003).

The rest of the chapter is organised as follows. In Section 2, we review the system architecture, describing each node, their functionality, and how data flows between the different actors involved. In Section 3, we describe a case scenario of a taxi company using OFELIA framework for tracking passengers, which can be quite useful and helps to illustrate all the messages exchange that has to occur between the consumer and the taxi company to accomplish the task at hand. In Section 4, we described what was accomplished, some preliminary conclusions for the work we have developed thus far for OFELIA, our future plans to the next steps and some development notes about libraries and software that we used to implement our scenario.

ARCHITECTURE

In this section, we describe in the detail the main components of the OFELIA architecture and discuss the reasons behind some of the options and compromises we had to take to make our vision work into mobile world.

We also take time to describe the flow of data and their important aspects like the protocols and services we have used to build our current secure communication infrastructure. For this stage of development we have decided to limit the OFELIA architecture to the development of two types of services, one for the attributes requester (RP or Requester Service) and other for the data owner (identity digital wallet or Endpoint), assuming that the data and its owner are both engaged in the same mobile device. Figure 1 shows the architecture currently being used for this approach.

XMPP: Extensible Messaging and Presence Protocol

XMPP is an open technology for real-time communication that uses the eXtensible Markup Language (XML) as a base format for exchanging information encapsulated into small pieces of XML documents. These XML documents are sent from one entity to other (Saint-Andre, Smith, & Troncon, 2009), using an appropriate application level transport protocol, normally HTTP, through the means of a rendezvous XMPP server that relays these messages to the end-points engaged in communication. XMPP servers provide a high standard set of services that can be used by all kind of client applications.

In OFELIA, our messaging infrastructure relies on the following XMPP instant messaging core services (Saint-Andre, 2004):

- **One-to-One Messaging:** This service, allows the exchange of peer-to-peer XML messages. In OFELIA, currently the peers are the Requester Service and the Endpoint Service (mobile attribute digital wallet).

Figure 1. OFELIA architecture

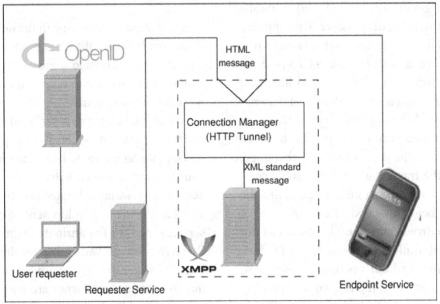

- **Authentication:** This service ensures that both Request Service and Endpoint Service are authenticated by the XMPP server before start any communication over network, the server acts like a gatekeeper for XMPP network access.

- **Presence:** This service, grants OFELIA the capacity of checking entity communication availability. This allows the infrastructure to make different decisions based on entity availability. For example the RP can determine whether the user Digital Wallet is on on-line and optional to send an off-channel message (for example an SMS) to ask the device that holds the Digital Wallet to wake up and go on-line to process some urgent asynchronous request.

- **Contact Lists:** This service allows OFELIA participants to manage a list of trusted entities and thus help a peer to authorise and verify the other peers availability and trustability.

- **Peer-to-Peer Media Sessions:** This service is currently not being used by our

prototype, but this XMPP service, allows a peer to negotiate and manage a media session with another peer, can be really interesting for the future of OFELIA as it enables mobile dynamic attributes to be composed of large and complex audio/video data streams creating new types of usage.

Arguably, in the mobile world, there is some difficulty in directly addressing and communicating with an Internet enabled mobile device. In the mobile world, an implicit direct communication with the device is almost impossible due to the shortage of public IPs addresses faced by Internet service providers. In the near future as we can see in Stallings (1996), IPv6 is supposed to solve this problem; however, it is our strong belief that the mobile Telecommunications operators (Mobicomms) will still not allow for this kind of direct communication to mobile phones due to their very inflexible business plans, where the mobile phone is nowadays mostly regarded simply as a consumer device, not a provider of services, in fact most Telecommunications operators restrict even the ports available to initiate communications and the most greedy of them only allows communication over port 80 (HTTP port).

A neutral rendezvous point on the Internet where both RP and Digital wallet can both meet to exchange messages was thus obviously necessary. Towards this end, XMPP proved to be an almost ideal communication infrastructure for OFELIA architecture because of its core services, namely:

1. Almost real time messaging, essential to maintain our dynamic data types exchange between Request Service and Endpoint Service. Dynamic data requests a constantly and almost instant data exchange.
2. Its ability to operate over HTTP connection by the means of the BOSH (Bidirectional-streams Over Synchronous HTTP) protocol (Paterson & Saint-Andre, 2010), which allow us to bypass the connectivity problems imposed by the overly restricted mobile Internet access from the mobile Telecommunications operators.
3. Its capacity to store and forward messages in case any of the nodes becomes offline, which is proving to be essential for asynchronous communications. At the beginning of the project, asynchronous communications was an important task due the mobile phones sometimes has bad reception of signal resulting on communication problems.
4. Its scalability to avoid bottleneck problems and the fact that it is a mature fully supported and approved Internet standard, widely deployed and an important part of the communication operations and infrastructure of large Internet operators like for example *Google, Facebook, Blizzard,* and *Steam.*

OAuth: Open Authorization

OAuth is an authentication and authorization protocol originally developed for Web applications that provides a standard method for clients to access server resources on behalf of a resource owner. It also provides a process for end-users to authorise third-party access to their server resources without sharing their credentials, using user-agent redirections (Hammer-Lahav, 2010). The most common analogy to this protocol is the valet key, in other words OAuth works look like a valet key for data access, the one who possess the key have temporary and restricted access to the valet key emitter data.

There are three actors involved in an OAuth transaction: The *data owner* (User), a *third party Web application* (TP), and the *User Data Storage* (UDS). Usually a user wants to provide a TP with an authorisation to access his data that resides on a certain UDS. To achieve this, the TP redirects the user user-agent to the UDS with a formalised request where the user is asked to authorise it, this request includes the data that the TP desires to obtain and for how long time TP wants to access it. After authorisation the UDS returns to the TP a signed authorisation token that allow the TP to access the requested data by presenting then, these tokens can be revoked at anytime by user. The security processes involved in the creation and management of authorisation tokens relies on valid digital signatures and on a shared secret between the OAuth consumer (TP) and the OAuth provider (UDS). An example process fully explained and described can be found in Hammer-Lahav (2008).

Currently, in OFELIA both the user and the UDS are at the same place and communicate locally on the same mobile device. Thus, in this case, Oauth communication security is built upon the TP digital X509 certificate and on a session unique key established between the TP and the UDS (Digital Wallet).

This co-location of both the User and the UDS on the same device also have some deep implications in the way the authorisation request and granting process is managed by the means of the OAuth protocol. Since in OFELIA, both user and UDS meet and are located in the same node (the mobile device), when the TP requests access to some identity attribute, an authorisation request appears on the user node showing on whose behalf the authenticated TP is making an access request, what attributes are being requested and for how much time that access must be provided. The user then has to decide whether to grant authorisation, and this can be done in an asynchronous way. Once the authorisation is granted, OAuth will generate and share an access token and a token secret with the TP that must be presented every time it wants to access the authorised user identity attributes. This continues until the OAuth tokens expires or are revoked by the user on the UDS.

OpenID: Open Identity

OpenID provides a decentralized protocol for user authentication. It is used as an Identity Manager (Recordon & Reed, 2006) that allows a user to sign into multiple websites with the same account and at the same time control how much of that account user identity attributes can be shared with the OpenID consumer.

Every time a user authenticates into a website (*Relying Party* [RP]) using OpenID, he is redirected to his OpenID provider, where he is then asked to login and authorise the identity attribute exchange requested by the website (RP). After that, the user is again redirected to the originating RP. In order to standardise and define appropriate semantics for a useful set of user attributes that could be universally recognised by all RPs, the full set of standardised and widely recognised identity attributes for OpenID is substantially reduced. This decreases the usefulness of the protocol and has so far limited its deployment almost exclusively to the authentication domain.

In OFELIA we employ OpenID as an authenticator for the RP (Requester) service. Both the user requester at the Requester (RP) and the user at the UDS need to have a registered OpenID identity that is used in OFELIA to authenticate both identities on the RP. This provides a common account creation and registration process that allows both

endpoints to have a common and coherent way of acquiring and verifying identity data.

Requester Web Service (RWS)

The requester Web service is an integral component of the Rely Party and is composed by a database, an OpenID consumer library, and a XMPP HTTP client library. It uses two XML Schemas to authenticate and validate XMPP communications with the UDS and at the same time maintain appropriate data semantics. It also employs two X509 certificates, both emitted by a common trusted PKI, as a way to assure both endpoints (RP and UDS) identity and establish session keys.

When on behalf of a user requester, an OFELIA RP tries to access someone identity attributes, held on an OFELIA digital wallet, the user requester is first asked to login and authenticate himself using an OpenId account. If this is the user requester first login on the RP, this action initiates an auto-enrolment process where the RWS stores, in its database, the requester OpenID address, name, jabber address, user certificate and mobile number, if they exist as OpenID attributes. This account information can then later be enriched with OFELIA OAuth tokens for some identity attributes being held in remote digital wallets, owned by this same requester or somebody else. If the requester has already been enrolled into the RP, he is just authenticated via OpenID and his OpenID identity attributes can then be transparently updated. After login, the RP, on behalf of the current user, can request and try to get identity data from a remote Digital Wallet by the means of the digital wallet endpoint jabber address. If this jabber address is not yet registered onto the RWS, a XMPP message is sent to this address, requesting registration. If the digital wallet jabber endpoint is not reachable, the RWS can nevertheless send an asynchronous request authentication to the digital identity wallet jabber address. This message is held by the XMPP communication infrastructure until the digital wallet comes online. If there is a mobile phone number available for the digital wallet, the RP can send a SMS to the smart phone where the digital wallet resides, requesting this endpoint to have his digital wallet to connect into the XMPP infrastructure as soon as possible in order to receive the pending OFELIA requests that have been sent by the RP on behalf of the requester. This sms scenario is quite essential since fast battery drain is still one of the smartphone problems (Falaki, Mahajan, & Kandula, 2010).

RWS must have a secure storage, because of storing Oauth tokens could be danger if keys fallen in wrong hands. The security details about authentication between the endpoints and the data exchanged are explained at subsection 2.7 and exemplified at section 3 on subsections 3.1 and 3.2.

Endpoint Web Service (EWS)

The Endpoint service was developed to be deployable on android mobile devices and must take into consideration that the data owner has to personally intervene as a human, during the authorisation process to authorise or decline any request made by a RWS. The EWS is currently composed by a database, both an OAuth consumer and an OAuth provider, a XMPP connector, one X509 certificate to ascertain his identity and two XML Schemas for communication security and OFELIA semantics.

The digital wallet at the EWS must be logged into the XMPP infrastructure with its jabber id and then wait for OFELIA access requests or can be waiting for a sms asking to connect to receive the pending communication. When a request is eventually received, the EWS must validate it against an appropriate XML Schema and process it. In case the requester does not exhibit a valid OAuth token, the digital wallet owner will be asked, by the means of an appropriate GUI, to authorise or deny the access request. This data access requests always contain information about how long RWS wants to access data and a set of

specific data that RWS wants to have access. All granted tokens are stored in a database at the EWS along with identity information of whom they have been emitted to, together with an expiration date determined by the wallet owner that can revoke at anytime any token previous granted. Once a token expires, their rights are revoked and the only way to renew is through a new data access request from RWS.

Thus, in order for the EWS to receive OFELIA requests from an authenticated RWS, it is mandatory for the RWS to have had a remote user authenticated by OpenID, on behalf of which the OFELIA request is being made and provide the EWS with the relevant identity information needed by the wallet owner to make an informed authorisation decision.

The security details about authentication between the endpoints and the data exchanged are explained at subsection 2.7 and exemplified at section 3 on subsections 3.1 and 3.2.

XML Schema

XML Schema allows us to define the structure and data types for XML documents, in our project, we use OFELIA XML Schemas to help maintain system interoperability between services and be able in the future to decouple endpoint services for different OFELIA implementations (McLaughlin & Edelson, 2006). For our framework we employed two different OFELIA XML Schemas, one to handle authentication processes allowing a session key exchange (OfeliaAuth) and the other (OfeliaDataEx) to handle the data exchange and token exchange, it takes place every time a data is requested.

In section 3, we present in more detail an XML exchange flow to better elucidate the documents interchange that can occur in the OFELIA identity infrastructure making it easier to understanding it usage.

*OfeliaAuth*As we can see in Figure 2, the XML Schema employed for session key establishment and user authentication, consists of a root element called *OfeliaAuth* composed by three sub-elements: *Header, User,* and *Authentication.*

The *Header* element carries information about the state of the authentication and the type of the OFELIA request allowing a clear understand of each communication step. The *User* element contains personal user information: a *Jabber id* and an *OpenId identity* to allow EWS verify user requester identity and the RWS *Public key* to exchange a *session symmetric key* in a secure channel. The *Authentication* element is composed by a *challenge* string, ciphered with the Endpoint public key to prove its identity and a blank attribute (*Session Key*) used to return a ciphered *session symmetric key.*

OfeliaDataEx

As we can see in Figure 3 the XML Schema employed for identity data exchange consists of a root element called *OfeliaDataEx*, once again composed by three elements: *Header, User* and *Data.*

At the *Header* element we keep information about the *state* of the data exchange and the *type* of the *OFELIA* request allowing a clear understand of each communication step like on OfeliaAuth. At the *User* element, we have the user *Jabber id,* his *OpenId Address* and *OAuth Tokens,* composed by three attributes: *AuthorizationToken, TokenSecret* and *ExpireDate*, the usage of these attributes was explained on section 2 at subsection 2.2. The *Data* element is composed by optional elements, describing the nature of the dynamic identity attribute being described. Currently we have a *GPS* element defined with *latitude, longitude,* and a *timestamp.*

We are currently defining several other elements to describe other dynamic attributes like *heartbeat, blood pressure*, etc. That could prove to be useful for remote monitoring Web applications. The *Data* element can thus contain highly diverse types of formalised dynamic data types, to cover a highly diverse range of application areas.

In other words, we can provide for all kind of personal dynamic attributes so long as its data type is formalised in the OfeliaDataEx XML Schema. It is also mandatory that all dynamic

Figure 2. XML schema for OfeliaAuth

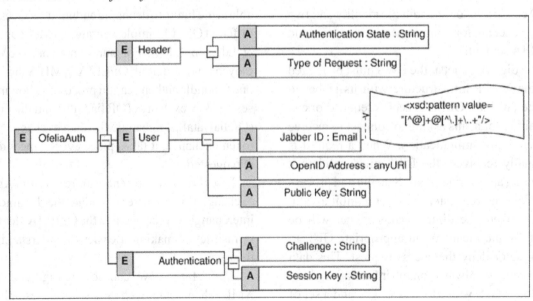

Figure 3. XML schema for Ofelia data exchange

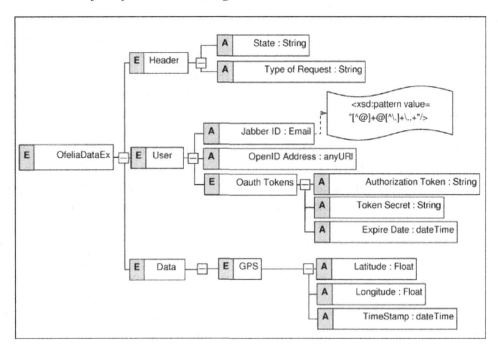

type elements have a valid *timestamp* attribute, not only to be able to maintain an historic value for its values but also to prevent the resending of the same value during different data exchanges.

Data Flow

OFELIA data flow interactions are divided into two main different operational phases:

1. The *OfeliaAuth* handles the authentication process, and it works by exchanging a symmetric session key, using a challenge-response cryptographic scheme ciphered with RWS and EWS public keys, that is then employed to set a secure tunnel between the RWS and the EWS.
2. The *OfeliaDataEx* phase handles the creation and management of OAuth access tokens and the subsequent identity data consultation.

Assuming both Web services have already been logged on into a trusted XMPP messaging infrastructure and that at every step, XML data documents are validate by the appropriate XML Schema, the data flow for authentication and the establishment of a secure communication channel are accomplished by the following three steps:

•   The RWS generates an *OfeliaAuth* XML data document, generates a random challenge string ciphered by the EWS public key from the mandatory previous register on RWS and completes the others attributes leaving only the *session key* in blank. It then sends the XML filled document to EWS by XMPP established connection as can be seen in Figure 4a under subsection 3.1.

•   The EWS verifies the requester data, deciphers the challenge and ciphers it again with the RWS public key received on XML. It then generates a session key to set on the attribute *Session Key* and sends it back to the RWS, ciphered with the RWS public key. This is illustrated on Figure 4b under subsection 3.1.

- The RWS deciphers the challenge and if is valid, it stores and sets the received attribute *Key* as a session key to secure the subsequent communication phase of OFELIA. Now RWS and EWS can communicate via a secure channel using the established symmetric session key.

The data flow for OAuth tokens management and data exchange are accomplished in six simple steps, four steps for OAuth token management and the others two steps for identity data consultation.

These six steps are ciphered and deciphered with the established session symmetric key obtained in the previous phase, resulting in a secure channel of communication between the RWS and EWS:

- The RWS presents an *OfeliaDataEx* document, with a valid *User* element and with an appropriate *Header* to request the identity data and sends it by XMPP to the EWS. This is illustrated by the Figure 5a under subsection 3.2.
- On receiving an *OfeliaDataEx* document, the EWS updates the *header*, sets the *data* types available with an empty value and sends it back to the RWS. This is illustrated by the Figure 5b under subsection 3.2.
- On receiving the partially filled *OfeliaDataEx* document, the RWS updates the *header*, deletes any identity attribute it does not want to consult, sets the attribute *ExpireDate* and sends the updated *OfeliaDataEx* document to the EWS. This is illustrated by the Figure 6a under subsection 3.2.
- On receiving an *OfeliaDataEx* document with the the attribute *ExpireDate* set, the EWS uses the information provided by the document to ask the owner of the identity attributes whether he authorises the consultation of these attributes by the entity whose

identity is described in the *OfeliaDataEx* document. If the authorisation is granted the EWS then updates the *header*, generates OAuth tokens for the requested attributes and fill then into the *AuthorizationToken* and *TokenSecret* attributes. It then sends the updated *OfeliaDataEx* document back to RWS. This is illustrated by the Figure 6b under subsection 3.2.

- On receiving an *OfeliaDataEx* document with OAuth *tokens*, the RWS updates the *header* for data request, stores the tokens and their expire date, set the timestamps with the last timestamp received for the requested data and sends the just updated *OfeliaDataEx* document with OAuth *tokens* back to the EWS. This is illustrated by the Figure 7a under subsection 3.2.
- On receiving an *OfeliaDataEx* document with OAuth *tokens* and a *timestamp*, the EWS updates the *header*, verifies the validity of the presented OAuth *tokens*, and fills the data element of the *OfeliaDataEx* with an array of dynamic type elements with the historic set of values the dynamic type has assumed on the Digital Wallet since the *timestamp* just received on the *OfeliaDataEx* document. It then sends the document back to RWS. This is illustrated by the Figure 7b under subsection 3.2.

USAGE CASE SCENARIO

In this section, we are going to describe a concrete case scenario to help a better understanding and illustrate how the OFELIA XML Schemas can be used within the XMPP infrastructure for a RP to get access authorisation and then subsequently present authorisation tokens to monitor dynamic attributes from a remote digital wallet held on a mobile device. For illustration purposes, we are going to explore a real case scenario where a

Web application is authorised to monitor a user by the means of the GPS device he has on its mobile phone.

Let us assume that a taxi company—let us name it "We know where you are"—decides to use our system to implement an innovative service on the Internet for its customers.

The taxi company releases a mobile application with our endpoint OFELIA Web service for smart phones to track clients GPS data. Every time a passenger needs a taxi he utilizes the application to request the service, after that the company cloud application requests the passenger for authorisation, using the OFELIA infrastructure to have for the next quarter of an hour temporary access to the costumer digital wallet to track the costumer geographic location thus allowing the nearest taxi driver to find him. This solves problems like unknown roads and moving costumers. Since the tracking authorisation is temporary the costumer privacy is protected because that information is only disclosed when the costumer is in need of service and everything is kept under his own control in other words the passenger can revoke the authorization to access their location at any time.

For a better comprehension of the data flow we are going to present a simplified XML OFE-LIA flow of documents for this scenario, the taxi company Internet cloud application acts as an OFELIA RP and the mobile application on the costumer phone acts as an OFELIA digital wallet.

XML Data Flow for Authentication

A customer decides to request a taxi using the mobile application. The taxi company then acts as a requester Web service and sends a XML document request with a challenge, the mobile processes the XML document request and replies with a *symmetric session key* that will be used to secure all future communication, as illustrated in Figure 4.

XML Data Flow of Data Exchange

After the establishment of an OFELIA session, the taxi company application sends a request to determine what types of dynamic identity attributes the costumer holds in his identity wallet. The mobile phone processes the request and sends the XML document back with a response, where the *Data* entity is properly filled with the relevant information. This process is illustrated in Figure 5.

Figure 4. OFELIA XML data from authentication method

```
<OfeliaAuth>
  <HEADER>
    <AuthState>INITIAL</AuthState><TypeReq>REQ</TypeReq>
  </HEADER>
  <USER>
    <JabberID>taxiservice@jabeber.com</JabberID>
    <OpenID>http://taxiservice.openids.com</OpenID>
    <PubKey>...</PubKey>
  </USER>
  <Authentication>
    <Challenge>1f3rw23fggec65fab916e2b6bheu2kl9u3</Challenge>
    <SessionKey></SessionKey>
  </Authentication>
</OfeliaAuth>
```

(a) Request

```
<OfeliaAuth>
  <HEADER>
    <AuthState>ACCEPTED</AuthState><TypeReq>ASW</TypeReq>
  </HEADER>
  <USER>
    <JabberID>taxiservice@jabeber.com</JabberID>
    <OpenID>http://taxiservice.openids.com</OpenID>
    <PubKey>...</PubKey>
  </USER>
  <Authentication>
    <Challenge>23mkqwdjbiu3basdu3fvwviu3ubugyw87ugf</Challenge>
    <SessionKey>6f803f09cy5fdg916edwsd2b6bd9953d549e</SessionKey>
  </Authentication>
</OfeliaAuth>
```

(b) Response

The taxi company requester now deletes from the XML response every data type supported by the remote digital wallet, except for the GPS dynamic identity attribute. It then sends the updated document back to the mobile phone, requesting access OAuth tokens with an appropriate small expiration date. On reception, the customer is asked by the mobile phone application to accept the request and grant access to the GPS. The mobile phone then sends the response back to the company application with valid OAuth tokens. Figure 6 illustrates this process.

With the tokens now stored on the company application, the taxi company now sends an OFELIA request each 5 seconds to monitor the costumer GPS location data. If the OAuth authorisation tokens are correct and correspond previously established session, the costumer mobile replies with an XML response with the GPS entity data correctly filled with updated data. This information is the relayed to the nearest taxi driver that can thus temporarily track the costumer and find him in the shortest possible time. This can be observed on Figure 7.

Reverse Taxi Scenario

Let us assume that the taxi company "We know where you are" made a huge success with this system and now they are studying the possibility of a reverse scenario, in other words both taxi and client will know their current position. As we already saw in our case scenario this case is completely possible.

The taxi company will have to update both the company cloud application and the mobile application; these applications will have to do EWS and RWS service at same time at both nodes to allow mutual tracking.

Every time a passenger needs a taxi, he starts the taxi company mobile application to request the service. At the same time, the mobile application demands access to the taxi GPS data. Now the company cloud application requests the passenger for authorisation to track his position for the next quarter of an hour or until both nodes find each other in a single point, after passenger grants permission the company cloud application have to assign the nearest taxi and authorise GPS data track of the assigned taxi to the passenger. Now both the passenger and the taxis driver can locate

Figure 5. OFELIA XML data from data list request

```
<OfeliaDataEx>
  <HEADER>
    <State>DATALIST</State><TypeReq>REQ</TypeReq>
  </HEADER>
  <USER>
    <JabberID>taxiservice@jabeber.com</JabberID>
    <OpenID>http://taxiservice.openids.com</OpenID>
    <OauthTokens>
      <AuthToken></AuthToken>
      <TokenSecret></TokenSecret>
      <ExpireDate></ExpireDate>
    </OauthTokens>
  </USER>
  <Data></Data>
</OfeliaDataEx>
```

```
<OfeliaDataEx>
  <HEADER>
    <State>DATALIST</State><TypeReq>ASW</TypeReq>
  </HEADER>
  <USER>
    <JabberID>taxiservice@jabeber.com</JabberID>
    <OpenID>http://taxiservice.openids.com</OpenID>
    <OauthTokens>
      <AuthToken></AuthToken>
      <TokenSecret></TokenSecret>
      <ExpireDate></ExpireDate>
    </OauthTokens>
  </USER>
  <Data>
    <GPS>
      <Latitude></Latitude>
      <Longitude></Longitude>
      <TimeStamp></TimeStamp>
    </GPS>
  </Data>
</OfeliaDataEx>
```

(a) Request

(b) Response

Figure 6. OFELIA XML data from tokens request

```
<OfeliaDataEx>
  <HEADER>
    <State>TOKENS</State><TypeReq>REQ</TypeReq>
  </HEADER>
  <USER>
    <JabberID>taxiservice@jabeber.com</JabberID>
    <OpenID>http://taxiservice.openids.com</OpenID>
    <OauthTokens>
      <AuthToken></AuthToken>
      <TokenSecret></TokenSecret>
      <ExpireDate>2012-05-30T09:00:00</ExpireDate>
    </OauthTokens>
  </USER>
  <Data>
    <GPS>
      <Latitude></Latitude>
      <Longitude></Longitude>
      <TimeStamp></TimeStamp>
    </GPS>
  </Data>
</OfeliaDataEx>
```

(a) Request

```
<OfeliaDataEx>
  <HEADER>
    <State>TOKENS</State><TypeReq>ASW</TypeReq>
  </HEADER>
  <USER>
    <JabberID>taxiservice@jabeber.com</JabberID>
    <OpenID>http://taxiservice.openids.com</OpenID>
    <OauthTokens>
      <AuthToken>6d03af09c65fab916e2b6bd8853d549e</AuthToken>
      <TokenSecret>884f1e27f15050586881b952c1c2b711</TokenSecret>
      <ExpireDate>2012-05-30T09:00:00</ExpireDate>
    </OauthTokens>
  </USER>
  <Data>
    <GPS>
      <Latitude></Latitude>
      <Longitude></Longitude>
      <TimeStamp></TimeStamp>
    </GPS>
  </Data>
</OfeliaDataEx>
```

(b) Response

Figure 7. OFELIA XML data from data exchange

```
<OfeliaDataEx>
  <HEADER>
    <State>DATA</State><TypeReq>REQ</TypeReq>
  </HEADER>
  <USER>
    <JabberID>taxiservice@jabeber.com</JabberID>
    <OpenID>http://taxiservice.openids.com</OpenID>
    <OauthTokens>
      <AuthToken>6d03af09c65fab916e2b6bd8853d549e</AuthToken>
      <TokenSecret>884f1e27f15050586881b952c1c2b711</TokenSecret>
      <ExpireDate>2012-05-30T09:00:00</ExpireDate>
    </OauthTokens>
  </USER>
  <Data>
    <GPS>
      <Latitude></Latitude>
      <Longitude></Longitude>
      <TimeStamp>2011-04-01T09:00:00</TimeStamp>
    </GPS>
  </Data>
</OfeliaDataEx>
```

(a) Request

```
<OfeliaDataEx>
  <HEADER>
    <State>DATA</State><TypeReq>ASW</TypeReq>
  </HEADER>
  <USER>
    <JabberID>taxiservice@jabeber.com</JabberID>
    <OpenID>http://taxiservice.openids.com</OpenID>
    <OauthTokens>
      <AuthToken>6d03af09c65fab916e2b6bd8853d549e</AuthToken>
      <TokenSecret>884f1e27f15050586881b952c1c2b711</TokenSecret>
      <ExpireDate>2012-05-30T09:00:00</ExpireDate>
    </OauthTokens>
  </USER>
  <Data>
    <GPS>
      <Latitude>41.152544</Latitude>
      <Longitude>-8.640651</Longitude>
      <TimeStamp>2011-04-01T09:05:00</TimeStamp>
    </GPS>
  </Data>
</OfeliaDataEx>
```

(b) Response

each other, and if passenger wishes he can walk to into taxis direction to speed up the encounter.

CONCLUSION

In this chapter, we have described how the OFELIA XMPP communication infrastructure implements a user empowering way of disclosing sensitive dynamic attributes held on mobile devices. The whole process relies as much as possible on standard well established services and protocols like OAuth, XMPP and openID, thus allowing for a simpler implementation and rapid service deployment. We are currently developing a working prototype composed of a Rely Party and a digital wallet held on a Android mobile devices that uses the *Google* XMPP messaging service to exchange documents in a secure and private way. Our prototype allow the Rely Party to track the mobile phone user real time GPS position after a previous authorisation by mobile device user and plots its location using the *Google* map service for the periods of time authorised by the user.

We introduced a new concept of data type that we named Dynamic Identity Attribute (DIA). This new type of data opened a whole new range of opportunities and possibilities due the ability to allow data be Processed as Requested (PaR). In other words, every time a rely party requests the digital attribute storage wallet a DIA, this data value is processed in real time, for static attributes DIA does not present great advantages (unless data is sensitive), since static attributes do not constantly update but still have the advantage of the user being its own data storage and sharing information only with third parties of its trust. However, this scenario has a considerable change and becomes essential when we use DIA with volatile data, because of its high constant value change, PaR becomes mandatory to keep a coherent timeline of data requested.

This digital identity infrastructure comes at a time where there is a real need for the users to gain back some control of their own privacy and only disclose their most sensitive identity attributes when they need a service from the Internet that really requires access to this data to work, and this for only a very limited period of time, kept under strict control by the user data owner.

With our OFELIA prototype, we have also proved that XMPP, with its very rich set of working extension services, constitutes an excellent choice for network communication, allowing us to quickly set up a system ready to manage and implement complex data exchange processes in almost real time. With XMPP problems like connection restrictions, offline messages, or security are readily solved in a standard way, as has been previously described at section 2 on subsection 2.1

Future Work

In the near future, OFELIA will have planned several tasks to implement, namely:

- **EWS on Mobile Phone:** OFELIA is still running on desktop computers, with the digital wallet set to run on an Android emulator. The next step will be to deploy the EWS directly into a real android mobile phone with a GPS. We have already done feasibility studies and experiments about running Web services on Android devices and found the Web container called i-jetty (I-Jetty Community, 2011) to be a good choice to run the EWS on a mobile phone.

- **RWS and EWS as One:** At this moment our identity digital wallet only generate and manage their own access tokens working only as a personal secure data storage but in a near future we plan to expand the wallet as a data requester too, allowing users to request data too. This expansion is quite interesting and important to OFELIA success; users will have the possibility to request other users for their data letting users share information like GPS position in real time, problems like lost friends in roads will never happen anymore.

- **More Dynamic Identity Attributes XML Schemas:** We want to expand OFELIA to other application areas. The eHealth sector (Marchibroda, 2007) is one area where there is a real need to remote monitor patients in a secure privacy oriented way. This is currently done with highly expensive equipment with no provision at all for the patient privacy. With OFELIA we want to be able to the same thing in a better way, by taking care of the patients privacy and the same time provide remote monitoring services with much less expensive equipment, mainly composed of Android phones and Bluetooth compatible body sensors capable of monitoring the patient heart beat, body temperature, blood pressure, etc.

- **Define Others Authentication Methods:** After some research, we are studying new possibilities of authentication like the Mobile Secure Card (MSC). This microSD card brings the usual flash memory plus a smart card chip giving us a strong authentication due the advantages of a smart-card explained in Poitner (2008). We are studying too a possibility of the usage of Portuguese citizen card via a Bluetooth to authenticate.

- **RWS as an API:** To allow for good extensibility, usability, and portability of the system, it is essential in the future to program the RWS with the help of an easy to use decoupled API for an easy integration of monitoring services into many different Web applications without the programmer having to know about the intricate details of the OFELIA XML document interchange and OAuth tokens.

- **Symbolic Links to Sensitive Data:** As we already said, we want to establish a formal way for this symbolic links aiming standardization over network. After a service get a symbolic link it will be possible to that service know what type of data it is requesting and what is the next hop it needs to ask about the desired data.

Development Notes

As already mentioned, to implement OFELIA architecture we relied on some libraries and software. In this sub-section, we exposed the libraries, their versions, and their respective links:

OpenID Consumer Library:

- Openid4java;
- Version: 0.9.5.593;

- Download link: http://openid4java.google-code.com/files/openid4java-full-0.9.5.593.tar.gz.

OAuth provider and consumer libraries:

- Oauth - API needz authorized?
- Revision: 8278;
- Download link: http://code.google.com/p/google-web-toolkit/source/browse/tools/lib/oauth/?r=8278.

XMPP BOSH Client Connector:

- Ignite realtime SMACK API;
- Revision: 12894;
- Svn link: http://svn.igniterealtime.org/svn/repos/smack/branches/bosh/.

XMPP Test Server:

- Ignite Realtime Openfire;
- Version: 3.6.4;
- Linux download link: http://www.igniterealtime.org/downloads/download-landing.jsp?file=openfire/openfire_3_6_4.tar.gz.

ACKNOWLEDGMENT

This work is funded by the ERDF through the Programme COMPETE and by the Portuguese Government through FCT – Foundation for Science and Technology, project OFELIA ref. PTDC/EIA-EIA/104328/2008 and is being conducted with the institutional support provided by DCC/FCUP and the facilities and research environment gracefully provided by the CRACS (Center for Research in Advanced Computing Systems) research unit, an INESC TEC Porto associate of the Faculty of Science, University of Porto.

REFERENCES

Anderson, R. (2011). *Can we fix security economics of federated authentication?* Cambridge, UK: University of Cambridge. doi:10.1007/978-3-642-25867-1_4

der Kinderen, G. (2011). *Openfire XMPP server.* Retrieved April 14, 2011, from http://bit.ly/openfireServer

Falaki, H., Mahajan, R., & Kandula, S. (2010). Diversity in smartphone usage. In *Proceedings of the 8th International Conference on Mobile Systems, Applications, and Services.* New York, NY: ACM Press.

Gollmann, D. (2010). *Computer security.* New York, NY: John Wiley & Sons, Inc.

Hammer-Lahav, E. (2008). *Security architecture.* Retrieved April 14, 2011, from http://bit.ly/OAuthToken

Hammer-Lahav, E. (2010). *The OAuth 1.0 protocol (RFC5849).* Retrieved April 14, 2011, from http://tools.ietf.org/html/rfc5849

Harold, E. R., & Means, W. S. (2002). *XML in a nutshell.* Sebastopol, CA: O'Reilly & Associates, Inc.

I-Jetty Community. (2011). *I-jetty: Webserver for the android mobile platform.* Retrieved April 14, 2011, from https://code.google.com/p/i-jetty

Igniterealtime.org. (2011). *Smack API.* Retrieved April 14, 2011, from http://www.igniterealtime.org/projects/smack/

Java OAuth Library. (2011). *OAuth API needz authorized?* Retrieved April 14, 2011, from http://bit.ly/OAuthLib

Jensen, M., Schwenk, J., Gruschka, N., & Iacono, L. (2009). On technical security issues in cloud computing. In *Proceedings of the IEEE International Conference on Cloud Computing,* (pp. 109-116). IEEE Press.

Lahlou, S. (2008). Identity, social status, privacy and face-keeping in digital society. *Social Science Information.* Retrieved from http://ssi.sagepub.com/content/47/3/299.abstract

Marchibroda, J. M. (2007). Health information exchange policy and evaluation. *Journal of Biomedical Informatics,* 40(6), S11–S16. doi:10.1016/j.jbi.2007.08.008

McLaughlin, B., & Edelson, J. (2006). *Java and XML.* New York, NY: O'Reilly.

Paterson, I., & Saint-Andre, P. (2010). *XEP-0206: XMPP over BOSH.* Retrieved April 14, 2011, from http://bit.ly/xep0206

Poitner, M. (2008). Mobile security becomes reality. *The Mobile Security Card.* Retrieved April 14, 2011, from http://www.ctst.com/CTST08/pdf/Poitner.pdf

Recordon, D., & Reed, D. (2006). OpenID 2.0: A platform for user-centric identity management. In *Proceedings of the Second ACM Workshop on Digital Identity Management,* (pp. 11-16). ACM Press.

Roussos, G., Peterson, D., & Patel, U. (2003). Mobile identity management: An enacted view. *International Journal of Electronic Commerce,* 8(1), 81–100.

Saint-Andre, P. (Ed.). (2004). *Extensible messaging and presence protocol (XMPP): Core.* RFC 3920. Retrieved from http://www.ietf.int

Saint-André, P., Smith, K., & Tronçon, R. (2009). *Definitive guide series.* New York, NY: O'Reilly.

Song, D., & Bruza, P. (2003). Towards context sensitive information inference. *Journal of the American Society for Information Science and Technology, 54*, 321–334. doi:10.1002/asi.10213

Stallings, W. (1996). IPv6: The new internet protocol. *IEEE International Communications Magazine, 34*, 96–108. doi:10.1109/35.526895

Tracy, K. (2008). Identity management systems. *IEEE Potentials, 27*, 34–37. doi:10.1109/MPOT.2008.929295

Chapter 3
Making Programming Exercises Interoperable with PExIL

Ricardo Queirós
CRACS and ESEIG/IPP, Porto, Portugal

José Paulo Leal
University of Porto, Portugal

ABSTRACT

Several standards have appeared in recent years to formalize the metadata of learning objects, but they are still insufficient to fully describe a specialized domain. In particular, the programming exercise domain requires interdependent resources (e.g. test cases, solution programs, exercise description) usually processed by different services in the programming exercise lifecycle. Moreover, the manual creation of these resources is time-consuming and error-prone, leading to an obstacle to the fast development of programming exercises of good quality. This chapter focuses on the definition of an XML dialect called PExIL (Programming Exercises Interoperability Language). The aim of PExIL is to consolidate all the data required in the programming exercise lifecycle from when it is created to when it is graded, covering also the resolution, the evaluation, and the feedback. The authors introduce the XML Schema used to formalize the relevant data of the programming exercise lifecycle. The validation of this approach is made through the evaluation of the usefulness and expressiveness of the PExIL definition. In the former, the authors present the tools that consume the PExIL definition to automatically generate the specialized resources. In the latter, they use the PExIL definition to capture all the constraints of a set of programming exercises stored in a learning objects repository.

DOI: 10.4018/978-1-4666-2669-0.ch003

INTRODUCTION

The concept of Learning Object (LO) is fundamental for producing, sharing, and reusing content in eLearning (Friesen, 2005). In essence a LO is a container with educational material and metadata describing it. Since most LOs just present content to students, they contain documents in presentation formats such as HTML and PDF, and metadata describing these documents using mostly Learning Objects Metadata (LOM) or other generic metadata format. When a LO includes exercises to be automatically evaluated by an eLearning system, it must contain a document with a formal description for each exercise. The Question and Tests Interoperability (QTI) (IMS Global, 2012) is an example of a standard for this kind of definitions that is supported by several eLearning systems. However, QTI was designed for questions with predefined answers and cannot be used for complex evaluation domains such as the programming exercise evaluation (Queiros & Leal, 2009). A programming exercise requires a collection of files (e.g. test cases, solution programs, exercise descriptions, feedback) and special data (e.g. compilation and execution lines). These resources are interdependent and processed in different moments in the lifecycle of a programming exercise.

The lifecycle comprises several phases: in the creation phase the content author should have the means to automatically create some of the resources (assets) related to the programming exercise such as the exercise description and test cases and the possibility to package and distribute them in a standard format across all the compatible systems such as Learning Management Systems (LMS) and Learning Object Repositories (LOR); in the selection phase the teacher must be able to search for a programming exercise based on its metadata from a repository of learning objects and store a reference to it in a learning manage-

ment system; in the presentation phase the student must be able to choose the exercise description in its native language and a proper format (e.g. HTML, PDF); in the resolution phase the learner should have the possibility to use test cases to test an attempt to solve the exercise and the possibility of automatically generating new ones; in the evaluation phase the evaluation engine should receive specialized metadata to properly evaluate the learner's attempt and return enlightening feedback. All these phases require a set of interdependent resources and specialized metadata whose manual creation would be time-consuming and error-prone.

This chapter focuses on the definition of an XML dialect called PExIL (Programming Exercises Interoperability Language). The aim of PExIL is to consolidate all the data required in the programming exercise lifecycle, from when it is created to when it is graded, covering also the resolution, the evaluation and the feedback. We introduce the XML Schema used to formalize the relevant data of the programming exercise lifecycle. The validation of this approach is made through the evaluation of the usefulness and expressiveness of the PExIL definition. In the former, we use a PExIL definition to generate several resources related to the programming exercise lifecycle (e.g. exercise descriptions, test cases, feedback files). In the latter, we check if the PExIL definition covers all the constraints of a set of programming exercises stored in a learning objects repository.

The remainder of this chapter is organized as follows. Section 2 traces the evolution of standards for LO metadata and packaging. In the following section, we present the PExIL schema with emphasis on the definitions for the description, test cases, and feedback of the programming exercise. Then, we evaluate the definition of PExIL and conclude with a summary of the main contributions of this work and a perspective on future research.

LEARNING OBJECT STANDARDS

The increasing popularity of programming contests worldwide resulted in the creation of several contest management systems. At the same time Computer Science courses use programming exercises to encourage the practice on programming. The interoperability between these types of systems is becoming a topic of interest in the scientific community. In order to address these interoperability issues several problem formats were developed such as CATS[1], FreeProblemSet (FPS)[2], Mooshak Exchange Format (MEF)[3], and Peach Exchange Format (PEF)[4]. However several issues were found regarding their expressiveness and proliferation over the Web. The majority of the formats only describe how the program should be compiled and executed and how the statement is composed. The latter issue is due to the fact that these formats are deeply related with the contest management systems that adopted them. Thus, they do not comply with any generic standard for describing, packaging, and deployment of the exercises such as the concept of learning objects.

Current LO standards are quite generic and not adequate to specific domains, such as the definition of programming exercises. The most widely used standard for LO is the IMS Content Packaging (IMS CP) (IMS Global, 2012). This content packaging format uses an XML manifest file wrapped with other resources inside a zip file. The manifest includes the IEEE Learning Object Metadata (LOM) standard (IEEE, 2002) to describe the learning resources included in the package. However, LOM was not specifically designed to accommodate the requirements of automatic evaluation of programming exercises. For instance, there is no way to assert the role of specific resources, such as test cases or solutions. Fortunately, IMS CP was designed to be straightforward to extend, meeting the needs of a target user community through the creation of application profiles. When applied to metadata the term Application Profile generally refers to "the adaptation, constraint, and/or augmentation of a metadata scheme to suit the needs of a particular community" (IMS Global, 2012). A well-known eLearning application profile is SCORM (ADL Net, 2012) that extends IMS CP with more sophisticated sequencing and Contents-to-LMS communication.

The creation of application profiles aims to meet the needs of the target user community, aid integration and enhance interoperability between tools and services of the community. The creation is based on one or more of the following approaches (Friesen, 2004):

1. Selection of a core sub-set of elements and fields from the source schema;
2. Addition of elements and/or fields (normally termed extensions) to the source schema, thus generating the derived schema;
3. Substitution of a vocabulary with a new, or extended vocabulary to reflect terms in common usage within the target community;
4. Description of the semantics and common usage of the schema as they are to be applied across the community.

Following this extension philosophy, the IMS Global Learning Consortium (GLC) upgraded the Question and Test Interoperability (QTI) specification (IMS Global, 2012). QTI describes a data model for questions and test data and, from version 2, extends the LOM with its own metadata vocabulary. QTI was designed for questions with a set of pre-defined answers, such as multiple choice, multiple response, fill-in-the-blanks and short text questions. It supports also long text answers but the specification of their evaluation is outside the scope of the QTI. Although long text answers could be used to write the program's source code, there is no way to specify how it should be compiled and executed, which test data should be used and how it should be graded. For these reasons, we consider that QTI is not adequate for automatic evaluation of programming exercises (Queiros

& Leal, 2009), although it may be supported for sake of compatibility with some LMS. Recently, IMS GLC proposed the IMS Common Cartridge (CC) (IMS Global, 2012) that bundles the previous specifications.

The IMS Common Cartridge specification defines an open format for the distribution of rich Web-based content. Its main goal is to organize and distribute digital learning content and to ensure the interchange of content across any Common Cartridge conformant tools. The latest revised version (1.1) was released in May 2011. The IMS CC package organizes and describes a learning object based on two levels of interoperability: content and communication as depicted Figure 1 (Queiros & Leal, 2012). In the content level, the IMS CC includes two types of resources:

- **Web Content Resources (WCR):** Static Web resources that are supported on the Web such as HTML files, GIF/JPEG images, PDF documents, etc.
- **Learning Application Objects (LAO):** Special resource types that require additional processing before they can be imported and represented within the target

system. Physically, a LAO consists of a directory in the content package containing a descriptor file and optionally additional files used exclusively by that LAO. Examples of Learning Application Objects include QTI assessments, Discussion Forums, Web links, etc.

In the communication level, the cartridge describes how the target tool of the cartridge (usually a LMS) should communicate with other remote Web applications using the IMS Basic Learning Tools Interoperability (LTI) specification (IMS BLTI, 2010). The LTI is a common interoperability specification that is increasingly supported by major LMS vendors. It provides a uniform standards-based extension point in LMS allowing remote tools and content to be integrated into LMSs. The main goal of the LTI is to standardize the process for building links between learning tools and the LMS. The IMS launched also a subset of the full LTI v1.0 specification called IMS Basic LTI. This subset exposes a unidirectional link between the LMS and the application. However, there is no provision for accessing run-time services in the LMS and only one security policy[5] is supported.

Figure 1. Common cartridge content hierarchy

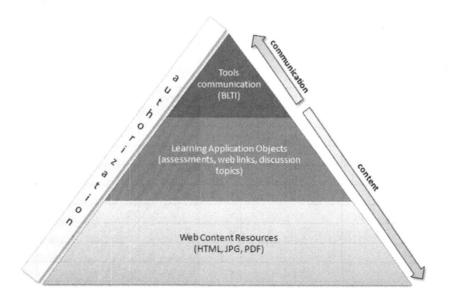

PExIL

In this section we present PExIL—Programming Exercises Interoperability Language—an XML dialect that aims to consolidate all the data required in the programming exercise life-cycle. This covers all the programs that receives data from the standard input and, after data process, send the results for the standard output. This dialect is formalized through the creation of a XML Schema. In the following subsections, we present the PExIL XML Schema organized in three groups of elements:

- **Textual**: Elements with general information about the exercise to be presented to the learner (e.g. title, date, challenge);
- **Specification**: Elements with a set of restrictions that can be used for generating specialized resources (e.g. test cases, feedback);
- **Programs**: Elements with references to programs as external resources (e.g. solution program, correctors) and metadata about those resources (e.g. compilation, execution line, hints).

Textual Elements

Textual elements contain general information about the exercise to be presented to the learner. This type of elements can be used in several phases of the programming exercise life-cycle: in the selection phase as exercise metadata to aid discoverability and to facilitate the interoperability among other systems such as LMS or even Integrated Development Environments (IDE); in the presentation phase as content to be presented to the learner (e.g. exercise description); in the resolution phase as skeleton code to be included in the student's project solution.

Table 1 presents the textual elements of the PExIL schema and identifies the phases where they are involved.

The title element represents the title of the programming exercise. This mandatory element uses the xml:lang attribute to specify the human language of the element's content. The definition of this element in the XML Schema has the maxOccurs attribute set to unbound allowing the same information to be recorded in multiple languages. The creation element contains data on the authorship of the exercise and includes the following sub-elements: author with information about the name(s) of the author(s); date which includes the date of the generation of the exercise, event which describes the event for which the

Table 1. Textual elements

Element	Selection	Presentation	Resolution	Evaluation
title	x	x		
creation/author	x	x		
creation/date	x	x		
creation/event	x	x		
creation/institution	x	x		
context		x		
challenge		x		
keywords	x	x		
skeleton		x	x	

exercise was created and institution which describes where the exercise will be used. The context element is an optional field used to contextualize the student with the exercise. The challenge element is the actual description of the exercise. Its content model is defined as mixed content to enable character data to appear between XHTML child-elements. This XML markup language will be used to enrich the formatting of the exercises descriptions. The keywords element is used to describe the subject(s) inherent to the exercise. The skeleton element refers to a resource containing code to be included in the student's project solution.

Specification Elements

The goal of defining programming exercises as learning objects is to use them in systems supporting automatic evaluation. In order to evaluate a programming exercise the learner must submit a program in source code to an Evaluation Engine (EE) that judges it using predefined test cases - a set of input and output data. In short, the EE compiles and runs the program iteratively using the input data (standard input) and checks if the result (standard output) corresponds to the expected output. Based on these correspondences the EE returns an evaluation report with feedback.

In the PExIL schema, the input and output top-level elements are used to describe respectively the input and the output test data. These elements include three sub-elements: description, example, and specification. The description element includes a brief description of the input/output data. The example element includes a predefined example of the input/output test data

file. Both elements comply with the specification element that describes the structure and content of the test data.

This definition can be used in several phases of the programming exercise life-cycle as depicted in Table 2: by (1) the content author to automatically generate an input and output test example to be included on the exercise description for presentation purposes and others (private) test cases to be used by the evaluator for evaluation purposes; (2) the learner to automatically validate his attempt against the public test cases generated previously; (3) the Evaluation Engine to evaluate a submission using the test cases.

The specification element (Figure 2) contains two attributes and two top-level elements. The attributes line_terminator and value_separator define respectively the newline and space characters of the test data. The two top-level elements are: line which defines a test data row and repeat which defines an iteration on a set of nested elements. The number of iterations is controlled by the value of the count attribute.

The line element defines a data row. Each row contains one or more variables. A variable in the specification model must have a unique name, which is used to refer values from one or more places in the specification element. A variable is represented in the PExIL schema by the data element containing the following attributes:

- **Id:** Defines the name of the variable. To access a variable one must use the id attribute preceded by the character $ to enable the further resolution and evaluation of XPath expressions while processing the specification model;

Table 2. Specification elements

Element	Selection	Presentation	Resolution	Evaluation
input/specification		x	x	x
output/specification		x	x	x

Figure 2. The specification element

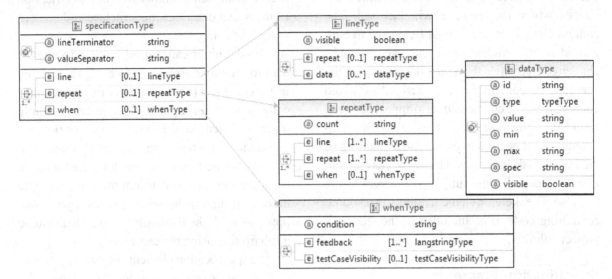

- **Type:** Defines the variable data type (e.g. integer, float, string, enum). In the case of an enumeration the values are presented as a text child node;
- **Value:** Represents the value to be included in the input/output test file. If filled the variable acts as a constant. Otherwise, the value can be automatically generated based on a set of constraints—the type, min, max, or spec attributes;
- **Min/Max:** Represents value constraints by defining limits on the values. The semantic of these attributes depends exclusively on the data type: may represent the ranges of a value (integer and float), the minimum/maximum number of characters (string) or a range of values to be selected from an enumeration list;
- **Spec:** Regular expression for generating/matching strings of text, such as particular characters, words, or patterns of characters.

The following XML excerpt shows the specification elements for the input and output test data of an exercise. The exercise challenge is *given*

three numbers to verify that the last number is between the first two.

Example of the input test description: "The input begins with a single positive integer on a line by itself indicating the number of the cases following." This line is followed by a blank line, and there is also a blank line between two consecutive inputs. Each line of input contains three float numbers (num1, num2, and num3) ranging values between 0 and 1000 (see Algorithm 1).

Example of the output test description: "The output must contain a boolean for each test case separated by a blank line between two consecutive outputs" (see Algorithm 2).

As said before, the EE is the component responsible for the assessment of an attempt to solve a particular programming exercise posted by the student. The assessment relies on predefined test cases. Whenever a test case fails a static feedback message (e.g. "Wrong Answer," "Time Limit Exceed," and "Execution Error") associated with the respective test case is generated. Beyond the static feedback of the evaluator, the PExIL schema includes a when element in the specification element. This element defines a dynamic feedback message to be presented to the student

Algorithm 1. Example of the input test description

```
<specification line_terminator="\n" value_separator=" ">
 <line><data id="numTestCases" type="int" value="3"/></line>
 <line/>
  <repeat count="$numTestCases">
  <line>
        <data id="num1" type="float" min="0" max="1000"/>
        <data id="num2" type="float" min="0" max="1000"/>
        <data id="num3" type="float" min="0" max="1000"/>
  </line>
  <line/>
  </repeat>
  <when condition="$num1>$num2">
<feedback xml:lang="en-GB">
Numbers can be given in descending order
</feedback>
  </when>
</specification>
```

Algorithm 2. Example of the output test description

```
<specification line_terminator="\n" value_separator=" ">
  <repeat count="$numTestCases">
    <line>
    <data id="result" type="enum" value="1">True False</data>
  </line>
  <line/>
</repeat>
</specification>
```

based on the evaluation of an XPath expression included in the condition attribute. This expression can include references to input and output variables or even dependencies between both. If the expression is evaluated as true then the element child node (feedback element) is used as the feedback message.

The PExIL definition supports the concept of incremental feedback to control the appearance of both types of feedback upon a submission of a student's attempt. The feedbackLevels element is a top-level child element, which defines a set of feedback levels that the exercise supports and when it is shown to the student. Algorithm 3 shows an example of a feedbackLevels element.

The levels attribute may have one or more feedback levels. The existent levels are:

- **Simple:** A feedback message indicating whether the student's attempt is correct or incorrect (e.g. "Wrong answer!");

Algorithm 3. Example of a feedbackLevels element

```
<pexil:feedbackLevels
    levels="simple|count_classifications|test_case_feedback_hint"
    incremental="2"
    showAllLevels="false"/>
```

- **Count_worst_classification:** A feedback message indicating the worst classification of all the tests (e.g. "1 test with wrong answer");
- **Count_classifications:** A feedback message indicating the classifications of all tests (e.g. "3 tests accepted and 1 test with wrong answer");
- **Test_case_feedback_hint:** A feedback message to be presented to the student based on the evaluation of a condition defined by the content author. This feedback level is pedagogical relevant since the teacher can cover common errors of his students and warn them with useful and contextual feedback (e.g. "Forgot to divide by the number of input elements");
- **Test_case_input_result:** A feedback message including the input data of an unsuccessful test case (e.g. "Unexpected output for the test with the input data: '5 6' ");
- **Test_case_input_output:** A feedback message with the input and the output data of an unsuccessful test case (e.g. "Unexpected output for the test with the input data: '5 6' and the output data: '5, 5' ").

The incremental attribute defines a value, which is used to control the appearance of the feedback levels. The showAllLevels attribute defines if the feedback to be presented to the student should accumulate with previous ones.

In the last example were defined three levels of feedback. Based on the incremental attribute value the two first students' unsuccessful attempts will receive a simple feedback, the next two a *count_classification* feedback and so on.

Program Elements

Program elements contain references to program source files as external resources (e.g. solution program, correctors) and metadata about those resources (e.g. compilation, execution line, hints). These resources are used mostly in the evaluation phase of the programming exercise life-cycle (Table 3) to allow the EE to produce an evaluation report of a students' attempt to solve a programming exercise.

A program element is defined with the programType type depicted in Figure 3.

This type is composed by seven attributes: id – a unique identifier for the resource; language – identifies the programming language used to code the resource (e.g. JAVA, C, C#, C++, PASCAL); compiler/executer – defines the name of the compiler/executer; version – identifies the version of the compiler; source/object – defines

Table 3. Program elements

Element	Selection	Presentation	Resolution	Evaluation
solution			x	x
corrector				x
hints	x			x

Figure 3. Program elements

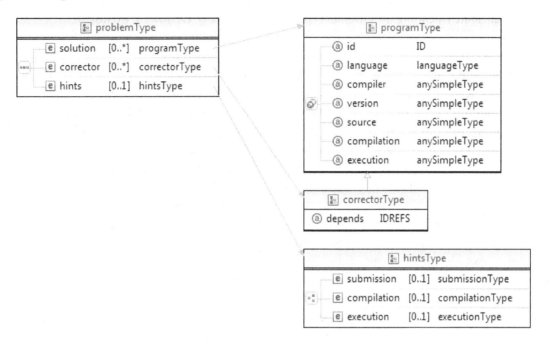

the name of the program source/object file; compilation – defines a command line to compile the source code; and execution – defines a command line to execute the compiled code.

There are two program elements in the PExIL schema: the solution and the corrector elements. The solution element contains a reference to the program solution file. Algorithm 4 shows an example of a solution element.

The corrector element is optional and refers to custom programs that change the general evaluation pattern for a given exercise. The corrector element is optional and refers to custom programs that change the general evaluation pattern for a given problem. There are two types of correctors: static and dynamic correctors. The static corrector is invoked immediately after compilation, before any execution. The corrector can be used to compute software metrics on the source code, judging the quality of source code; perform unit testing on the program; check the structure of the program's source code. The dynamic corrector is invoked after each execution with a test case. Deals with non-determinism (e.g. the solution is a set of unordered values, in this case the corrector normalizes the outputs before comparing them). A single programming exercise may use an arbitrary number of correctors. The

Algorithm 4. Example of a solution element

```
<solution
    id="solution" language="JAVA"
    compiler="javac" executer="java"
    version="1.6" source="solution.java" object="solution"
    compilation="$compiler $source"
    execution="$executer $object">
```

order in which they are executed is defined by the depends attribute extending the programType type.

The metadata about the program type resources is consolidated in the hints element aggregating a set of recommendations for the submission, compilation, and execution of exercises. These recommendations can be used by the EE to improve the evaluation and feedback process. The hints element is composed by three sub-elements: submission, compilation, and execution elements.

The submission element defines guidelines to follow in submission process. It is composed by the following attributes: time-solve – time limit for solving the exercise; time-submit – time limit for submitting the exercise; attempts – maximum number of attempts for submitting the problem; code-lines – maximum number of code lines in the user's code; length – maximum length in the user's code.

The compilation element defines guidelines to follow in compilation process. It is composed by the following attributes: time – time limit to compile the exercise; size – maximum size of the execution code.

The execution element defines guidelines to follow in execution process. It is composed by the following attributes: time – time limit for executing the exercise.

USING PExIL

In this section, we validate the PExIL definition according to: its usefulness while using the PExIL definition as input of a set of tools related to the programming exercise life-cycle (e.g. generation of a IMS CC learning object package); and its expressiveness while using the PExIL definition to capture all the constraints of a set of programming exercises in a repository (e.g. description of crimsonHex (Leap & Queirosw, 2009) programming exercises).

Generating a IMS CC Learning Object Package

In this subsection, we validate the usefulness of the PExIL definition by detailing the generation of an IMS CC LO package based on a valid PExIL instance. An IMS CC object is a package standard that assembles educational resources and publishes them as reusable packages in any system that implements this specification (e.g. Moodle LMS).

A Generator tool (e.g. PexilUtils) uses the PExIL definition to produce a set of resources related with a programming exercise such as exercise descriptions in multiple languages or input and output test files. The LO generation is depicted in Figure 4. The generation of a LO package is straightforward. The Generator tool uses as input a valid PExIL instance and a program solution file and generates: (1) an exercise description in a given format and language, (2) a set of test cases and feedback files, and (3) a valid IMS CC manifest file. Then, a validation step is performed to verify that the generated tests cases meet the specification presented on the PExIL instance and the manifest complies with the IMS CC schema. Finally, all these files are wrapped up in a ZIP file and deployed in a Learning Objects Repository. In the following sub-subsections, we present with more detail these three generations.

Exercise Description Generation

For the generation of an exercise description (Figure 5) it is important to acquire the format and the human language of the exercise description. The former is given by the Generator tool and the latter is obtained from the total number of occurrences of the xml:lang attribute in the title element of the PExIL instance.

The Generator tool receives as input a valid PExIL instance and a respective XSLT 2.0 file and uses the Saxon XSLT 2.0 processor combined with the xsl:result-document element to generate

Figure 4. Learning object package generation

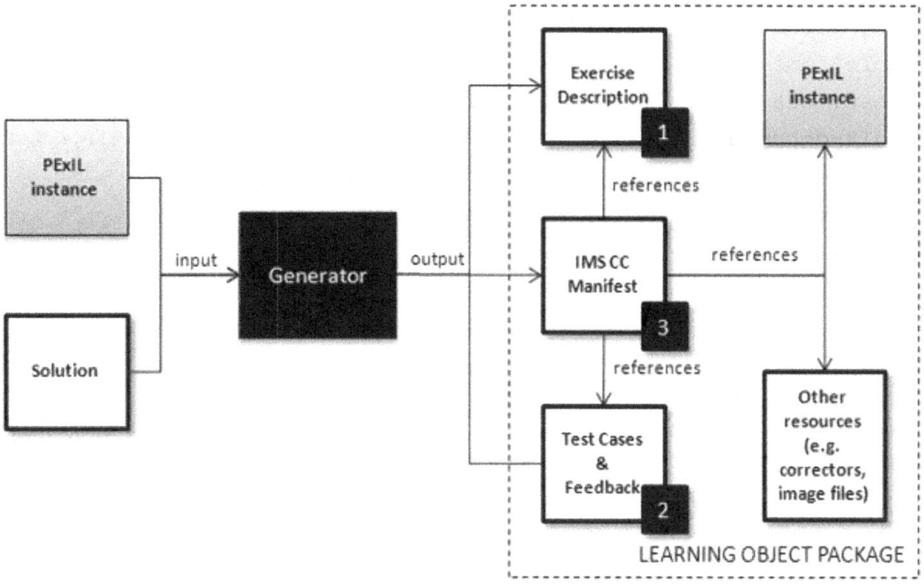

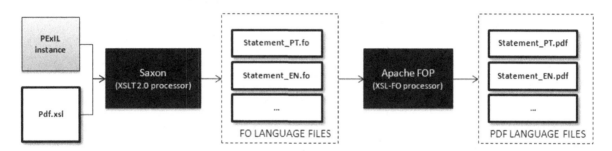

Figure 5. Generation of the exercise descriptions

a set of .FO files corresponding to the human languages values founded in the xml:lang attribute. The following code shows an excerpt of the Pdf.xsl file. Algorithm 5 generates the .FO files based on the textual elements of a PExIL instance.

In the next step, the .FO files are used as input to the Apache FOP formatter—an open-source and partial implementation of the W3C XSL-FO 1.0 standard—generating for each .FO file the corresponding PDF file.

The use of the PExIL definition to generate exercise descriptions does not end here since the PExIL definition is included in the LO itself making it possible, at any time of the LO life-

cycle, to regenerate the exercise description in other different formats. Figure 6 shows a typical exercise in PDF format.

The description also includes a description and an example of a test case. In the case of the absence of the input/description and input/example the Generator relies on the specification element to generate the test data and include it in the exercise description.

Test Cases and Feedback Generation

The generation of test cases and feedback relies on the specification element of the PExIL defi-

Algorithm 5. Stylesheet

```
<xsl:template match="pexil:title">
 <xsl:variable name="uri"
select="concat('desc',@xml:lang,'.fo')"/>
   <xsl:result-document href="resources/{$uri}">
        <fo:root xmlns:fo="http://www.w3.org/1999/XSL/Format">
         <!—apply templates over the textual elements --> ...
        </fo:root>
   </xsl:result-document>
</xsl:template>
```

Figure 6. A typical exercise statement

Problem C: Selfdescribing Sequence

Solomon Golomb's *selfdescribing sequence* $(f(1), f(2), f(3),\ldots)$ is the only nondecreasing sequence of positive integers with the property that it contains exactly $f(k)$ occurrences of k for each k. A few moments thought reveals that the sequence must begin as follows:

n	1	2	3	4	5	6	7	8	9	10	11	12
$f(n)$	1	2	2	3	3	4	4	4	5	5	5	6

In this problem you are expected to write a program that calculates the value of $f(n)$ given the value of n.

Input

The input may contain multiple test cases. Each test case occupies a separate line and contains an integer n ($1 \leq n \leq 2,000,000,000$). The input terminates with a test case containing a value 0 for n and this case must not be processed.

Output

For each test case in the input output the value of $f(n)$ on a separate line.

Sample Input

```
100
9999
123456
1000000000
0
```

Sample Output

```
21
356
1684
438744
```

nition. The Generator tool can be parameterized with a specific number of test files to generate. Regardless of this parameter, the tool calculates the number of test cases based on the total number of variables and the number of feedback messages. In the former, the number of test cases is given by the formula 2^n where the base represents the number of range limits of a variable and the exponent the total number of variables. Testing the range limits of a variable is justified since their values are usually not tested by students, thus with a high risk of failure. In the latter, the tool generates a test case for each feedback message found. The generation will depend on the successful evaluation of the XPath expression included in the condition attribute of the when element. Algorithm 6 helps to understand how the Generator calculates the test cases.

Suppose that the Generator tool is parameterized to generate 10 test cases. Using the previous example we can estimate the number of test cases and its respective input values as demonstrated in the Table 4.

The test values are: eight tests to cover the range limits of all variables ($2^3 = 8$); one test to represent the constraint included in the feedback message. Note that this test case will be executed only if the expression included in the condition attribute was not covered in the previous eight test cases; the remaining tests are generated randomly. Also, note that whoever is creating the programming exercise can statically define new test cases and use the PExIL definition for validation purposes.

Manifest Generation

An IMS CC learning object assembles resources and metadata into a distribution medium, typically a file archive in ZIP format, with its content described by a manifest file named imsmanifest.xml in the root level. The main sections of the manifest are: metadata which includes a description of the package, and resources which contains a list of references to other resources in the archive and dependency among them.

The metadata section of the IMS CC manifest comprises a hierarchy of several IEEE LOM elements organized in several categories (e.g. general, lifecycle, technical, educational). In order to achieve interoperability have defined a binding of the textual elements of the PExIL definition and the corresponding IEEE LOM elements. The Generator tool uses this binding to generate the LOM elements through a template pattern. Table 5 presents a binding of the PExIL textual

Algorithm 6. Example of how the generator calculates the test cases

```
<line>
        <data id="n1" type="float" min="0" max="1000"/>
        <data id="n2" type="float" min="0" max="1000"/>
        <data id="n3" type="float" min="0" max="1000"/>
  </line>
  <line/>
  </repeat>
  <when condition="$n1>$n2">
<feedback xml:lang="en-GB">
Numbers can be given in descending order
</feedback>
  </when>
```

Table 4. Specification elements

Var.	T1	T2	T3	T4	T5	T6	T7	T8	T9	T10
n1	0	0	0	0	1000	1000	1000	1000	Min=n2+1	R
n2	0	0	1000	1000	0	0	1000	1000	N2	R
n3	0	1000	0	1000	0	1000	0	1000	R	R

Table 5. Binding PExIL to IEEE LOM

Data Type	Schema	Element path
Title	LOM	lomcc:general/lomcc:title
	PExIL	exercise/title
Date	LOM	lomcc:lifecycle/lomcc:contribute[lom:role='Author']/lom:date
	PExIL	exercise/creation/date
Author	LOM	lomcc:lifecycle/lomcc:contribute[lom:role='Author']/lom:entity
	PExIL	exercise/creation/authors/author/v:VCard/v:fn
Event	LOM	lomcc:general/lomcc:coverage
	PExIL	exercise/creation/event

elements and the corresponding LOM elements, which will be used by the Generator tool to feed the IMS CC manifest.

By defining this set of metadata at the LOM side, eLearning systems continue to use the metadata included in the IMS CC manifest to search for programming exercises, rather than using a specialized XML dialect such as PExIL.

The resources section of the IMS CC manifest contains a list of references to other files in the archive (resources) and dependency among them. The resources element identifies a collection of resource elements. A resource is not necessarily a single file. It may be a collection of files internally referenced (within the package) or externally referenced through a URL. Internal files used by the resource are either directly enumerated by file elements or indirectly enumerated by using the dependency element to reference another resource. The file element may contain a metadata sub-element allowing content authors to describe additional metadata meaningful for searching or indexing in a repository (e.g. the file statements

could have a LOM language element identifying the human language of the statement). The dependency element identifies a single resource (based on the identifierref attribute) which can be used as a container for several files that this resource depends upon. Rather than having to list all resources each time they are needed, the dependency element allows content authors to define a container of resources and to simply refer to that dependency element instead of individual resources.

In this example (Figure 7) the resources section starts with a LAO resource (1) pointing to the PEXIL descriptor. This file is responsible for the automatic generation of all the other files included in the package (with the exception of the solution program and images). The description of the exercise is included on the manifest as a WCR resource (2). This type of resource can be automatically rendered by the browser without any additional processing. The program solution (3) is associated with metadata since this resource should not be made visible in player mode to the

Figure 7. Structure of the IMS CC manifest file

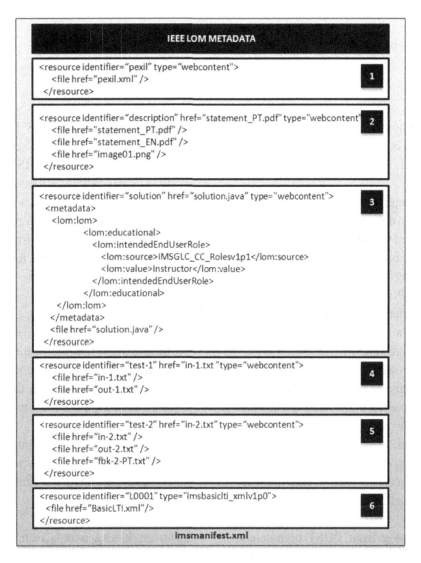

students and will be used only to regenerate test cases and in the evaluation phase of the programming life-cycle. The test cases are defined with a pair of input and output files (and feedback files) as resource objects (4 and 5). Finally, the BLTI link is included as a LAO resource (6). This link points to a XML file that includes all the data needed to integrate the cartridge in a LMS-Web application communication. This XML file contains information to create a link in a Tool Consumer (e.g. LMS). Upon the user's click on the LMS, the execution flow passes to a Tool Provider along with contextual information about the user and Consumer. The Basic LTI link is defined in the resource section of an IMS Common Cartridge, as shown in Algorithm 7.

The href attribute in the resource entry refers to a file path in the cartridge that contains an XML description of the Basic LTI link. A BLTI link contains several elements. The most important are: the title and description elements contain generic information about the link; the custom and extensions elements allow the Tool Consumer to extend the basic communication data;

Algorithm 7. Basic LTI link

```
<resource identifier="MyBLTILink" type="imsbasiclti_xmlv1p0">
   <file href="BasicLTI.xml"/>
</resource>
```

the launch_url element contains the URL to which the LTI invocation is sent; the secure_launch_url element is the URL to use if secure HTTP is required.

The LTI message signing is performed by a security mechanism designed to protect POST and GET requests called OAuth. OAuth 1.0 specifies how to construct a base message string and then sign that string using a secret. The signature is then sent as part of the POST request and is validated by the Tool Provider using OAuth. The signing process produces a set of values added to the launch request (Algorithm 8).

The value of the oauth_consumer_key depends on which credentials are being used. The oauth_consumer_key is passed in the message as plain text and identifies which Tool Consumer is sending the message allowing the Tool Provider to look up the appropriate secret for validation. The oauth_consumer_secret is used to sign the message. Both systems (TP and TC) should support and use the HMAC-SHA1 signing method with OAuth fields coming from POST parameters. Upon receipt of the POST, the TP will perform the OAuth validation using the shared secret it has stored for the oauth_consumer_key. The timestamp should also be validated to be within

a specific time interval (IMS BLTI, 2010). In order to validate the IMS CC cartridges previously generated we use the IMS validator[6]. This service validates cartridges for conformance with the IMS Common Cartridge v1.0 and/or v1.1 specification. In the validation process, the IMS CC Validator tests the whole cartridge (or just the XML manifest) verifying the following type of constraints:

- **Static:** The parameters (e.g. file names) are fixed in the profile (e.g. imsmanifest.xml must exist at the root of the package)
- **Dynamic:** The parameters are taken from an instance document in the package (e.g. href attribute of a resource element must point to a QTI file)
- **Conditional:** The constraint depends on a condition (e.g. if parameter 'contenttype' is 'question' then the href attribute must point to a QTI file).

The cartridges generated from PExIL instances using the methodology presented in the previous sub-section passed all tests performed by the validator.

Algorithm 8. Set of values added to the launch request

```
oauth_consumer_key=b289378-f88d-2929-lmsng.school.edu
oauth_signature_method=HMAC-SHA1
oauth_timestamp=1244834250
oauth_nonce=1244834250435893000
oauth_version=1.0
oauth_signature=Xddn2A%2BjzwjgBIVYkvigaKxCdcc%3D
```

Describing CrimsonHex Programming Exercises

In this subsection, we validate PExIL expressiveness by using the PExIL definition to cover the requirements (e.g. the input/output constraints of the exercise) of a subset of programming exercises from a learning objects repository.

For the evaluation process we randomly selected 24 programming exercises (1% of a total of 2393 exercises) from a specialized repository called crimsonHex (Leap & Queiros, 2009). We checked manually if the PExIL definition covers all the constraints of the input/output data. The evaluation results, depicted in the Figure 8, shows that in most cases (21 – 88%), PExIL was expressive enough to cover the constraints of the exercise test data. In just one case, we had to make a minor change in the PExIL definition to capture alternative content models.

Finally, two exercises were not completely covered by the PExIL definition. This means that using only the standard data types of PExIL we were able to define the input and output files, and these definitions can be used to validate them. However, these definitions cannot be used to generate a meaningful set of test data. In these cases the programming exercise author would

Figure 8. Evaluation of PExIL expressiveness

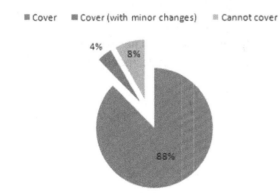

have to produce test files by some other means (either by hand or using a custom made generator). In our opinion, the data types required be these exercises are comparatively rare and do not justify their inclusion in the standard library. However, PExIL does not restrict data types and PexilUtils can be extended with generators for other data types, if this proves necessary.

CONCLUSION

In this chapter, we present PEXIL—a XML dialect for authoring LOs containing programming exercises. Nevertheless, the impact of PExIL is not confined to authoring since these documents are included in the LO itself and they contain data that can be used in its lifecycle, to present the exercise description in different formats, to regenerate test cases or to produce feedback to the student.

For evaluation purposes, we validate the PExIL definition by using it as input for the generation of an IMS CC learning object package through a set of tools and by using it to capture all the constraints of a set of programming exercises stored in a learning objects repository called crimsonHex.

In its current status, the PExIL schema[7] is available for test and download. Our plans are to support in a near future this definition in the crimsonHex repository. We are currently finishing the development of the generator engine to produce a LO compliant with the IMS CC specification. This tool could be used as an IDE plug-in or through command line based on a valid PExIL instance and integrated in several learning scenarios where a programming exercise may fit from curricular to competitive learning.

REFERENCES

Friesen, N. (2004). Semantic and syntactic interoperability for learning object metadata. In Hillman, D. (Ed.), *Metadata in Practice*. Chicago, IL: ALA Editions.

Friesen, N. (2005). Interoperability & learning objects: Overview of elearning standardization. *Interdisciplinary Journal of Knowledge and Learning Objects*. Retrieved from http://www.ijello.org/Volume1/v1p023-031Friesen.pdf

Global, I. M. S. (2010). *IMS basic learning tools interoperability specification – v.1.0 final specification*. Retrieved from http://www.imsglobal.org/lti/blti/bltiv1p0/ltiBLTIimgv1p0.html

Global, I. M. S. (2012a). *IMS-QTI - IMS question and test interoperability: Information model, version 1.2.1 final specification*. Retrieved from http://www.imsglobal.org/question/index.html

Global, I. M. S. (2012b). *IMS-CP – IMS content packaging, information model, best practice and implementation guide, version 1.1.3 final specification*. Retrieved from http://www.imsglobal.org/content/packaging

Global, I. M. S. (2012c). *IMS application profile guidelines overview, part 1 – Management overview, version 1.0*. Retrieved from http://www.imsglobal.org/ap/apv1p0/imsap_oviewv1p0.html

Global, I. M. S. (2012d). *IMS common cartridge profile, version 1.1 final specification*. Retrieved from http://www.imsglobal.org/cc/index.html

IEEE. (2002). *IEEE LTSC lom learning technology standards committee: Draft standards for learning object metadata, 2002: Final 1484.12.1 LOM draft standard document*. Retrieved from http://ltsc.ieee.org/wg12/files/LOM_1484_12_1_v1_Final_Draft.pdf

Leal, J. P., & Queirós, R. (2009). CrimsonHex: A service oriented repository of specialised learning objects. In *Proceedings of ICEIS 2009: 11th International Conference on Enterprise Information Systems*. Milan, Italy: ICEIS.

Net, A. D. L. (2012). *ADL SCORM overview*. Retrieved from http://www.adlnet.gov/Technologies/scorm

Queirós, R., & Leal, J. P. (2009). Defining programming problems as learning objects. In *Proceedings of ICCEIT*. Venice, Italy: ICCEIT.

Queirós, R., & Leal, J. P. (2012). Using the common cartridge profile to enhance learning content interoperability. In *Proceedings of ECEL - 10th European Conference on e-Learning*. Brighton, UK: ECEL.

ENDNOTES

[1] http://imcs.dvgu.ru/cats/docs/format.html

[2] http://code.google.com/p/freeproblemset/

[3] http://mooshak.dcc.fc.up.pt/

[4] http://peach.win.tue.nl/

[5] OAuth – http://oauth.net

[6] http://validator.imsglobal.org

[7] http://www.dcc.fc.up.pt/~rqueiros/projects/schemaDoc/examples/pexil/pexil.html

Chapter 4

GuessXQ:
A Query-by-Example Approach for XML Querying

Daniela Morais Fonte
University of Minho, Portugal

Daniela da Cruz
University of Minho, Portugal

Pedro Rangel Henriques
University of Minho, Portugal

Alda Lopes Gancarski
Institut Telecom, France

ABSTRACT

XML is a widely used general-purpose annotation formalism for creating custom markup languages. XML annotations give structure to plain documents to interpret their content. To extract information from XML documents XPath and XQuery languages can be used. However, the learning of these dialects requires a considerable effort. In this context, the traditional Query-By-Example methodology (for Relational Databases) can be an important contribution to leverage this learning process, freeing the user from knowing the specific query language details or even the document structure. This chapter describes how to apply the Query-By-Example concept in a Web-application for information retrieval from XML documents, the GuessXQ system. This engine is capable of deducing, from an example, the respective XQuery statement. The example consists of marking the desired components directly on a sample document, picked-up from a collection. After inferring the corresponding query, GuessXQ applies it to the collection to obtain the desired result.

DOI: 10.4018/978-1-4666-2669-0.ch004

INTRODUCTION

In this chapter, we address the problem of accessing information in structured documents annotated in eXtensible Markup Language (XML). Those documents, being structured, are accessed using specific query languages where the interesting structural components are specified, as well as restrictions over them if needed.

The bigger the worldwide collection of XML documents gets, the more relevant is the existence of an efficient search engine. These engines should be aware of the explicit structure of the documents. This problem has raised a research area called Structured Document Retrieval (Lu, 1990). In this area, the specification of a query that yields valid results strongly depends on the user-friendliness of the search engine interface.

The standard query language for XML is XQuery (Boag, et al., 2005). XQuery queries are powerful but complex to write (the user must have a deep knowledge of the query language as well as the document structure). To help the user in the task of specifying his queries, some specialized editors have been developed (XMLSpy [Kim, 2002], EditiX[1], Oxygen[2]), but still requiring a good knowledge level of the query language.

"Example is always more efficacious than precept." This statement, by Samuel Johnson (1999), led Human-Computer Interaction researchers to suggest a new interaction paradigm called Query-by-Example (QBE). Born in the context of database querying (Ramakrishnan & Gehrke, 2007), typical QBE systems are based on the "fill in the blanks" approach. Zloof (1975) defined QBE as "a query language for use by non-programmers querying a relational database." QBE is based on the concept that the user formulates his query by filling in the appropriate skeleton tables the fields and/or restrictions on fields (relational selection concept) he intends to search.

Due to the complex nature of XML documents querying, the QBE concept was adapted to XML retrieval by showing the XML Schema Definition

(XSD)[3] instead of the relational table skeleton (see for instance Tulchinsky, et al., 2008; Bohere, et al., 2003; Zhang, et al., 2002; Li, et al., 2007; Braga & Campi, 2005; Newman & Ozsoyoglu, 2004). XSD consists in a XML Schema Language usually used to express a set of rules to which an XML document must conform in order to be considered *valid* or *well formed* (according to that schema). Other very well known notation to define document families' structure is the Document Type Definition (DTD), which uses a formal syntax to declare rigorously the elements and references that may be used in the documents of the family and which content type the elements can have. Despite its simplicity and wide use, DTD is being replaced by XSD for two main reasons: XSD is written in XML and it is much more powerful and rigorous, allowing a more complete definition.

The system we present here called GuessXQ, also displays the XML Schema tree representation to the user. Moreover, the user has the chance to go through a sample (a XML document extracted from the repository) and mark over it the components he wants to retrieve from the overall collection. Element selections and restrictions are done directly on the sample document, giving the user a clear indication of the information he is searching for (Ferreira, et al., 2007; Cruz, et al., 2009; Fonte, et al., 2010).

This chapter describes how we implement the QBE concept in a Web-application for information retrieval from a collection of structured documents, the GuessXQ system. In essence, we propose an engine capable of deduce, from a specific example, the respective XQuery statement. Thus, instead of specifying the desired components of the documents and eventual restrictions in a query, the user exemplifies those components marking them directly on a sample document, picked-up from the collection. After inferring the generic statement, GuessXQ system applies it to all documents in the collection to perform the desired retrieval.

This chapter is organized as follows. The introduction briefly presents XML querying and the QBE paradigm. Then, the chapter presents the following GuessXQ aspects: the XML and XSD Repository used for testing the GuessXQ system; the collection and sample document selection; the GuessXQ user interface; the Visual Query Specification process that supports the query generation process; the Information Retrieval; how the system displays the result of the information retrieval process; the Repository Access Interface module, which allows the other modules to access the Repository in a systematic and simple way; some examples to illustrate the query specification process and show the respective retrieved results; how XAT (XML Archive for Testing) (Fonte, et al., 2010) came to live from the need to test the GuessXQ system through XML Benchmarking. Finally, the chapter concludes about our work and gives directions for future work.

XML Querying

Queries for XML retrieval allow the access to certain parts of documents based on content and structural restrictions. Examples of such queries are those defined by XPath language (Berglund, et al., 2005) and XQuery, the standard proposed by the W3C. These languages are very expressive, allowing the specification of sophisticated structural and textual restrictions.

XQuery is formed by different kinds of expressions, including XPath location paths and FLWOR expressions based on typical database query languages, such as Structured Query Language (SQL):

```
for ... let ... where ... order by ... return
```

Variables are used to pass information from one operator to another.

As an example, assume a document that stores information about articles, including title, author, and publisher. The following query returns articles of author Kevin ordered by the respective title.

```
for $a in document ('articles.xml')/
article
    where $a/author = 'Kevin'
    order by $a/title
    return  $a
```

XQuery operates in the abstract, logical structure of an XML document, rather than its surface syntax. The corresponding data model represents documents as trees where nodes may correspond to a document, an element, an attribute, a text, a namespace, a processing instruction, or a comment. Each node has a unique identity provided by the use of a path notation as in URLs, for navigating through the hierarchical structure of an XML document. XPath gets its name from this use. In addition to addressing, XPath can also be used for testing whether or not a node matches a pattern. This explains why it is required to know XPath to write XQuery expressions: the *location path* selects a set of nodes relative to the context node and can recursively contain expressions that are used to filter sets of nodes.

A *location path* is a sequence of one or more *location steps* separated by "/". It can be *relative* to the current element in the document structure or *absolute* with respect to the root element in the structure; to mark the difference, the second one starts with a "/". A "/" by itself will select the root node of the document containing the context node; if it is followed by a relative location path, then it selects the set of nodes that would be selected by the relative location path, with regard to the root node of the document.

Steps in a relative location path are composed together from left to right. Each step selects a set of nodes relative to a context node: the initial sequence selects a set of nodes relative to the current node (the root in an absolute path); and then each node in that set is used as a context node for the following step. If the path is intended to start from any descendant of the root, not only from a direct child, it starts by "//" instead of "/".

Although precisely defined, structured queries construction is not always an easy process because, among other reasons, the user may not have a deep knowledge of the query language or of the documents collection structure. Moreover, after specifying a query, the user may not get the expected result; this means that he usually needs to rephrase the query, spending more time and effort.

To solve these problems, many researchers are working on friendly graphical user-interfaces that aid in the task of query specification. The adoption of the Query-by-Example paradigm is one of the promising directions deserving further investigation.

Query-by-Example in the Relational Model

Ma and Tanaka (2004) define the QBE paradigm as a "method to create queries that allows the user to search for documents based on an example in the form of a selected text string or in the form of a document name or a list of documents." Once the QBE system formulates the actual query, it is easier to learn than formal query languages, such as the standard SQL, while still enabling powerful searches. Basically, in terms of database management systems, QBE can be seen like a "fill-in-the blanks" method of query creation. Microsoft Access Query Design Grid is an example of that: to conduct a search for field data matching some particular conditions, the user enters criteria into the form, creating search conditions for the desired fields. Automatically, a query is generated to search the database for matching the corresponding data.

Suppose for example the user is interested to search in a database composed of set of books, each one defined by a title, an author, a publisher, a set of pages and a publication year. If the user wants to find all the books published in 2008 by the publisher *Ignatius Press*, he just has to search the title of books which have the field publishing year equal to 2008 AND a publisher named *Ignatius Press*. Criteria specified for different

fields in the "Criteria" row are combined by using the AND operator. Then, only records that meet all the defined criteria are included in the result.

Now, suppose the user is interested in the list of book titles written by *W. Shakespeare* or *Joseph Pearce*. In other words, the author represents alternative criteria because only one of the conditions needs to be met: the result list can contain titles written by any of them. When the user has to specify sets of independent criteria, the user uses both the "Criteria" and the "or" rows in the design grid. Criteria specified in the "Criteria" and "or" rows are combined using the OR operator, as shown in Figure 1.

This "fill-in-the blanks" method for query creation abstracts the user from the SQL query used to query the database, thus no requiring a deep knowledge of the query language. In the next section, we show how this concept was adopted to XML and introduce our proposal.

Query-by-Example in XML

The idea of generating queries through an example seems the perfect solution for the problem of searching particular information in a document, without the need of learning a new query language. Most of the works adapt the relational QBE model by showing the XML Schema Definition (XSD) tree instead of the table skeleton (e.g. Braga & Campi, 2005; Li, et al., 2007; Newman & Ozsoyoglu, 2004).

We propose a system called GuessXQ that not only displays the XML Schema tree representation to the user, but also a sample document from the collection. In GuessXQ, element selection and restriction is done directly in the sample document, giving the user a complete indication about the information he is searching for. Moreover, GuessXQ focuses on a subset of XQuery functionalities used by common real users.

As an example, suppose a collection of book documents composed of a title, an author, a publisher, a set of pages and a publication year.

Figure 1. Example QBE specification

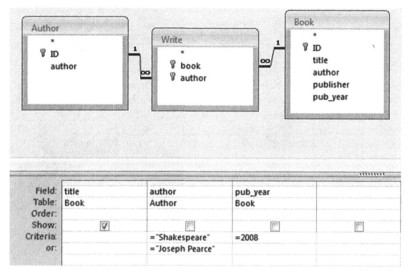

Suppose the user is interested to search all books of the famous *J.R.R. Tolkien* author. If the user knows XQuery language, he is able to write a query like the one bellow.

To get the desired results, the query is executed for each file corresponding to a book in the collection, replacing *book i* by the corresponding file name. Using the QBE principle, instead of specifying the query in textual form, the user selects, in a sample document, an author element and associates to it the *J.R.R. Tolkien* value in the query form. The associated query result should be all the Book nodes, where the author attribute has J.R.R. Tolkien value (for instance, the Books with titles *The Fellowship of the Ring* and *The Hobbit*). It is important to notice that all the documents that belong to some collection share a common structure formally described by a schema. This *family schema* is also taken in consideration in our approach.

Our system allows the choice of a XSD schema representing the collection of documents from where the user wants to retrieve information. After this, GuessXQ picks up a sample document from the collection and presents it to the user to specify the intended query. Then, the system shows the inferred query and (total or partially) displays the retrieved documents.

As can be seen in Figure 2, the process of query creation using GuessXQ starts with the Collection Selection followed by the Sample Document Choice. After this, the XML document picked up is displayed in an interface adapted to the Visual Query Specification. The Visual Annotations made in this interface are then translated into XQuery by a Query Generator. The generated query is processed by the Information Retrieval Engine, which searches in the collection all the documents specified in the query. The returned components are given back to the user in a Document Viewer interface.

In the remaining of this chapter, we detail each module of the GuessXQ architecture by presenting its role in the system.

XML AND XSD REPOSITORY

The Repository is a collection of XML files grouped by their schema (XSD). By now, it is composed of documents belonging to Web accessible collections like the Medical Subject Headings

Figure 2. GuessXQ system architecture

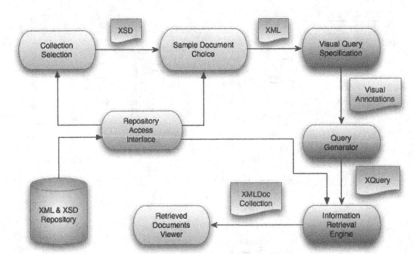

vocabulary files (MESH), the complete plays of Shakespeare, Eurovoc—a multilingual thesaurus covering the fields in which the European communities are active, and a set of miscellaneous documents collected from different sources. These documents were collected during the development of our XML Archive for Testing (XAT) (Fonte, et al., 2010).

COLLECTION SELECTION AND SAMPLE DOCUMENT CHOICE

The Collection Selection module offers an appropriate interface to allow the user to choose a XSD document from the Repository and to visualize it. The system displays the XSD selected only in a textual mode, but as future work, we intend to offer alternative ways to present the Schema, like *tree*, *graph,* and *table* views.

The Sample Document Choice module offers an appropriate interface to allow a manual or random choice of the *sample document* and its visualization. This choice is a crucial point in our approach to QBE since the user specifies his needs over that document.

Actually, we propose to implement a system capable to suggest a sample document that better represents the collection selected. For this, there must be a well-founded logic behind the selection of the sample document from the collection. We have identified several criteria, which should be taken into account when choosing the sample document (document size, number of different elements, diversity of values, among others).

Criteria for the Sample Document Choice

The choice of the sample document plays a major role in the user interaction with the search system. At present, the sample document is randomly picked from the collection. The user may also choose it manually. However, we are implementing a document choice component in the system based in the following criteria.

- **Document Size:** Files with a big size can slow down the system; also, files with a smaller size can contain too little information or elements to aid the user selection. This criterion can be used as a delimiter to complement the others by not allowing a file bigger than a predefined size.

- **Number of Elements/Attributes:** Taking into account the number of elements and attributes in the sample document is important. In one hand, if the file has too many components (elements or attributes), it can be too cluttered for the user to select his desired example. On the other hand, if the document has few components, it may not contain all those ones the user needs.

- **Number of Different Elements/ Attributes:** To counteract some of the shortcoming of the previous criterion, it may be interesting to look at the number of different elements and attributes in a file. This way, if a file contains almost all the elements and attributes present in the schema, the user gets a more complete variety of elements to specify his needs.

- **Diversity of Values:** As stated before, the capacity of the user to see example data and not just the structure (schema) of the queried documents is the main innovation of our QBE approach. Therefore, a criterion guaranteeing the diversity of data in the sample document is important. Having different values for the same element (or attribute) allows the user to better understand the fields in the document he is querying. However, similar to the other criteria, if there is too much diversity, the sample document may become too big.

As seen, each criterion has its own merits and shortcomings, so they must be used together in a meaningfully way. The sample document should be diverse, which means that it must have a rich subset of the elements, attributes, and possible values from the schema. However, it also must be a file contained in a predefined size. We intend to make a ranked list of possible sample documents, thus making easy for the user to retrieve the "second best choice" when the previous document suggested by the QBE system is not suitable.

GuessXQ USER INTERFACE

GuessXQ system intends to offer a simple and intuitive user interface that allows the visual specification of XQuery queries, without the need of an advanced knowledge of this *query* language. By exemplifying over the sample document what kind of information he is searching for in the collection, the user describes, with a few clicks, the restrictions to the needed XPath filters.

Figure 3 presents the GuessXQ GUI interface, which is composed of a Command-Area on the left-hand side and a Work-Area, on the centre and right-hand side of the useful system application area. The first one is used to control the application working options, while the second one is the main visual stage of the query specification and inference process. With this approach, we get a lighter design and navigability, without forgetting future improvements (like applying Web 2.0 technologies, to agile the application and delegate to the client-side more heavy tasks). Thus, we improve the proposed concepts by offering not only a simple and intuitive way of visually specify a query, but also a versatile, complete and efficient way to obtain the desired query and results.

The three different stages that compose the Work-Area are a XSD tab, responsible for the XSD documents visualization; a XML tab, which supports the XML sample document visualization and the visual query specification process; a Results tab, which provides an organized way to consult the generated query and the results of its inference process.

VISUAL QUERY SPECIFICATION

We describe now the interaction between the system and the user through this interface, in order to explain the proposed QBE concept. As previously said, the user starts by selecting the intended working collection choosing a Schema and the system shows its content in the XSD Tab. In this way, the user may analyse the Schema and

Figure 3. GuessXQ XML tab: sample document and visual query specification

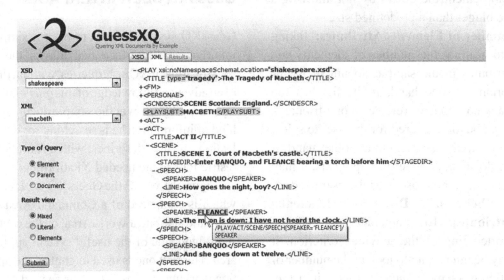

get a better knowledge about the structure of this collection. After the XSD selection, GuessXQ allows for the choice of a sample XML document belonging to this family. The system displays then its content in the XML Tab.

To specify his information need, the user directly selects it in the sample document by clicking on the desired components. To improve the interaction, each time a component is selected, its colour is changed. Thus, the user can easily see which document nodes are already selected, and have a better perception of the restrictions imposed by his selection. This enhancement is obtained using different colours to highlight the items selected according to their types, as depicted in Figure 3: elements are highlighted in blue; attributes, in green; PCDATA content, in red; and the attribute values, in yellow. The user can also unselect a previously highlighted component, by simply clicking again on it.

To improve the perception of restrictions implied by each selected item (i. e. its meaning in terms of the final query), GuessXQ interfaces can show the XPath expression corresponding to each selection. For that, the user just has to put the mouse cursor over the selected node; then,

a tooltip with the inferred XPath expression is shown (as seen in Figure 3).

To simplify the navigation and the search of the components to select, the system provides a feature to expand or retract blocks inside the document, more specifically elements with children nodes. Figure 3 illustrates this feature: by clicking on "-" (*minus*) sign, the corresponding block retracts, and only its element name is displayed, preceded now by a "+" (*plus*) sign. To expand again the element, the user just clicks on the "+" sign, and the entire element sub-tree will be displayed again (this feature provided by the XSLT file applied to present the document to user). When the user finishes the direct selection of one or more items over the sample document, he must submit the inferred query from the "example," so that GuessXQ starts the search applying this query to the entire collection. Before the submission, the user must select the type of view he wishes for the retrieved answer.

As future work, we intend to improve this feature to intelligently support the specification of more complex queries, by allowing the comparison of values with the selected components. Next section is devoted to the explanation of the current approach along the Query Generation process.

QUERY GENERATOR

Our approach combines the power of the XQuery language with the simplicity of the visual specification, in order to simplify and optimize the query building process.

After selecting the desired components, GuessXQ generates the corresponding XQuery query based on the following query pattern:

```
for $x in document (j)
return ⋃ⁿᵢ₌₀ $x / pathᵢ
```

The *return* clause of the query corresponds to the union of the paths generated for each selected component. GuessXQ assigns these paths to each document node according to three different modes of querying: *element-oriented, ancestral-oriented,*

and *document-oriented*. Figure 4 helps to understand the difference between each mode: it shows for each type of selected component the XPath expression corresponding to each query mode.

In the *element-oriented* mode, the path is generated based on the selected component: the path reflects the corresponding *absolute* location path from the root node to selected node. This query-mode is useful when the user expects results only with the specific components that he selects. The output of this generation mode is illustrated in Figure 4 by the first path associated with each component. For example, if we select the element *address*, the corresponding path in this mode is /*xml/shiporder/shipto/address*. The result is the list of *address* elements that match this absolute location path.

In the *ancestral-oriented* mode, the generator assigns to each component the *absolute* path from the root node to its ancestral. This query-mode is adequate when the user looks for results which reflect the ancestral element of the selected com-

Figure 4. Query mode: the different XPath expressions associated to each component

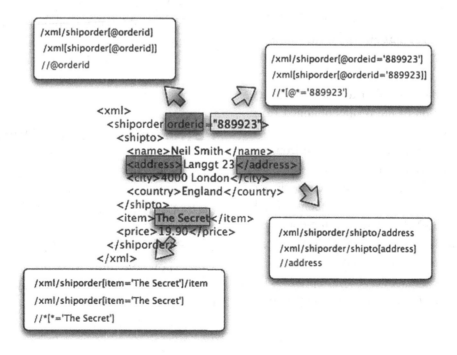

ponent. This mode is illustrated in Figure 4 by the second path associated with each component. For example, by selecting the element *address* the user gets the entire element *shipto* having an element *address* and matching the path */xml/shiporder/shipto*.

In the *document-oriented* mode, the generated XPath expression allows the search for the selected component in the entire document, independently of its position in the document tree. This query-mode searches in the collection ignoring the context of the selected node. For example, if the user only needs to find all the elements *address* of each document, the associated path is simply *//address*. Figure 4 illustrates this mode with the third path associated with each component.

The different querying modes are implemented in XSLT which allow, not only for the pretty visualization of the sample document, but also for the computation of the respective XPath for each document node, enabling a quicker and efficient query generation process.

INFORMATION RETRIEVAL ENGINE

To create an easy and automated way to query all the documents of the collection, with a simple specification drawn over only one sample XML document, our retrieval engine accesses all the documents in the collection to build the query result as the union of the results obtained from each document.

The complete (final) query inferred from the direct selections made over the sample document is the union of the XPaths generated for each selected node. Thus for each query component (XPath fragment), GuessXQ searches all the document parts that match it, gathering these answers with those obtained for the other query components. In the algorithm below, we describe this process: the retrieved results (*ir*) are obtained from the union

Algorithm 1. Complete query

```
var ir, res_i;
ir = ε;
for doc_i in Collection do
  res_i = ε;
  for $x in Query do
    res_i.append ([$y ← doc_i.match($x)]);
  end
  ir.append(res_i);
end
return ir;
```

of the partial results (*res_i*) extracted from each document, by concatenating the list of the document parts (*y*) that match each query component (*x*) (see Algorithm 1).

This approach allows for obtaining more than the textual data present in each document that matches the query: it enables to present richer and more illustrative results by retrieving complete parts of each XML document.

Furthermore, this enables GuessXQ to aggregate the partial results by document, separated by query component; this offers a more direct and perceptible way to view the query process results. However, we think that it could be interesting in the future to explore new aggregation possibilities, in order to offer different modes to explore the built results.

RETRIEVED DOCUMENT VIEWER

Concerning the visualization of the answer retrieved by the search engine, the user can choose one out of three modes: only the correspondent node names (*elements*); only the *literal* (PCDATA) values; or a *mixed* of both *elements* and *literals*, which shows the entire XML document resulting from the search. By default, the system outputs the results in *mixed* mode.

These three modes are implemented with XSL technologies, which allow the user to easily switch between them without needing to re-infer the query. With a future inclusion of Web 2.0 technologies, this will also allow the switch between modes without a page resubmission, by once again applying XSL directly on the client-side. The search results are shown in the Results Tab, as depicted in Figure 5.

After the *query specification* submission, GuessXQ shows in the Results Tab (1) the generated query, (2) the results of applying that query to the sample document (e.g. *macbeth* in Figure 5), and (3) the query results found in the collection (e.g. *a_and_c* in Figure 5). Each result is loaded into a selector. To improve the usability, the user can expand or retract the selector by clicking on it. The user can expand as many selectors as he needs and easily compare results between documents. To easily distinguish the sample document selector from the others, it is displayed in green, whereas other ones are displayed in light brown.

The system also allows for expanding/collapsing all the selectors with just one click and offers

the chance to copy the *query* to the clipboard. In this way, we aim at offering a versatile and user-friendly interface. As future work, we intend to explore new results visualization options to improve navigability through more extensive output, like restricting the number of documents presented at a time. We also intend to explore new ways of selecting, ordering and creating documents from the results.

REPOSITORY ACCESS INTERFACE

The Repository Access Interface module allows other modules to access the Repository in a systematic and simple way. It allows the selection of a XSD, a collection of documents, a single document, or document components.

It uses a database to associate each XML document with the corresponding Schema, without the need to search this relation inside the document. This is particularly useful when executing a query: only documents associated with that Schema are analysed, without needing to navigate through

Figure 5. GuessXQ GUI (results tab): retrieved document viewer

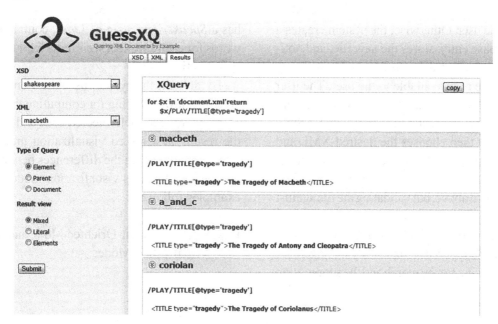

the *Repository*. The system also stores for each document its *md5*[4], a cryptographic hash function that we use to provide a unique identifier for each document and detect duplicated files.

The Repository Access Interface module is composed of a set of fetch methods for retrieving documents from the Repository: it works as an abstraction layer, allowing the system to change the Repository model in the future without a major architecture modification.

Currently, this module is also responsible for the Repository support by offering a simple way to upload new files to the Repository and a method to manage them, guaranteeing their validity.

The user can upload new XSD documents into the Repository, validating it as follows. First, the system tests if the uploaded file is a valid XML file against the XSD W3C Recommendation, through a XML Schema[5] validator: if not, the system notifies the user; otherwise, the system computes its *md5* and compares it to all the XSD stored in the system Database to determine if the XSD document is already in the Repository. If so, the name of the uploaded document may be different from the existing one, in which case the name is updated.

If the both name and *md5* of the new XSD document are already in the system, GuessXQ notifies the user. Otherwise, the system creates a new database entry, stores the new file, and notifies the user about the operation success, being the XSD file now available to the user. The user can also easily upload new XML documents into the system, after selecting the respective XSD.

The user then chooses the desired XML and the system uploads the file for proceeding to its validation in a similar process to the XSD validation described above, but validating the file against the selected XSD.

As future work, we intend to offer an easy interface to fully support the Repository management by also allowing for the search and the suppression of files. We also aim to include in this module a simple platform to allow the user to import to GuessXQ system an external Repository and to query its files. This platform intends to classify each file and to allow the inclusion in the system only valid collections of XML documents, which guarantees the efficiency of the query inference process.

USING GuessXQ

After the presentation of each module of the GuessXQ architecture and its features, we describe the full GuessXQ system capabilities and features. For this, suppose an example of XML collection composed of the plays of William Shakespeare. His complete work is divided in four categories: Comedies, Tragedies, Histories, and Poetry.

Suppose the user uploads the complete set of Shakespeare plays in XML format, grouped in a collection named *Shakespeare*. Each play of this collection is composed of a *title*, a *characters* list divided by groups, a *scenario description*, a *subtitle,* and a list of *Acts*. Each *Act* is composed of a *title* and a list of *Scenes*. Each *Scene* is divided though *Speeches* and has a *title* and *Stage directions* describing the scene. Finally, each *Speech* has a *Speaker* and a set of *Lines*, containing the words for each speaker (see Figure 5 for the XSD specification).

By default, the system uses the element-oriented mode of querying for computing the XPath corresponding to each selected node and presents the results in a mixed visualization mode. For better understanding the differences between the querying and results visualization modes, some examples follow.

Example 1: Element-Oriented Mode and Mixed Visualization Mode.

Suppose the user is interested in the complete list of the tragedies. For this, after choosing the *Shakespeare* collection in the Command-Area, the user selects the famous *Macbeth* tragedy, as depicted in Figure 3. Each play includes the attribute *type* defining the type of the play contained in that XML file. Thus, the user has to select the *"tragedy"* specific value for this attribute, obtaining the query and results depicted in Figure 5.

Example 2: Parent-Oriented Mode for Querying and Mixed Visualization Mode.

Suppose now the user is interested in the speeches of a specific *Speaker*—the *First Witch*. The user is not able to represent this restriction in the element-oriented mode. In fact, if the user selects the *PCDATA* value "First Witch" of the element *Speaker*, the system returns all the *Speaker* elements in the collection with having content "First Witch." Moreover, if he also selects the *Speech* element, the inferred query if the union of these two restrictions (in the element-oriented mode), yielding the complete list of all the *Speech*

elements together with all the *Speaker* elements in the collection.

As we can see in Figure 6, if the user switches to the parent-oriented mode, the XPath associated to each document node matches the node's ancestral. By selecting the PCDATA value "First Witch" in the *Speaker* element, the user gets all *Speech* corresponding ancestral elements.

Example 3: Document-Oriented Mode and Literal Visualization Mode.

Suppose the user needs all the titles presented in the set of plays. All the *Play*, *Act* and *Scene* elements have an associated *Title*. As easily deduced, the parent-oriented mode does not support this type of restriction. The choice of element-oriented mode forces the user to select the *Title* element in its three different contexts (plays, acts, and scenes) to reach the desired results. To avoid this situation, the document-oriented mode allows the search for the selected component in the entire document, independently of its hierarchical position in the document, as we can see in Figure 7.

Figure 6. Example 2: visual query specification process

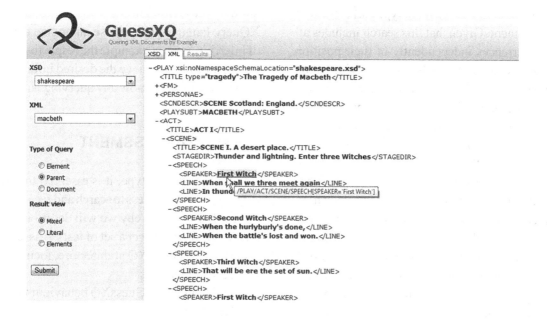

Figure 7. Example 3: visual query specification process

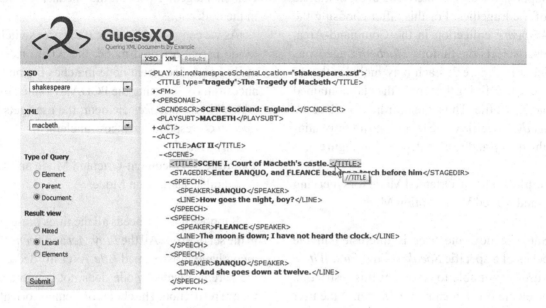

This mode allows the matching with all the *Title* elements present in each document of the collection.

Example 4: Document-Oriented Querying Mode and Element Visualization Mode.

Imagine now the user wants to search for all the occurrences of the character name *Macduff*, independently of the element type and context in the document. Given that this search includes all the occurrences independently of their position on the document hierarchy, the querying mode that better fits this need is the document-oriented mode. The main difference from example 3 is that the literal results visualization mode only displays the word *Macduff* as many times as its number of occurrences on the entire *Shakespeare* collection, which is obviously not meaningful. Therefore, for this situation, the best is the results visualization elements mode, which allows for viewing only the XML tags of the matching results, having in the content implicitly always the word *Macduff*. This is particularly useful to notice the different types of occurrences of the desired string, as depicted in Figure 8.

As we can see, the *MACDUFF* character has two different types of occurrence: speakers and simple words from the speech in *Line* elements.

Examples 1, 2, 3, and 4 show that GuessXQ current version offers a simple and versatile way to specify different types of information needs by choosing the adequate combination of the query specification mode with the results visualization mode. GuessXQ system allies the facilities offered by the QBE concept with the power of the XQuery language to propose an engine capable of inferring from an example the respective query statement, and to retrieve the desired information without the need to know any querying language.

GuessXQ ASSESSMENT

As with every prototype, it is essential to assess the system effectiveness to search and fix eventual system failures. Thereby we will describe in this Section how we project a set of tests to assess the robustness of GuessXQ architecture, focusing on its goals and features.

We intend to test GuessXQ behaviour in three main directions:

Figure 8. Example 4: results obtained for element visualization mode

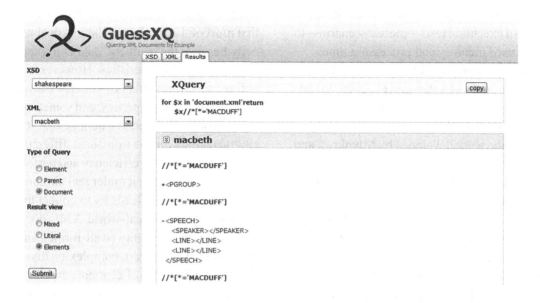

- Performance when working with files of different sizes;
- Ability for dealing with malformed XML files;
- Ability to process XML files having a great diversity of elements, attributes, text data, or a complex deepness.

Concerning the first direction, the aim is to compare the execution time for large or small files. For this comparison, it is important to collect as many information as possible to ensure the system is able to work with large files in a reasonable time. Therefore, with the emphasis in document size, we have defined five categories:

- **C1:** From 0Kb to 10Kb;
- **C2:** From 10Kb to 100Kb;
- **C3:** From 100Kb to 1Mb;
- **C4:** From 1Mb to 1Gb;
- **C5:** Higher than 1Gb.

These categories illustrate the diversity of file sizes that each XML collection may have. Larger files require more time to extract the query results. Therefore, it is important not only to focus the analysis in the ability of displaying the entire XML document and generate correct results, but also in the querying efficiency for collections with several larger files. They may slow down the system and it is also crucial to ensure the correctness of the query results generated in more extreme situations.

Concerning the second direction, our tests will help to model the behaviour of the application when facing an unexpected input. The aim is to guarantee that GuessXQ prototype is able to recognize malformed XML files, and prevent a system failure when processing it.

Finally, concerning the third direction, the objective is to test the system response facing the diversity of information that can be present in a XML file, ensuring the reliability of the produced output. If the system response is correct, it certifies GuessXQ main purpose: the information access from structured documents with the QBE assistance.

In order to perform the required tests, a large number of files that fit those criteria are need.

Usually, XML Benchmarking systems are for such propose: they consist of XML test collections and a set of execution tests—the test scenario—to measure used memory and processing time.

Nowadays, many works address this thematic (Mlýnková, 2009; Mlynkova, et al., 2006; Vranec & Mlýnková, 2009) and, more specifically, there exists a large set of XML Query Benchmarks. According to the work developed by Mlýnková and Vranec (2009) the seven best-known representatives are XMark (Busse, et al., 2003), XOO7[6], XMach-1 (Bohme & Rahm, 2002), MBench[7], XBench (Yao & Ozsu, 2003), XPathMark[8], and TPoX[9]. However, there are many other ones: for example, XML Test[10] is an XML processing test developed at Sun Microsystems (Sun Microsystems, 2009) aiming at comparing XML processing performance in Java and .NET.

For our testing proposes it is important to distinguish benchmarks from the point of view of the type of data: benchmarks involving real-world data from ones involving synthetic data (Mlýnková, 2009). According to a statistical analysis of real XML data collections (Mlýnková, 2006), we can conclude that they are usually very simple and do not cover all constructs allowed by XML specifications; can contain a huge number of errors or are not well-formed; are often available without any associated schema. These characteristics imply that important features of the tools under assessment could not be covered by the test sets. This statement led some people to defend the use of synthetic data, like Mlýnková. Synthetic data is created by the benchmark generator; based on user-specific characteristics (amount of documents and size of data), the generator produces documents covering as much as possible the various features of XML. These generators deal with marginal problems such as where to get the textual data or the elements/attributes name, to obtain data as natural as possible.

In opposition to Mlýnková approach, oriented towards synthetic data sets to build benchmarks, we decide to follow a more pragmatic approach oriented towards real-world test collections. We believe those collections better represent the data that most of the XML applications deal with, exactly because the synthetic data is limited to the user-specific characteristics. However, as stated before, real-world data does not have always the same and desired properties, and sometimes they have errors. However, we believe that it is possible to take advantage from those differences and errors, and assess the efficiency and performance of our tool by testing it under real circumstances (i.e. real data). This leads us to collect and rank a large number of real-world XML documents concerning their validity (well-formed and compliant with the schema), complexity, diversity in the number and size of elements and the size of the document, in order to provide an easy way to find the real-data document that fits the user needs for his/her specific benchmark. (XML Archive for Testing – Fonte, et al., 2010).

To build our XML collection, we searched for XML query benchmarks (publicly available and well described) which provide a set of testing collections and the respective operations. We collect and classify documents from the following list of available XML collections:

- MESH[11], Medical Subject Headings vocabulary files;
- Shakespeare[12], the complete plays of Shakespeare;
- Eurovoc[13], a multilingual thesaurus covering the fields in which the European communities are active; it provides a means of indexing the documents in the documentation systems of the European institutions and of their users;
- Miscellaneous (Religion[14], etc.), a set of diverse documents collected from different sources.

The Shakespeare and Religion sets are composed of larger files, excellent for performance tests. Eurovoc documents containing some usual errors are appropriate to analyse the system behaviour with malformed files. Mesh files are diverse in their content, so good to test the system response facing the diversity of information that can be present in XML files.

The several informal tests made during the development phase allowed us to conclude that our system is capable of working with large files without significant increase in the time needed to display the file. Moreover, GuessXQ is capable of displaying XML files with several MB without major problems. We also emphasize the system ability to identify any type of malformed documents, by validating each uploaded file against its respective XSD file, preventing system failures. We also noticed that GuessXQ coped appropriately with documents with diverse content components producing rich and interesting answers.

We intend now to test rigorously the system, as described above, and analyse the obtained answers in order to conclude if the prototype is ready to be deployed to end-users to be submitted to real tests—this will be a topic for future work.

CONCLUSION AND FUTURE WORK

This chapter presents new contributions for XML query specification in a user friendly interface, based on the traditional QBE approach. Existing works apply QBE to XML retrieval by showing the XML Schema to the user in order for him to select the needed information. Our system improves this by showing the user a sample document from the collection, giving a better indication of the information he can find in the collection. The GuessXQ prototype is fully detailed in a Technical Report (Fonte, 2010).

As future work, besides some ideas, which we gave along the descriptions of the system's architecture modules, we plan to implement a method for choosing an adequate sample document from the collection. There are two points of view to use those metrics in order to measure how much a document is an adequate sample document, i.e. how much it is representative of the collection: a common document – a document with a structure and contents similar to the majority of the documents; an including document – a document including as much as possible the Schema components and sub-trees. We defined algorithms for documents ranking using both points of view. Next step is to implement them and verify which one is more adequate for real case studies.

We think about the Portuguese Emigration Museum[15] as a real application for making experiments with real users. This museum is a Web-museum that wants to make easily accessible to the general public the rich cultural heritage characterizing the Portuguese emigration phenomenon, and the impress left by the Portuguese people around the world.

REFERENCES

Berglund, A., Boag, S., Chamberlin, D., Fernández, M., Kay, M., Robie, J., & Siméon, J. (2010). *XML path language (XPath) 2.0 (second edition).* W3C Working Draft. Retrieved February 22, 2012, from http://www.w3c.org/xpath20

Boag, S., Chamberlin, D., Fernández, M., & Florescu, D. Robie, & Siméon, J. (2010). *XQuery 1.0: An XML query language (second edition).* W3C Working Draft. Retrieved February 22, 2012, from http://www.w3c.org/TR/xquery

Bohere, K., Liu, X., McLaughlin, S., Schonberg, E., & Singh, M. (2003). Object oriented XML query by example. *Lecture Notes in Computer Science, 2814,* 323–329. doi:10.1007/978-3-540-39597-3_32

Böhme, T., & Rahm, E. (2002). XMach-1: A benchmark for XML data management. In *Database Systems in Office, Engineering and Science* (pp. 264–273). Berlin, Germany: Springer-Verlag. doi:10.1007/978-3-642-56687-5_20

Braga, D., & Campi, A. (2005). XQBE: A graphical environment to query XML data. *World Wide Web (Bussum)*, *8*(3), 287–316. doi:10.1007/s11280-005-0646-x

Cruz, D., Ferreira, F. X., Henriques, P. R., Gançarski, A. L., & Defude, B. (2009). GuessXQ: An inference web-engine for querying XML documents. In *Proceedings of INForum 2009 - Simpósio de Informática*, (pp. 322-325). Lisboa, Portugal: Faculdade de Ciências da Universidade de Lisboa.

Ferreira, F. X., Cruz, D., Henriques, P. R., Gançarski, A. L., & Defude, B. (2009). *A query by example approach for XML querying*. Paper presented at WISA - Workshop on Intelligent Systems and Applications, Iberic Conference on Information Systems and Technologies. Povoa de Varzim, Portugal.

Fonte, D. (2010). *GuessXQ: A query-by-example approach for XML querying. Technical report.* Braga, Portugal: Universidade do Minho.

Fonte, D., Carvalho, P., Cruz, D., Gançarski, A. L., & Henriques, P. R. (2010). XML archive for testing: A benchmark for GuessXQ. In *Proceedings of XATA 2010 - XML, Associated Technologies and Applications*, (pp. 127-138). Vila do Conde, Portugal: XATA.

Fonte, D., Cruz, D., Henriques, P. R., & Gançarski, A. L. (2010). GUI for XML documents access using query-by-example paradigm. In *Proceedings of Interacção 2010: Interacção Humano-Computador* (pp. 89–93). Aveiro, Portugal: Universidade de Aveiro.

Johnson, S. (1999). Query-by-example (QBE). In Ramakrishnan, R., & Gehrke, J. (Eds.), *Database Management Systems*. New York, NY: McGraw-Hill Publisher.

Kim, L. (2002). *The XMLSPY handbook*. New York, NY: John Wiley & Sons, Inc.

Li, X., Gennari, J. H., & Brinkley, J. F. (2007). XGI: A graphical interface for XQuery creation. In *Proceedings of the American Medical Informatics Association Annual Symposium*, (pp. 453-457). American Medical Informatics Association.

Lu, X. (1990). Document retrieval: A structural approach. *Information Processing & Management*, *26*(2), 209–218. doi:10.1016/0306-4573(90)90026-X

Ma, Q., & Tanaka, K. (2004). Topic-structure based complementary information retrieval for information augmentation. In Yu, J. X., Lin, X., Lu, H., & Zhang, Y. (Eds.), *Advanced Web Technologies and Applications* (pp. 608–619). Berlin, Germany: Springer. doi:10.1007/978-3-540-24655-8_66

Mlýnková, I. (2009). *XML benchmarking - The state of the art and possible enhancements*. Hershey, PA: IGI Global.

Mlýnková, I., Thoman, K., & Pokorny, J. (2006). Statistical analysis of real XML data collections. In *Proceedings of the 13th International Conference on Management of Data*. COMAD.

Newman, S., & Ozsoyoglu, Z. M. (2004). A tree-structured query interface for querying semi-structured data. In *Proceedings of the International Conference on Scientific and Statistical Database Management*. IEEE.

Schmidt, A., Waas, F., Kersten, M., Carey, M. J., Manolescu, I., & Busse, R. (2002). XMark - An XML benchmark project. In *Proceedings of the 28th VLDB Conference*. Hong Kong, China: VLDB.

Sun Microsystems. (2009). *The XML performance team: XML processing performance in Java and. NET*. Retrieved February 22, 2012, from http://java.sun.com/performance/reference/whitepapers/XML_Test-1_0.pdf

Tulchinsky, V. G., Yushchenko, A. K., & Yushchenko, R. A. (2008). Graph queries for data integration using xml. *Cybernetics and Systems Analysis, 44*(2), 292–303. doi:10.1007/s10559-008-0029-2

Vranec, M., & Mlýnková, I. (2009). FlexBench: A flexible XML query benchmark. In *Proceedings of DASFAA*, (pp. 421-435). DASFAA.

Yao, B. B., & Ozsu, M. T. (2003). *XBench - A family of benchmarks for XML DBMSs*. Retrieved from http://se.uwaterloo.ca/ ddbms/projects/xbench/

Zhang, S., Wang, J. T. L., & Herbert, K. G. (2002). XML query by example. *International Journal of Computational Intelligence and Applications, 2*(3), 329–337. doi:10.1142/S1469026802000671

Zloof, M. M. (1975). Query-by-example: The invocation and definition of tables and forms. In *Proceedings of the 1st International Conference on Very Large Data Bases*, (pp. 1-24). ACM Press.

KEY TERMS AND DEFINITIONS

Information Retrieval: Information Retrieval (IR) is the area of study concerned with searching for documents, for information within documents, and for metadata about documents, as well as that of searching structured storage, relational databases and the World Wide Web. The Web search engines are the most visible IR applications, and many universities and public libraries use IR systems to provide access to books, journals and other documents, intending to reduce the "information overload."

Query-by-Example: Query by Example (QBE) is a database query language for relational databases. It was devised by M. Zloof at IBM Research during the mid 1970s, in parallel to the development of SQL. It is the first graphical query language, using visual tables where the user would enter commands, example elements and conditions. Many graphical front-ends for databases use the ideas from QBE today.

Sample Suggestion: The automatic extraction of a sample document, picked-up from the XML document collection using an algorithm that chooses the most adequate according to a given criterion.

Visual Query Specification: The visual process of selecting components directly on the sample document, in order to generate the desired query.

Web User Interface: A user interface, in the field of human–machine interaction, is the space where interaction between humans and machines occurs. The goal of this interaction is effective operation and control of the machine, and feedback from the machine. Web user interfaces accept input and provide output by generating Web pages, which are transmitted via the Internet and viewed by the user using a Web browser program.

XML: Extensible Markup Language (XML) is a markup language that defines a set of rules for encoding documents in a format that is both human-readable and machine-readable. It is defined in the XML 1.0 Specification produced by the W3C, and several other related specifications, all free open standards.

XQuery: XQuery, an XML Query Language, is a query and functional programming language that is designed to query collections of XML data. XQuery 1.0 was developed by the XML Query working group of the W3C.

ENDNOTES

[1]   http//www.editix.com
[2]   http//www.oxygenxml.com
[3]   http://www.w3.org/XML/Schema
[4]   http://tools.ietf.org/html/rfc1321
[5]   http://www.w3.org/2001/XMLSchema.xsd
[6]   http://www.comp.nus.edu.sg/ebh/XOO7.html

7   The michigan benchmark http://www.eecs. umich.edu/db/mbench

8   http://users.dimi.uniud.it/massimo.france-schet/xpathmark

9   http://tpox.sourceforge.net/

10 XML_Test_1.1 downloadable at http://java. sun.com/performance/reference/codesa-mples/

11 http://www.nlm.nih.gov/mesh/xmlmesh. html.

12 http://xml.coverpages.org/bosakShake-speare200.html.

13 http://europa.eu/eurovoc.

14 http://www.ibiblio.org/pub/sun-info/stan-dards/xml/eg/

15 http://www.museu-emigrantes.org/

Section 2
Learning Environments

Chapter 5
On Quality Assessment of Learning Technology Specifications

José Janssen
Open Universiteit, The Netherlands

Adriana J. Berlanga
Open Universiteit, The Netherlands

Rob Koper
Open Universiteit, The Netherlands

ABSTRACT

Specifications can be considered "hidden" technology: they are deployed in tools and applications without being directly visible. This poses a challenge regarding quality assessment of this type of technology. This chapter describes a framework for quality assessment of learning technology specifications and how it was used to evaluate and improve a case in point: the Learning Path Specification. However, although the importance of raising the quality of a specification is beyond question, this in itself is no guarantee for its (wider) adoption. The final section of this chapter discusses how quality assessment of the Learning Path Specification at best informs us on its chances of gaining adoption, but by no means suffices to establish it. For this discussion, the authors draw on Rogers's work regarding five perceived characteristics of innovations influencing their diffusion: relative advantage, compatibility, complexity, triability, and observability.

INTRODUCTION

Considerable efforts are directed towards the development of specifications and standards to enable reuse and exchange of particular solutions (Hodgins, et al., 2003; McClelland, 2003; Sloep, 2004). The impact of this 'hidden' technology is far less tangible than that of a concrete tool. Moody (2005) makes a similar observation regarding the evaluation of conceptual models, stating that a finished product can be easily evaluated against initial requirements, while evaluation of a conceptual model involves tacit needs, desires and expectations as well.

DOI: 10.4018/978-1-4666-2669-0.ch005

The Learning Path Specification (Janssen, Hermans, Berlanga, & Koper, 2008) is a case in point: rather than a "finished product," it is a model to describe learning paths: sets of one or more learning actions that help attain a particular learning goal. Development of the Learning Path Specification was inspired by the question 'How can we support lifelong learners in finding learning actions and learning paths that best meet their needs?' Efficient and effective lifelong learning requires that learners can make well-informed decisions regarding the selection of a learning path and the best way to proceed along a chosen path. In order to support these processes a Learning Path Specification was developed, which enables transparent descriptions of possible ways to attain a particular learning goal, so that:

1. It becomes easier for learners to compare and select learning paths;
2. It becomes possible to automate navigation support for a chosen learning path;

3. It becomes easier to see which parts of a learning path (i.e. which learning actions) can be substituted by other learning actions (e.g. prior learning).

Figure 1 describes various tools that are envisaged to deploy the Learning Path Specification.

The Learning Path Specification is meant to support way finding in formal, non-formal, and informal learning. The benefits of using the specification would augment if the Learning Path Specification became more widely adopted, as this would offer the added value of exchange of learning paths between institutions and systems. Discussing ways forward for lifelong learning, Colardyn (2002) states that not only the visibility but also the portability and transferability of any form of learning should be ensured to further the European lifelong learning agenda. The Learning Path Specification could support this agenda if it became widely used, i.e. if it were to develop into a standard.

Figure 1. Tools building on the learning path specification

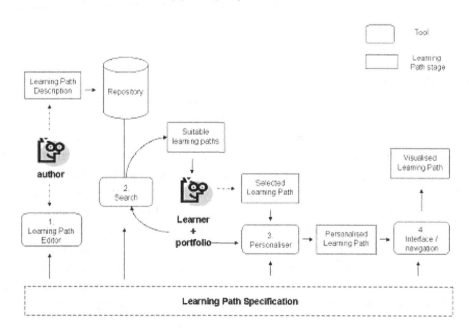

The following section briefly describes the Learning Path specifications. Next, a quality framework will be described that was developed with the aim to inform and guide quality assessment of the specification (Janssen, Berlanga, & Koper, 2011). This quality framework draws on general theories of model quality as related work regarding standards and software quality focuses on quality criteria like 'compliance,' 'reliability,' 'maintainability,' 'performance,' etc. (Côté, Suryn, & Georgiadou, 2007; Ortega, Pérez, & Rojas, 2003; Pfleeger, Fenton, & Page, 1994), which are typical for existing standards or software tools, but less suitable for the evaluation of a specification. The introduction of the quality framework is followed by a brief description of three studies, which were carried out to evaluate the quality of the Learning Path Specification based on this framework. The chapter continues by discussing how the results of these studies may not exactly guarantee wider adoption of the specification, but can nevertheless be used to assess the prospects of wider adoption and possible development into a standard. For this discussion, we draw on Rogers's (1995) five perceived characteristics of innovations that affect their chances of adoption: relative advantage, compatibility, complexity, triability, and observability.

THE LEARNING PATH SPECIFICATION

Requirements for the Learning Path Specification were drawn from literature in the field of curriculum design and lifelong learning, as well as recent initiatives to enhance comparability and exchangeability of learning actions (Janssen, Berlanga, Vogten, & Koper, 2008). We started from a learner (consumption) perspective, rather than a provider (provision) perspective. This approach has led the Learning Path Specification to distinguish itself from other specifications that aim to describe learning opportunities or learning objects to support retrieval and reuse of learning opportunities or learning objects, such as Learning Object Metadata (2002), Dublin Core Metadata Initiative – Education Application (2006), eXchange of Course Related Information (2006), and Metadata for Learning Opportunities Advertising (2008).

In sum, the requirements state that the Learning Path Specification should enable description of: learning outcomes and entry requirements, modular and nested compositions, mandatory and optional parts, ordering of parts, alternatives, completion requirements, and conditions. Further technical requirements were that the specification should enable to describe learning paths in a formal and interoperable way.

A conceptual model of the Learning Path Specification (Figure 2) was developed in UML.

The model states that a learning path has a start and a finish, which are defined in terms of competences at particular levels of proficiency. A learning path further defines one or more learning actions that lead from the start to the finish. Both the learning path and its actions are further described by a set of metadata specifying content, process, and planning information (e.g. title, description, assessment, tutoring, delivery mode, attendance hours). These metadata are assumed to play a role in the process of choosing a learning path.

The UML model was subsequently implemented in a binding using XML, so as to meet the technical requirements of formality and interoperability (Janssen, Hermans, Berlanga, & Koper, 2008). The Learning Path XML schema is based on the UML conceptual model but is not an 'exact match.' For instance, the attributes from the UML model have been regrouped in a container element 'Metadata.' Start, Finish and Learning Actions have been grouped in an element 'LearningPathDesign.' Thus, at the highest level, the schema distinguishes:

Figure 2. Learning path conceptual model

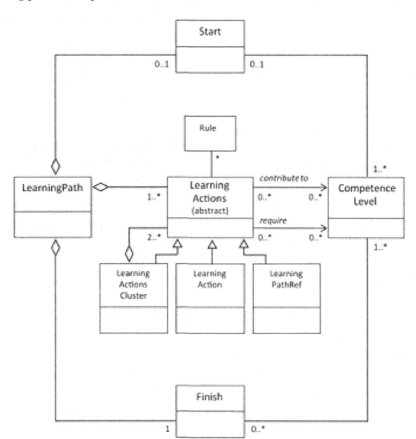

1. **Metadata:** Providing information about the Learning Path;
2. **LearningPathDesign:** Describing the structure of the Learning Path;
3. **CompetenceLevels:** The stepping stones constituting a blueprint for the design;
4. **LearningActions:** The actual steps the Learning Path proposes to the learner, in an order specified in the LearningPathDesign.

In other words, CompetenceLevels and LearningActions constitute the 'ingredients' of the LearningPathDesign, which in turn can be considered the 'recipe' that describes how and in which order the ingredients are mixed.

The following stakeholders can be identified in relation to the Learning Path Specification:

- Lifelong learners;
- Learning path designers;
- Providers;
- Software developers.

Now someone interested in finding suitable learning paths is likely to focus on different aspects of the Learning Path Specification than someone interested in designing learning paths or in developing tools to support these processes. Consequently, evaluation of the specification requires input from these different perspectives.

FRAMEWORK FOR QUALITY ASSESSMENT

The framework developed for the evaluation of the Learning Path Specification (Table 1) distinguishes three aspects of quality:

1. **Syntactic Quality:** Does the specification express what it intends to express in a correct way, i.e. in accordance with the syntax rules of the modeling language?
2. **Semantic Quality:** Does the specification represent essential features?
3. **Pragmatic Quality:** The specification easily comprehended and used by the stakeholders for its intended purpose?

Syntactic quality is at stake mainly in the process of modeling the specification in UML and in translating the specification to a binding, and is to a certain extent covered by validations provided through the modeling tools.

Regarding semantic quality Krogstie (1998) makes an interesting distinction between semantic quality and perceived semantic quality:

To build a model, one has to go through the participant's knowledge regarding the domain, and to check the model, one has to compare with the participant's interpretation of the externalized model. Hence, what we observe at quality control is not the actual semantic quality of the model, but a perceived semantic quality, based on comparisons of the two imperfect interpretations (Krogstie, 1998, p. 87).

Pragmatic quality, finally, can be further split into technical pragmatic quality and social pragmatic quality (Nelson, Poels, Genero, & Piattini, 2005), indicating whether the model is easily interpreted by tools and human users, respectively.

The quality, more particularly semantic and pragmatic quality, of the Learning Path Specification was enhanced through three successive stud-

ies. In these studies, the focus of attention gradually shifted from semantic to pragmatic quality, as it makes sense only to evaluate pragmatic quality after semantic quality has been sufficiently tested, because poor semantic quality will inevitably result in poor pragmatic quality.

ASSESSING AND IMPROVING THE LEARNING PATH SPECIFICATION

First, a case study was carried out to investigate the question whether the metadata included in the specification are clear and whether they reflect the characteristics that play a role in lifelong learners' choice processes (Janssen, et al., 2011). More particularly, the study addressed the following quality aspects relating to the purpose of enabling comparison and selection of learning paths:

1. Is the information provided by the model clear?
2. Is the specification complete: does the model contain all essential information lifelong learners' desire/need to select suitable learning paths?
3. Is the specification minimal: does the model contain information, which is not considered relevant by lifelong learners?

In order to answer these questions, choice processes were studied retrospectively through semi-structured interviews with learners (n=15) who recently decided upon a learning path having compared at least two different options. The interviews focused on identifying characteristics that played a role in the comparison and selection of learning paths, relying first on spontaneous recall, followed by a more structured approach of aided recall. Results indicated that the specification does not contain any redundant information. Rather the study led to further refinement of scheduling information, through addition of an element contact time, thus improving the specification's semantic

Table 1. Framework for the evaluation of the learning path specification

Quality dimensions	Description	Sub-characteristics	Description	Evaluation methods	Metrics
Syntactic quality	Does the model correctly express what is meant to be expressed in accordance with UML syntax rules?	proper notation of association, aggregation, generalization, multiplicity etc.		• Submit model to peer/ expert review • Validity checks through software	• Number and type of errors, ambiguities, etc.
Semantic quality	Does the model represent essential features of the phenomenon under study?	adequate[1] orthogonal/independent [3,5] valid [2,4]	The model adequately reflects the domain, i.e., independent aspects are captured by different concepts and relations are adequately represented.	• Explain the model to lifelong learners and learning path providers to see whether they find it adequate on points relevant to them • Analyse lifelong learners' learning path choice processes to establish learning path characteristics essential in this process • Map existing learning paths on model	• Number and type of issues open to debate • Number of changes made to the model • Number and type of frictions in mapping learning paths
		complete [1,3,4,5] nothing missing what is expected [2]	The model describes all essential features.		
		minimal [1] parsimonious [3,5] nothing unexpected presented [2]	The model does not contain irrelevant aspects and relations		
Pragmatic quality Social and Technical	Is the model easy to understand/ interpret correctly?	unambiguous [1,3]	Concepts and relations have a clear single meaning	• Establish whether the specification is adequate to develop tools. • Establish whether tools developed are considered useful	• Perceived ease of use • Perceived usefulness • Intention to use
		internally consistent [1,3]			
		general	Concepts should be as independent as possible from any specific application(domain)	• Map informal and non-formal learning paths from different domains	

[1] van Lamsweerde (2000) [2] Leung & Bolloju (2005) [3] Teeuw & van den Berg (1997) [4] Krogstie (1998) [5] Moody et al. (2002)

as well as pragmatic quality. Interestingly, the study also showed a need for subjective metadata: information on other learners' experiences with a particular learning path. However, information on learner experiences cannot be included in the specification, because the description of learning paths is made by the provider and the information on experiences is only of value when it is provided completely independently.

Further evaluations focused on pragmatic quality, i.e. the question whether stakeholders can understand and use the specification (Janssen, et al., 2010). In this, we distinguish first-order and second-order pragmatic quality, relating to two different types of users and usage of the specification. Firstly, software developers who use the specification directly in the process of implementing the specification in tools and secondly, end-users of these tools. As is illustrated by Figure 1 there is a chronological order, starting with the description of learning paths by means of a Learning Path Editor, and ending with an interface that provides navigational support. Hence, for the evaluation of pragmatic quality, development of a tool that enables description of learning paths was the most likely context to start with.

The Learning Path Editor was developed to function as a portlet within the Liferay environment (Liferay, 2000) and consists of three different 'views' that correspond to different tasks related to the description of learning paths:

1. Handling of learning paths, i.e. keep an overview, choose to change existing learning paths or to create a new learning path (Master view);
2. Describing the characteristics of a learning path (Metadata view);
3. Modelling a learning path (Design view).

In the Metadata view (Figure 3), the author enters a title and short description of the learning path and selects the competence levels which are attained upon completion of the learning path. The competence levels displayed in the metadata view are predefined and made available through another portlet within the Liferay Environment.

Additional characteristics of the learning path used by learners in the process of searching a suitable learning path, e.g. language, costs, delivery mode, etc., are specified through a form. When the necessary information has been provided, the author clicks 'save' and returns to the Master view, which now includes the newly created learning path. For the actual modeling of the learning path, the author clicks 'Design.'

In the Design view, the author can add actions or existing learning paths and group them in clusters to specify particular subsets, e.g. sequential ordering, choice options, etc. To add an Action the author clicks the 'Add action' button. A dialogue box appears which asks to provide a title and a Web address for the action. To group actions and/ or existing learning path descriptions into a cluster the author clicks 'Add Cluster.' A dialogue box appears, in which she can specify what type of cluster she wants to create: Free-order, Sequence or Parallel (Figure 4). Once the cluster has been added the author can drag and drop the required actions to the cluster.

The second study involving six software developers working more or less closely with the specification in developing the Learning Path Editor, led to three minor and three more profound adaptations of the specification, which all contributed to improved pragmatic quality of the specification in the sense that these changes made it easier for software developers to read, understand, and implement the specification (Janssen, et al., 2010). Minor changes are changes concerning the translation of the specification into this specific schema rather than the specification itself. The term 'specification' is somewhat confusing in this respect, as it is used both for conceptual models (e.g. a UML model) and the technical implementation of these models in a schema us-

Figure 3. Learning path editor metadata view: competence levels

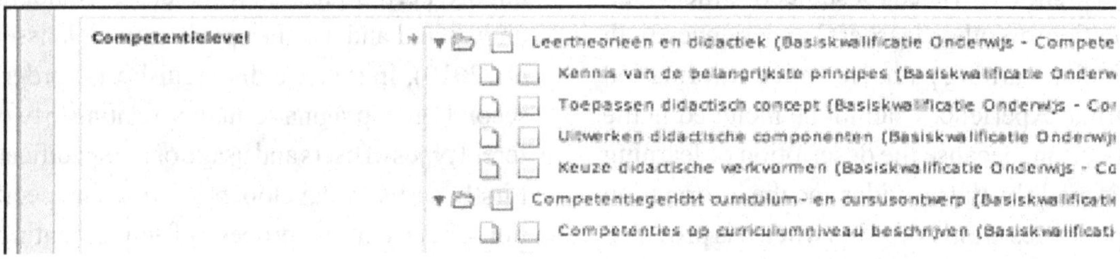

Figure 4. Learning path editor design view: add cluster

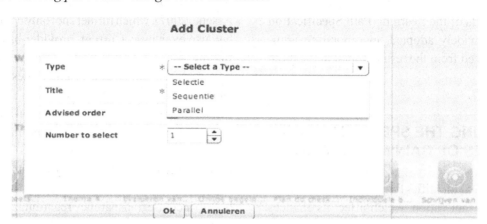

ing a particular syntax, in our case XML (cf. Klein, Fensel, Harmelen, & Horrocks, 2000). As is the case in natural language, the things we want to express can be made explicit in many different ways grammatically, representing different nuances perhaps, but still bearing the same message/meaning. Similarly, the minor adaptations made to the schema represent 'grammatical' or 'syntactical' changes. Nevertheless, even if we call these changes minor, they clearly brought about an important improvement in terms of pragmatic quality, in the sense that these changes made it easier for software developers to read, interpret, and deploy the specification.

Finally, a third evaluation was carried out to assess second-order pragmatic quality through a number of workshop sessions involving 16 prospective end users, occupying the job of study advisors and educational technologists (Janssen, et al., 2010). The workshop sessions entailed a video explaining the purposes of the Learning Path Specification including a demo of the Learning Path Editor. The demo was needed to communicate the purpose and intended use of the specification. Next, participants gained some hands-on experience with the Editor through three small tasks involving the adaptation of the learning path description they had watched being created in the demo. Finally, they were

asked to evaluate their experiences taking a broad perspective: i.e. considering the entire approach of describing learning paths through a learning path specification in the proposed way and its intended effects. The evaluation was carried out using an online adaptation of the Desirability Toolkit (Storm & Börner, 2009). Drawing on the product reaction cards methodology the toolkit allows respondents to select six cards (from a set of 118 cards containing positive and negative adjectives) which best express their experiences and evaluation of the proposed approach. It is not so much the precise set of selected adjectives, as the motivations provided along with them, which clarify users' views on both usability of the tool and desirability of the approach suggested by the Learning Path Specification. Results indicate that the nested structure of learning actions clusters within the learning path as an overall cluster, posed somewhat of a challenge. However, participants were confident this was only a matter of practice and developing some routine. As some participants found the term selection (indicating a particular type of cluster) confusing, a final change was made to the specification, replacing this term by 'free order.' Participants' motivations provided along with selected cards underlined that they consider the approach to increase transparency and efficiency, both for providers and learners.

In the final section of this chapter we assess the prospects of the Learning Path Specification becoming widely adopted, incorporating arguments derived from the results found in the three studies.

ASSESSING THE SPECIFICATIONS CHANCES OF GAINING ADOPTION

Rogers (1995) identifies five perceived characteristics of an innovation, which affect its chances of gaining adoption:

1. **Relative Advantage:** The innovation is perceived as having an advantage compared to the current situation.
2. **Compatibility:** The innovation is perceived as consistent with existing values, past experiences and needs of potential adopters.
3. **Complexity:** The degree to which an innovation is perceived as difficult to understand and use.
4. **Triability:** The degree to which an innovation may be experimented with
5. **Observability:** The degree to which the results of an innovation are visible.

We will discuss the Learning Path Specification with respect to these characteristics, drawing both on our own findings and related research areas.

Relative Advantage

The approach proposed by the Learning Path Specification has several advantages over the current situation and indeed related specifications. The first and principal advantage of the Learning Path Specification is that it facilitates comparison (hence selection) of a learning path as well as navigation through a learning path in an automated way. A second advantage lies in the fact that the Learning Path Specification proposes to draw on standard competence descriptions

(Kickmeier-Rust, Albert, & Steiner, 2006; Van Assche, 2007), which furthers not only comparison but also exchange. Current, provider-based, way finding support focuses on catalogue information such as course titles, subject descriptions, and difficulty levels. It is also led by marketing considerations: providers of education and training seek niche markets to distinguish themselves from others. Though this may help to cover the needs of the knowledge society and its demands for increased provision and diversity, it does not help to increase transparency regarding exchangeability of offerings.

Thirdly, the learning path metadata provide scheduling information. As the results of our first study indicate, this information is paramount in establishing suitability of a learning path. Existing metadata standards like Learning Object Metadata (2002) and the Dublin Core Education Application Profile (2006) do not include scheduling information. Other specifications that enable descriptions of learning opportunities—eXchanging Course Related Information (2006) and Metadata for Learning Opportunities Advertisement (2008)—do include scheduling information, but focus on the selection of formal courses and programmes rather than on provision of navigation support through a programme, as the Learning Path Specification does.

This brings us to the fourth distinguishing characteristic of the Learning Path Specification: it is sufficiently generic to include informal and non-formal learning. The generality of the specification becomes clear, for instance, in the use of element labels such as 'workload' to express the number of hours it takes to complete a learning path, rather than 'study hours' or 'credits.' Equivalent credits can easily be derived from the hours it takes to complete the learning path (European Credit Transfer System, 2009). The specification does of course require that learning paths are described in terms of specific competences and proficiency levels which they help to attain. Even learning that was not intentional, could in hindsight be described in terms of the actions that contributed to particular learning outcomes. The advantages of documenting informal learning paths, or learning paths that consist of a combination of formal, non-formal, and informal learning, could serve a variety of purposes, such as storage in an e-portfolio, as learning evidence, or storage in a repository in order to make them available as an example to others.

Studies in the field of knowledge management and workplace learning use the term codification (Bartholomaei, 2005; Foray & Lundvall, 1998; Kessels, 1999; Sørensen & Snis, 2001; Unwin, et al., 2007): "Where pedagogical practices are visibly encouraged and valued in workplaces, they may be underpinned by the codification of relevant knowledge and skills into a workplace curriculum" (Unwin, et al., 2007, p. 339). This could take the form of for instance a training manual.

The Learning Path Specification could be taken as an instrument to codify a particular kind of knowledge: knowledge about pathways to personal competence development. This way unarticulated, not yet codified, tacit knowledge becomes available as information to others (Boekhorst, Koers, & Kwast, 2000). Both the production and interpretation of codified knowledge requires a codebook (Bartholomaei, 2005). The Learning Path Specification could be considered just that: a codebook for the codification of learning paths. The added value of using a learning path specification for the codification of a workplace curriculum again lies in the fact that it provides links with formal competence descriptions, thus contributing to visibility and transparency of workplace learning. As Fuller and Unwin (2003) have pointed out, both the mapping of knowledge, skills and tasks in a workplace curriculum, and the codification of knowledge and competence in formal qualifications are important sources of reification (concretization) of learning.

Further research is needed to shed light on the question to what extent the Learning Path Specification is perceived to offer relative advantages by various stakeholders in the context of workplace learning, e.g. employers, employees, human resource managers, training providers.

Our evaluation of second-order pragmatic quality (the extent to which end users consider it desirable and doable to describe learning paths according to the specification) showed that potential end users of the Learning Path Editor clearly perceived relative advantages, especially the fact that a learning path specification enables comparison of learning paths on relevant characteristics as well as provision of automated navigational support. Some of them expressed a confidence that the benefits were obvious, judging by comments like: "Many will easily see the benefits," or "This is the innovation students have been waiting for." Several participants commented that description of learning paths in line with the specification will be time-consuming. However, in formal education the information needed to describe learning paths has to be provided for diverse purposes. When this information is described in XML, using the Learning Path Specification, it can be reused in many contexts, e.g. search engines, marketing, course catalogues etc. Some participants seemed to perceive this advantage by describing the approach as low maintenance pointing out that the structured and uniform description of this information makes it easier to update.

Compatibility

To what extent can the Learning Path Specification be considered as consistent with existing values, past experiences and needs of potential adopters? The need for navigational support became clear through other studies, most notably studies regarding student dropout (Janssen, et al., 2007). An initial solution, providing recommendations based on collaborative filtering, made clear that provision of navigational support helps to foster learner progress. Additionally the Learning Path Specification was developed to enable to describe learning paths and to define relations between learning actions.

Trying to establish to what extent the Learning Path Specification is consistent with needs of potential adopters is less straightforward, and carries a risk not uncommon to needs assessment generally. This is perhaps best illustrated by a well-known tale of a bygone era, which recounts of two employees of a shoe manufacturer, who are sent to Africa to investigate the market. Whereas the first employee reports back: 'In these parts people do not wear shoes, so no market for us here,' the second one concludes, 'People here hardly wear shoes, yet: great market potential!'

A similar ambivalence was visible in our study of lifelong learners' decision-making processes: if we had drawn conclusions solely on the base of an investigation of current practice of selecting a learning path, we would have underestimated lifelong learners' information needs, because quite regularly information was not taken into account simply because it was not available. Extending the investigation using aided recall and information needs more generally, led us to conclude that the learning path characteristics included in the specification are relevant. Besides, it made clear that additional scheduling information (contact-time) was required to further enhance the specifications compatibility with learners' information needs.

Finally, our evaluation of second-order pragmatic quality of the Learning Path Specification revealed that study advisors and learning designers clearly consider the specification to meet learners' needs for navigational support, both in selecting and following a learning path.

However, when it comes to adoption of the Learning Path Specification, learners, learning designers and study advisors are not the key agents at the outset. Rather, this will be experts and organisations that are directing the future of education and learning in Europe. Important questions concerning the role of these potential adopters are still unanswered. Given the fact that the knowledge economy encourages competitiveness too in the realm of educational and training, one question that arises is how reluctant providers will be to offer as much transparency as the Learning Path Specification requires. However, despite the competition, calls are heard as well for further collaboration, for example in a recent White Paper published jointly by CAUDIT, EDUCAUSE, JISC, and SURF (2010), "The Future of Higher Education: Beyond the Campus." This report mentions developments such as "above the campus" provisioning of technology and associated services, and increased openness and transparency of developing structures and sustainability models. According to the authors, some of these developments mean that institutions need to focus more on access than on ownership. Open educational resources potentially change the way higher education is delivered. Though the move towards open educational resources still faces some hurdles, for instance because the sources and oversight of resources vary considerably, it is expected to free institutions to shift their focus from developing educational content to programs and activities that improve competence development.

Trying to assess the compatibility of the Learning Path Specification with values and past experiences of potential adopters we cannot ignore the fact that so far, standards have not been uncontroversial:

On the one hand, cost-reduction, secure investments, and new market potentials are expected. On the other hand, there is the fear of limitations for creative solutions. Standards are often misunderstood, especially in the education community. They are perceived as restricting flexibility or creativity or huge additional effort (Ehlers & Pawlowski, 2006, p. 5).

Though this controversy was not paramount in our evaluation of second-order pragmatic quality, one of the study advisors did select the adjective 'patronizing,' explaining his choice by saying that it will become less easy to customize learning paths because of the use of standards.

With Ehlers and Pawlowski, we maintain that it is a misunderstanding to think that standards reduce flexibility. However, when stakeholders believe so, adoption will be more challenging. Therefore, it seems crucial to further probe these opposing views, and to ask what we and others mean by flexibility: flexibility of what and for whom? The fear that technology may restrict individual creativity and personal influence is to some extent understandable. Learning technology standards have been developed to increase flexibility, but with the further aim of increasing efficiency. This means that although the technology in itself increases flexibility, actual deployment policies often place the technology in the context of increasing efficiency, streamlining, etc. Computer-supported customization of learning paths is a case in point, leading to concerns such as: What happens when a learner wants to negotiate exceptions regarding specific learning actions? We would maintain that the Learning Path Specification and standards more generally, are not meant to deal with or solve exceptions. In this respect nothing changes: the learner will still have to get in touch with a study advisor, tutor, or other intermediary. However, this example also illustrates that it is a misunderstanding that standards are restrictive, though policies surrounding them might be, for instance, when the learner from our example has no one turn to with her request. The Learning Path Specification increases flexibility for learners, for instance in the sense that it facilitates exchange of learning actions and paths by linking them to standard competence descriptions. Besides, the specification offers flexibility in describing and combining formal, non-formal, and informal learning. This is not only a relative advantage, but also illustrates its compatibility with contemporary lifelong learning needs. Finally, the specification ensures that learning paths can be modeled in a flexible way because learning actions are not strictly connected with competences. This deliberately reflects the fact that in practice learning actions tend not to be linked to competences in a simple 'one on one'

base, and enables to even define learning actions that leave it to learners to decide upon the learning outcomes they want to achieve. Though internal validity of a learning path is of course a point of concern, research indicates that a rigid internal logic, which prevents integration of actors' interests, values, and beliefs potentially undermines external validity (Kessels & Plomp, 1999).

Paradoxically, enabling this kind of flexibility implies that in order to achieve a different kind of flexibility, e.g. automated adaptation of a learning path based on prior learning or exchange of particular elements between learning paths, relevant parts have to be modeled as learning paths within the overall learning path in order to enable strict matching based on attained competence levels.

In sum, the Learning Path Specification offers and supports flexibility in a variety of ways. Nevertheless, we should keep an open mind to potentially restrictive effects in the use of technology, e.g. in how a next step in a learning path is best presented (Janssen, et al., 2007). Although recommendations are optional, leaving it up to learners whether or not to the follow the advice provided (Drachsler, 2009), they may be restraining in other respects, which need further clarification. It is not really clear, for instance, whether learners would prefer to be presented a number of options, call it a 'prepared choice,' rather than a single recommendation. Nor is it clear how much information should be provided along with a recommended option and possible alternatives. As we have pointed out elsewhere (Janssen, Berlanga, & Koper, 2009), navigational support is meant to reduce learners' disorientation, but should still enable self-directed learning: "a form of study in which learners have the primary responsibility for planning, carrying out, and evaluating their own learning experiences" (Merriam & Caffarella, 1991, p. 41). The challenge is to present recommendations and learning paths in such a way that they help learners develop a structural representation of the knowledge domain (Chen, Fan, & Macredie, 2006).

Complexity

Our third study showed that prospective end-users do not consider the specification complex when it is explained to them, but tend to change their mind when they actually try to work with it. The clustering of learning actions, in combination with the fact that overall a learning path represents a cluster too, appeared somewhat difficult to grasp. However, participants tended to regard this indicative of a need for more examples and more practice to acquire some routine. The basic cluster types are fairly easy to understand. It is the nesting of clusters that proved challenging. In this respect it should be noted that the Learning Path Specification alone does not enable modelling of complex learning paths that require specification of rules (e.g. if learning action A is selected from cluster B, it should no longer be presented in cluster C). For this, a rule language is required in addition (Oussena & Barn, 2009).

Though the Learning Path Specification itself is not very complex, our experiences in the course of designing and piloting studies for the evaluation of the Learning Path Specification have made us aware that a description of informal learning paths is not an easy task to perform by learners themselves, due to the fact that it requires both sufficient distance to reflect on the learning path and the skills to distinguish between learning actions and learning outcomes, in sum learning design skills. However, learning paths might also be derived in a semi-automated way, for instance, from portfolios.

Triability

We expect perceived triability of the Learning Path Specification to be very low for a number of reasons. First of all, providers will be reluctant to try it out unless it becomes clear that a critical mass can be attained. Secondly, the Learning Path Specification does not stand on its own. This has become clear, in particular, in the description of the Learning Path Editor; its integration in a wider infrastructure, for necessary interactions with portlets (services) that have been developed for the description of competences and the presentation of learning paths to learners.

Triability would certainly increase if these services were provided 'above campus' (Caudit, et al., 2010) and made freely available. 'Above campus' provision will be a necessity at any rate as the way finding problem extends beyond a single institution and even country. Ideally, other services are provided alongside, e.g. services that enable enrolment, accreditation, development of joint programmes, etc. (Pawlowski & Adelsberger, 2002). Our first study investigating lifelong learners' information needs indicates that services enabling use of subjective metadata (Hodgins, 2006; Manouselis & Vuorikari, 2009) would be appreciated too.

Observability

As was stated in the introductory section, specifications and standards can be considered 'hidden technology.' Heddergot (2006) notes in this respect:

Discussing standards in e-learning means talking about a matter, that mostly cannot be recognised at first sight—from a learner or customer view, one is talking about an "invisible subject." Generally, most standards are for developers only. (...) this is because most benefits of standards indeed are created underneath in the thicket of markup languages (Heddergott, 2006, p. 185).

In fact, our research design demonstrates the fact that the observability of the Learning Path Specification is low. The lack of observability of the Learning Path Specification affected our evaluation of pragmatic quality. It led us to distinguish first-order and second-order pragmatic quality in relation to two types of users: software programmers who use the specification in a direct way and end users who engage with tools that are developed to deploy the specification. Besides, it led us to evaluate second-order pragmatic quality using both a demo and the Learning Path Editor.

CONCLUSION

The framework for the evaluation of the Learning Path Specification presented in this chapter, has proved valuable, especially in designing various complementary evaluation studies and in keeping sight of how they relate to one another, e.g. first-order pragmatic quality assessment (implementation) and second-order pragmatic quality assessment (user study) provide quite different results and insights.

A point of concern regarding the evaluation of second-order pragmatic quality was how to make sure that it would be an evaluation of the specification, rather than this specific implementation: the Learning Path Editor. Duval (2004) discusses this problem stating that "specifications cannot be validated with end users as such. Rather, the interoperability specifications will give rise to specifications of software tools that will offer a set of functionalities to the end user" (Duval, 2004, p. 37). The use of the tool by end users can be evaluated and has to be carefully analyzed to determine whether eventual problems are caused by the specification, the functionality of the tool, or the interface through which the functionality is provided.

Though we agree with Duval's problem analysis, we have not chosen to restrict our evaluation to use of the tool, but to extend the evaluation to the specifications wider purposes. This makes sense not only because use of the tool, the Learning Path Editor, represents only an 'intermediate' step (i.e. describing learning paths with a further aim), but is also in line with our perception of a specification as a conceptual model. After all, one of the purposes of a conceptual model is to enable communication (Moody, 2005). This approach

implies that the results of an innovation may not be observable yet, but might still be anticipated. Thus, our approach enabled us to gather data on usability as well as desirability.

We stated above that syntactic quality and semantic quality precede pragmatic quality. If a specification lacks clarity or completeness or if it is poorly expressed in UML, XML or any other language, this will affect pragmatic quality, i.e. whether the specification is (easily) understood. In other words, semantic quality and syntactic quality are a prerequisite (but not sufficient) condition for pragmatic quality. However, paradoxically, some semantic and syntactic flaws are likely to become visible only in the process of deploying the specification. This means that the evaluation of model quality is inevitably an iterative process.

The results obtained through the various studies provided valuable input for another assessment, namely of the Learning Path Specification's chances to become widely adopted. For this purpose, we used another framework: Rogers's (1995) five perceived characteristics of innovations, which affect an innovation's chances of adoption. Though these characteristics are clearly related to the concepts of quality and usability they extend the initial framework by including a much broader context of use, i.e. the wider world 'out there' and the way it will perceive the specification.

REFERENCES

Bartholomaei, M. (2005). *To know is to be: three perspectives on the codification of knowledge*. Sussex, UK: University of Sussex.

Boekhorst, A., Koers, D., & Kwast, I. (2000). *Informatievaardigheden*. Utrecht, The Netherlands: Uitgeverij Lemma.

Caudit, E. JISC, & Surf. (2010). *The future of higher education: Beyond the campus*. Retrieved 03-04-2010, from http://net.educause.edu/ir/library/pdf/PUB9008.pdf

Chen, S. Y., Fan, J.-P., & Macredie, R. D. (2006). Navigation in hypermedia learning systems: Experts vs. novices. *Computers in Human Behavior, 22*, 251–266. doi:10.1016/j.chb.2004.06.004

Colardyn, D. (2002). From formal education and training to lifelong learning. In Colardyn, D. (Ed.), *Lifelong Learning: Which Ways Forward?* (pp. 17–28). Utrecht, The Netherlands: Lemma.

Côté, M.-A., Suryn, W., & Georgiadou, E. (2007). In search for a widely applicable and accepted software quality model for software quality engineering. *Software Quality Journal, 15*, 401–416. doi:10.1007/s11219-007-9029-0

Drachsler, H. (2009). *Navigation support for learners in informal learning networks.* (Doctoral Thesis). Open Universiteit. Heerlen, The Netherlands. Retrieved from http://dspace.ou.nl/handle/1820/2098

Dublin Core Metadata Initiative. (2006). *Dublin core metadata initiative: Education application profile.* Retrieved from http://dublincore.org/educationwiki/DC_2dEducation_20Application_20Profile

Duval, E. (2004). Learning technology standardization: Making sense of it all. *Computer Science and Information Systems, 1*(1), 33–43. doi:10.2298/CSIS0401033D

Ehlers, U., & Pawlowski, J. M. (2006). Quality in European e-learning: An introduction. In Ehlers, U., & Pawlowski, J. M. (Eds.), *Handbook on Quality and Standardisation in E-Learning* (pp. 1–13). Berlin, Germany: Springer. doi:10.1007/3-540-32788-6_1

European Credit Transfer System. (2009). *ECTS users' guide.* Brussels, Belgium: Directorate General for Education and Culture.

eXchanging Course-Related Information. (2006). *Website.* Retrieved from http://www.xcri.co.uk/schemas/xcri_r1.0.xsd

Foray, D., & Lundvall, B.-Å. (1998). The knowledge-based economy: From the economics of knowledge to the learning economy. In Neef, D., Siesfeld, G. A., & Cefola, J. (Eds.), *The Economic Impact of Knowledge* (pp. 115–121). London, UK: Butterworth-Heinemann. doi:10.1016/B978-0-7506-7009-8.50011-2

Fuller, A., & Unwin, L. (2003). Learning as apprentices in the contemporary UK workplace: Creating and managing expansive and restrictive participation. *Journal of Education and Work, 16*(4). doi:10.1080/1363908032000093012

Heddergott, K. (2006). The standards jungle: Which standard for which purpose? In Ehlers, U.-D., & Pawlowski, J. M. (Eds.), *Handbook on Quality and Standardisation in E-Learning* (pp. 185–191). Berlin, Germany: Springer. doi:10.1007/3-540-32788-6_13

Hodgins, W. (2006). Out of the past and into the future: Standards for technology enhanced learning. In Ehlers, U.-D., & Pawlowski, J. M. (Eds.), *Handbook on Quality and Standardisation in E-Learning* (pp. 309–327). Berlin, Germany: Springer. doi:10.1007/3-540-32788-6_21

Janssen, J., Berlanga, A. J., Heyenrath, S., Martens, H., Vogten, H., & Finders, A. (2010). Assessing the learning path specification: A pragmatic quality approach. *Journal of Universal Computer Science, 16*(21), 3191–3209.

Janssen, J., Berlanga, A. J., & Koper, R. (2011). Evaluation of the learning path specification. *Journal of Educational Technology & Society, 14*(3), 218–230.

Janssen, J., Berlanga, A. J., Vogten, H., & Koper, R. (2008). Towards a learning path specification. *International Journal of Continuing Engineering Education and Lifelong Learning, 18*(1), 77–97. doi:10.1504/IJCEELL.2008.016077

Janssen, J., Berlanga, J., & Koper, R. (2009). How to find and follow suitable learning paths. In Koper, R. (Ed.), *Learning Network Services for Professional Development* (pp. 151–166). Berlin, Germany: Springer. doi:10.1007/978-3-642-00978-5_9

Janssen, J., Hermans, H., Berlanga, A. J., & Koper, R. (2008). *Learning path information model*. Retrieved from http://hdl.handle.net/1820/1620

Janssen, J., Tattersall, C., Waterink, W., Van den Berg, B., Van Es, R., & Bolman, C. (2007). Self-organising navigational support in lifelong learning: How predecessors can lead the way. *Computers & Education, 49*(3), 781–793. doi:10.1016/j.compedu.2005.11.022

Kessels, J. (1999). Het verwerven van competenties: Kennis als bekwaamheid. *Opleiding & Ontwikkeling, 12*(1-2), 7–11.

Kessels, J., & Plomp, T. (1999). A systemic and relational approach to obtaining curriculum consistency in corporate education. *Journal of Curriculum Studies, 31*(6), 679–709. doi:10.1080/002202799182945

Kickmeier-Rust, M. D., Albert, D., & Steiner, C. (2006). *Lifelong competence development: On the advantages of formal competence-performance modeling*. Paper presented at the International Workshop in Learning Networks for Lifelong Competence Development, TENCompetence Conference. Sofia, Bulgaria.

Klein, M., Fensel, D., Harmelen, F. V., & Horrocks, I. (2000). The relation between ontologies and schema-languages: Translating OIL-specifications to XML-schema. In *Proceedings of the Workshop on Application of Ontologies and Problem-Solving Methods*. Berlin, Germany: ECAI.

Krogstie, J. (1998). Integrating the understanding of quality in requirements specification and conceptual modeling. *ACM SIGSOFT Software Engineering Notes, 23*(1), 86–91. doi:10.1145/272263.272285

Learning Object Metadata. (2002). *Learning technologies standards committee of the IEEE 148.41.21*. Retrieved from http://ltsc.ieee.org/wg12/files/LOM_1484_12_1_v1_Final_Draft.pdf

Leung, F., & Bolloju, N. (2005). *Analyzing the quality of domain models developed by novice systems analysts*. Paper presented at the 38th Annual Hawaii International Conference on System Sciences. Hawaii, HI.

Liferay. (2000). *Liferay open source enterprise portal*. Retrieved from http://www.liferay.com

Manouselis, N., & Vuorikari, R. (2009). *What if annotations were reusable: A preliminary discussion*. Paper presented at the 8th International Conference Advances in Web Based Learning - ICWL 2009. Aachen, Germany.

McClelland, M. (2003). Metadata standards for educational resources. *Computer, 36*, 107–109. doi:10.1109/MC.2003.1244540

Merriam, S. B., & Caffarella, R. S. (1991). *Learning in adulthood: A comprehensive guide*. San Francisco, CA: Jossey-Bass.

Metadata for Learning Opportunities Advertising. (2008). *Website*. Retrieved from ftp://ftp.cenorm.be/PUBLIC/CWAs/e-Europe/WS-LT/CWA15903-00-2008-Dec.pdf

Moody, D. L. (2005). Theoretical and practical issues in evaluating the quality of conceptual models: Current state and future directions. *Data & Knowledge Engineering, 55*, 243–276. doi:10.1016/j.datak.2004.12.005

Moody, D. L., Sindre, G., Brasethvik, T., & Sølvberg, A. (2002). *Evaluating the quality of process models: Empirical analysis of a quality framework*. Paper presented at the 21st International Conference on Conceptual Modeling – ER 2002. Tampere, Finland.

Nelson, H. J., Poels, G., Genero, M., & Piattini, M. (2005). Quality in conceptual modeling: Five examples of the state of the art. *Data & Knowledge Engineering, 55*, 237–242. doi:10.1016/j.datak.2004.12.004

Ortega, M., Pérez, M., & Rojas, T. (2003). Construction of a systemic quality model for evaluating a software product. *Software Quality Journal, 11*, 219–242. doi:10.1023/A:1025166710988

Oussena, S., & Barn, B. (2009). *The Pspex project: Creating a curriculum management domain map*. Retrieved 29-07-2009 from http://www.elearning.ac.uk/features/pspex

Pawlowski, J. M., & Adelsberger, H. H. (2002). Electronic business and education. In *Handbook on Information Technologies for Education and Training* (pp. 653–672). Berlin, Germany: Springer-Verlag.

Pfleeger, S. L., Fenton, N., & Page, S. (1994). Evaluating software engineering standards. *Computer, 27*(9), 71–79. doi:10.1109/2.312041

Rogers, E. M. (1995). *Diffusion of innovations*. New York, NY: The Free Press.

Sloep, P. B. (2004). Learning objects: The answer to the knowledge economy's predicament? In Jochems, W., Koper, R., & Merriënboer, J. V. (Eds.), *Integrated E-Learning*. London, UK: Routledge/Falmer.

Sørensen, C., & Snis, U. (2001). Innovation through knowledge codification. *Journal of Information Technology, 16*(2), 83–97. doi:10.1080/026839600110054771

Storm, J., & Börner, D. (2009). *Online desirability kit*. Retrieved 08-02-2010, from http://desirabilitykit.appspot.com/

Teeuw, W. B., & Van den Berg, H. (1997). *On the quality of conceptual models*. Paper presented at the ER 1997 Workshop on Behavioral Models and Design Transformations: Issues and Opportunities in Conceptual Modeling. Los Angeles, CA.

Unwin, L., Felstead, A., Fuller, A., Bishop, D., Lee, T., & Jewson, N. (2007). Looking inside the Russian doll: The interconnections between context, learning and pedagogy in the workplace. *Pedagogy, Culture & Society, 15*(3), 333–348. doi:10.1080/14681360701602232

Van Assche, F. (2007). *Linking learning resources to curricula by using competencies*. Paper presented at the First International Workshop on Learning Object Discovery & Exchange (LODE 2007). Retrieved from http://ceur-ws.org/Vol-311/paper11.pdf

Van Lamsweerde, A. (2000). Formal specification: A roadmap. In A. Finkelstein (Ed.), *The Future of Software Engineering: 22nd International Conference on Software Engineering*. ACM Press.

KEY TERMS AND DEFINITIONS

Compatibility: The degree to which an innovations is perceived as consistent with existing values, past experiences and needs of potential adopters.

Complexity: The degree to which an innovation is considered hard to understand and use.

Learning Path: A set of one or more learning actions that help attain (a) particular learning goal(s).

Observability: The degree to which the results of an innovation are visible.

Pragmatic Quality: Indicates whether a model can be easily comprehended and applied for its intended purposes.

Relative Advantage: The degree to which an innovation is perceived as offering an advantage over the present situation.

Semantic Quality: Indicates whether a model represents essential features, i.e. no essential features are omitted and no non-essential features included.

Syntactic Quality: Indicates whether a model expresses that what is meant to be expressed in accordance with the syntax rules of the modeling language.

Triability: The degree to which an innovation lends itself for experimentation.

Chapter 6
MCEQLS Approach in Multi-Criteria Evaluation of Quality of Learning Repositories

Eugenijus Kurilovas
Vilnius University, Lithuania & Vilnius Gediminas Technical University, Lithuania

ABSTRACT

This chapter analyzes the quality of XML learning object repositories. Special attention is paid to the models and methods to evaluate the quality of learning repositories. Multiple criteria decision analysis and optimization methods are explored to be applied for evaluating the quality of learning repositories. This chapter also presents the results of several large-scale projects co-funded by EU research programs that have been implemented in the area of learning repositories. Learning repositories' technological quality model (system of criteria) and novel comprehensive model for evaluating the quality of user interfaces of learning repositories are presented in more detail. The general MCEQLS (Multiple Criteria Evaluation of Learning Software) approach is presented in this chapter. It is shown that the MCEQLS approach is suitable for evaluating the quality of learning repositories. The author believes that research results presented in the chapter will be useful for all educational stakeholder groups interested in developing learning repositories.

DOI: 10.4018/978-1-4666-2669-0.ch006

1. INTRODUCTION

LO Repositories (LORs), or learning repositories, are considered here as properly constituted systems (i.e. organised learning object collections) consisting of learning objects, their metadata and tools / services to manage them (Kurilovas, 2009c). Learning Object (LO) is referred here as "any digital resource that can be reused to support learning" (Wiley, 2000).

Authorities and/or companies in many countries have launched Web-based learning repositories in order to make it easier for teachers and students to find the best relevant LOs. The variety in the LORs across Europe reflects this situation: they are all Web based. However, some repositories are merely catalogues of LOs. They only contain descriptions of the learning content.

There has been a number of large scale LORs related EU-funded projects implemented in Europe during last few years. The largest of them are FP6 CALIBRATE, eContent*plus* ASPECT and eContent*plus* EdReNe projects. The author of this chapter acted as a manager of a Lithuanian team is all of those projects.

CALIBRATE and ASPECT projects were aimed at creation and development of European Learning Resource Exchange (LRE, 2011) system.

CALIBRATE (Calibrating eLearning in Schools) project (2005 – 2008) led to the design and implementation of an open source brokerage system that relies on open standards and open content to promote the exchange of LOs within a federation of e-learning systems. Its role is limited to carrying and routing messages exchanged by federation members rather than to facilitate semantic interoperability. With the system, semantic interoperability becomes the responsibility of the federation members that rely on "clients" to communicate with the brokerage system and to support the negotiation of common query languages and metadata formats. The system itself adopts a service-oriented architecture so that each service (e.g., LO discovery, digital rights management) can be used separately and combined with any (group) of the others. Current services include connection management, federated searching, and metadata harvesting.

CALIBRATE has produced tools to help developers to connect systems (e.g., repositories, search interfaces) to the federation. Tools include a test instance of the federation, a test repository, a test search interface, a "query watcher," a tool for monitoring connections, and a connection toolkit. CALIBRATE developed an Agent-Based Search System (ABSS) to help ranking search results according to the profiles of users. This was implemented in the CALIBRATE portal/ federation as follows: (1) the ABSS collects LRE metadata using the LRE harvesting service, (2) the CALIBRATE portal provides the ABSS with user profiles and Contextual Attention Metadata (CAM) using a SQI (Sequential Inquiry Interface) service, and (3) the ABSS is queried using the SQI service.

The ASPECT (Adopting Standards and Specifications for Educational Content) Best Practice Network (2008 – 2011) involved project partners and teachers using a version of the LRE service that enables schools to find open educational content from many different countries and providers. In ASPECT, a customised and password protected version of the LRE was developed for schools in the project that contained LOs from commercial providers and some additional search and retrieval features related to the exploration of the standards under investigation in the project.

In ASPECT, content providers from both the public and private sectors applied content standards to their LOs and made them available via the LRE. This represents a large-scale implementation of standards and specifications for content discovery and use.

As a result, the following elements, not directly linked to the quality of the specifications themselves, were identified as necessary for the successful adoption of the content standards:

- Availability and quality of tools for producing compliant content and metadata.
- Availability and quality of tools to test for compliance.
- Availability of solutions adapted to the different needs of content providers from both the public and private sectors.

CALIBRATE and ASPECT research results are analysed in detail by Kurilovas (2012).

EU EdReNe (Educational Repositories Network) was co-financed by the Commission in 2007 – 2010 and currently is funded by the network members. EdReNe has analysed that some repositories contain both content and a brief description of each title, meaning they have both data (the LO itself) and metadata. EdReNe has also analysed that it is certainly the case that the approaches taken by the various European countries differ. However, all countries share the objective of making LOs available and visible to the users, and face the same challenges of, e.g., reaching many users, managing rights, and adopting standards. The EdReNe partners together with the external experts have performed a LOR issues analysis that has shown that the high priority of the research of LOR user interfaces.

The educational sector needs high quality software (e.g., LORs) to provide students with qualitative education services. LORs are the main parts of any education institution's e-learning system and environment, and therefore the overall quality of the learning environment and learning services mostly depends on the quality of this kind of software.

The main players in the educational sector are the educational institutions themselves (schools, universities, etc.), educational authorities (ministries of education, regional and other agencies, etc.) and policy makers, as well as providers of the educational software (LOs publishers, LORs producers, etc.). Educational institutions are interested in using the high quality software. Therefore, they need proper approaches, models, and methods how to choose qualitative educational software in the market or to find free software. Publishers and vendors are interested in proposing such educational software to the institutions, and the policy makers are interested to be aware of these models and methods in order to formulate the education policy (e.g., while implementing the public tenders on providing the educational sector with LORs services). All these education sector stakeholders need to know for sure which kind of LORs are qualitative ones and which are not. Therefore, this problem is of very high practical relevance for the educational sector that needs clear and easy to use models and methods to evaluate the quality of the learning software in the market, both the proprietary and free one. Those proper quality evaluation models and methods have to fit all the aforementioned stakeholders' needs. Therefore, the problem of evaluation of the quality of LORs is high on the agenda of the international research and education systems.

The rest of this chapter is organised as follows. Section 2 presents what are XML repositories; Section 3 presents multiple criteria decision analysis and optimisation methods suitable to evaluate quality of LORs. The MCEQLS (Multiple Criteria Evaluation of Learning Software) approach to evaluate quality of LORs is presented in more detail. Section 4 presents both LOR general technological as well as user interface quality models (criteria systems), Section 5 offers further research trends, and conclusions are provided in Section 6.

2. XML REPOSITORIES

According to Dallas (2008), what all XML repositories have in common is the fundamental adoption of XQuery over SQL as the query language for content discovery and metadata management. This mechanism goes beyond simple support for API on top of a relational database architecture, integrating XQuery into the core of the system.

According to Bourret (2005), an XML document is a database only in the strictest sense of the term, i.e., it is a collection of data. As a "database" format, XML has some advantages. For example, it is self-describing (the mark-up describes the structure and type names of the data, although not the semantics), it is portable (Unicode), and it can describe data in tree or graph structures. It also has some disadvantages, i.e., it is verbose and access to the data is slow due to parsing and text conversion. A more useful question to ask is whether XML and its surrounding technologies constitute a "database" in the broader sense of the term—that is, a Database Management System (DBMS). The answer to this question could be "a sort of." On the one side, XML provides many of the aspects found in databases: storage (XML documents), schemas (DTDs, XML Schemas, RELAX NG, etc.), query languages (XQuery, XPath, XQL, XML-QL, QUILT, etc.), programming interfaces (SAX, DOM, JDOM), etc. On the other side, it lacks many of the things found in real databases such as efficient storage, indexes, security, transactions and data integrity, multi-user access, triggers, queries across multiple documents, and so on.

According to Shaffner (2001), an XML repository is a system for storing and retrieving XML data. This data is usually in the form of XML documents and their associated Document Type Definitions (DTDs) or XML Schemas. XML data lends itself to a hierarchical structure rather than a relational structure. Therefore, it may be difficult to store XML data in traditional relational database systems. The repository itself may be a relational database system, but it is more likely to be a custom storage system built exclusively for XML (or hierarchical) data. The data storage method will vary depending on the specific system being used. The process of storing and

retrieving data may also vary. Data can be stored and retrieved using a key-based indexing system or a query-based retrieval system. Finally, XML repositories may use a variety of access methods. Some systems use a proprietary API based on COM, CORBA, or Enterprise JavaBeans (EJB), while others use a more open ODBC standard. Most repositories provide good support for network access. According to Shaffner (2001), the process of storing XML data consists of two tasks: adding a new XML document to the repository and updating an existing document. Removing a document from the repository is considered a specialised example of updating an existing document. As far as XML data is not based on a traditional relational model, implementing XML repositories using such databases can be complex and cumbersome.

The method used to retrieve XML documents is related to the storage method. For relational systems, this will usually be through SQL or stored procedures. These methods have the disadvantage of accessing and returning data as a relational set rather than as an XML hierarchical structure. Hierarchical systems will usually provide an XQL or XPath method for accessing XML data. These technologies more accurately reflect the type of data queries made against XML data. They also provide the data in a hierarchical format (Shaffner, 2001).

According to Kellokoski (1999), XML enables many new technologies, including Internet Search Engines, Electronic Commerce, EDI, Self-describing BLOBS and Distributed Object file Systems, Data Repurposing, Content Personalisation (intelligent pull, agent accumulation, and push), Customized Bandwidth Allocation, Individual Content Cache, etc. All of the applications described above require data persistence, and these requirements are very different from the requirements of monolithic file storage. XML extends HTML's simple unidirectional linking, adding support for links to multiple targets, indirect addressing, and bidirectionality. Handling this rich linking requires a storage mechanism with far more powerful management of references between objects than that provided by the file system or relational databases. In order to effectively address the XML opportunity the storage mechanisms must also be able to understand the structure of XML content—which is composed of a dynamic number of objects—while scaling effectively to handle increased usage load and data volume. Furthermore, XML's object centric focus will create the need for an API that enables rich object-centric manipulation from object-oriented languages such as C++ and Java. In other words, what is needed is an XML-aware object repository. Only an object database management system can maintain information about XML document structure in a scalable manner while handling standard data types and BLOBs with rich hyperlinking and navigation in the database. HTML is stored as a monolithic block. Therefore, HTML storage management is almost always implemented using flat file storage. Using the file system this way provides acceptable functionality, and therefore wins out because it is extremely easy to implement.

According to Kellokoski (1999), the ideal XML repository should address the needs of XML as well as the needs of the associated applications. In evaluating the requirements of applications in this field, the following criteria are critical:

1. **Scalability:** Scalability will be very important since the XML applications described above will run on both the client and the server. It is important that the object database scale down as well as up, while leveraging the same APIs, to simplify application development.
2. **Language Support:** Language support is also important. Ease of programming is critical due to the compressed development cycles.
3. **Ease of Programming**; and
4. **Embeddability:** Embeddability encompasses two criteria—zero-management and

low memory footprint. Embeddability is an interesting issue since it has both short and long-term ramifications. In the short-term, embeddability it important because most initial XML applications, lacking sufficient XML support in the file system, will build-in this support. However, long-term the object database will replace the standard file manager running on top of the file system. This of course will make embeddability an absolute requirement.

3. QUALITY EVALUATION METHODS FOR LEARNING REPOSITORIES

3.1. What is Multiple Criteria Decision Analysis?

According to Oliver (2000), evaluation can be characterised as "the process by which people make judgements about value and worth." In the context of learning technology this judgement process is complex and often controversial. Although the notion of evaluation is rooted in a relatively simple concept, the process of judging the value of learning technology is complex and challenging.

Evaluation of quality is usually defined as "the systematic examination of the extent to which an entity (part, product, service, or organisation) is capable of meeting specified requirements" (ISO/IEC 14598-1:1999, 1999).

Expert evaluation is referred here as a multiple criteria evaluation of the learning software aimed at the selection of the best alternative based on score ranking results (Kurilovas & Dagiene, 2010a, 2009a, 2009b). Until today, a number of researchers have proposed several frameworks for the evaluation of quality of LORs, but the main problem of these frameworks is a high level of subjectivity of the expert evaluation. There are also a number of problems dealing with comprehensiveness and overall construction of quality evaluation models. The majority of researchers do not use any appropriate scientific approaches, principles and methods to establish the proper quality evaluation models and methods. The author believes that there are several scientific methods and models to minimise the subjectivity level and to improve the expert evaluation of quality of the learning software.

According to Dzemyda and Saltenis (1994), if the set of decision alternatives is assumed to be predefined, fixed and finite, then the decision problem is to choose the optimal alternative (of the learning software) or, maybe, to rank them. However, usually the experts (decision-makers) have to deal with the problem of an optimal decision in the multiple criteria situation where the objectives are often conflicting. Evaluation of the quality of LORs is a typical case where the criteria are conflicting, i.e., LORs could be very qualitative against a number of criteria, and not qualitative against the other ones, and vice versa. On the other hand, these evaluation criteria should reflect the opinion of all stakeholders (education policy makers, teachers, and publishers/vendors—providers of the learning software). In this case, according to Dzemyda and Saltenis (1994), "an optimal decision is the one that maximises the decision maker's utility."

According to Zavadskas and Turskis (2010), there is a wide range of Multiple Criteria Decision-Making (MCDM) problem solution techniques, varying in complexity and possible solutions. Each method has its own strength, weaknesses, and possibilities to be applied. However, according to Zavadskas and Turskis (2010), there are still no rules determining the application of multiple criteria evaluation methods and interpretation of the results obtained.

According to Ardito *et al.* (2006), despite the recent advances of the electronic technologies in e-learning, a consolidated evaluation methodology for the e-learning applications is not available. The evaluation of the educational software must consider its usability and more in general its accessibility, as well as its didactic effectiveness. According to Chua and Dyson (2004), despite the widespread use of the e-learning systems and the considerable investment in purchasing or developing them, there is no consensus on a standard framework for evaluating system quality.

A complex decision-making problem often requires to explicitly consider several points of view. The classical approaches in the field of operations research consider only a single objective function to be optimised. Hence, such a single criterion models one aspect of the decision problem, or aggregates relevant aspects into a single criterion.

Many multidimensional approaches have been proposed as the extensions of the classical ones. A first one was the so-called Multiple Criteria (or Multi-Criteria) Decision Making (MCDM), developed by the so-called American School. More recently, the European School has created a new type of approach to these problems, called Multiple Criteria Decision Aid (MCDA). Many real life applications have successfully validated the feasibility of this approach. MCDM / MCDA deal with different classes of decision problems (choice, classification, sorting, ranking), explicitly taking into consideration several points of view (multiple attributes or criteria, i.e. attributes with an ordered domain), in order to support the experts (decision-makers) in finding a consistent solution of the problem at hand (MCDM, 2011).

MCDM methods are used in many areas of human activities. MCDM is one of the most widely used decision methodologies in science, business, and governments, which are based on the assumption of a complex world, and can help to improve the quality of decisions by making the decision-making process more explicit, rational, and efficient.

According to Zavadskas and Turskis (2010), the problem of a decision-maker consists of "evaluating a finite set of alternatives in order to find the best one, to rank them from the best to the worst, to group them into predefined homogeneous classes, or to describe how well each alternative meets all the criteria simultaneously." There are many methods for determining the ranking of a set of alternatives in terms of a set of decision criteria. In a multiple criteria approach, the experts seek to build several criteria using several points of view. There is a number of well-known methods of multiple criteria optimisation and determination of the priority of the analysed alternatives. According to Zavadskas and Turskis (2010), it is hardly possible to evaluate the effect of various methods of a problem solution.

In the general case, the practical problem analysed in this chapter is how to choose the best LORs alternative in the market or create it. Here "the best" alternative means an alternative of the highest quality.

Therefore, the main scientific problem analysed in this chapter is creation of the proper models and methods for the expert evaluation of quality of LORs. The problem is how to elaborate approaches, models, and methods for choosing the qualitative alternatives of LORs that are quite objective, exact, and simple to use.

One of the main issues here is how to establish a proper (i.e., as objective as possible) set of LORs quality evaluation criteria which should reflect the objective scientific principles of constructing a model (criteria tree) for their quality evaluation. These issues have been analysed in the research works on the Multiple Criteria Decision Analysis (MCDA). There are a number of MCDA-based principles of identification of quality evaluation criteria elaborated by Belton and Stewart (2002). These principles will be presented below.

Another problem is the application of suitable MCDA methods in the numerical evaluation of quality of the learning software. The main problems of the existing approaches are a high level of expert evaluation subjectivity as well as their insufficient exactness, clarity, and usability.

3.2. The MCEQLS Approach for Evaluating the Quality of Learning Software

In his previous works, the author analysed several scientific methods, requirements and principles to minimise the problems of the evaluation of the quality of learning software and proposed to use the MCEQLS (Multiple Criteria Evaluation of Quality of the Learning Software) approach.

The MCEQLS approach was presented in Kurilovas and Dagiene (2010b) and refined in Kurilovas, Vinogradova, and Serikoviene (2011). In these papers, the author showed that the MCEQLS approach can significantly improve the quality of the expert evaluation of learning software and noticeably reduce the expert evaluation subjectivity level. Besides that, the MCEQLS approach can significantly reduce cost, time, and human resources necessary for the evaluation process.

While creating MCEQLS, the author had to analyse the following scientific methods, requirements and principles to minimise the aforementioned problems of the evaluation of the quality of learning software:

1. The principles of multiple criteria decision analysis for the identification of quality evaluation criteria,
2. Technological quality criteria arrangement principle,
3. Fuzzy group decision making theory to obtain final evaluation measures,
4. Normalisation requirement for the weights of the evaluation criteria, and, finally
5. Scalarisation (the experts' additive utility) function.

A proper approach to quality evaluation has to fit all the educational stakeholders' needs. This requirement leads to a shared problem understanding of the different stakeholders' groups such as educational institutions, policy makers, and software providers. In the author's opinion, MCEQLS approach fits all aforementioned stakeholders' needs. Besides that, the MCEQLS approach is clear and easy-to-use in real-life situations.

The MCEQLS approach consists of the complex application of the 5 aforementioned principles, methods and requirements. It is obvious that the first two principles deal with the problem of constructing a model (i.e. a set of criteria) for evaluating quality of the learning software, and the latter three methods deal with the process of the expert evaluation of the quality using the established models.

The more detailed analysis of each of these principles, methods, and requirements is separately provided in the next sub-sections.

3.2.1. Quality Model: Identification of Criteria

First of all, the author proposes to use MCDA principles of identification of the quality evaluation criteria.

Each alternative in a multiple criteria decision-making problem can be described by a set of criteria that can be qualitative and quantitative. According to Zavadskas and Turskis (2010), criteria usually have different units of measurement and a different optimization direction. Real-world decision-making problems are usually too complex and unstructured to be considered through the examination of a single criterion, or point of view that will lead to an optimum decision. According to Turskis *et al.* (2009), all new ideas and possible variants of decisions must be compared according to many criteria.

According to Zeleny (1982), decision criteria are rules, measures, and standards that guide decision-making. Bouyssou (1990) proposed a general definition of a quality criterion as a tool allowing comparison of alternatives according to a particular point of view. When building a criterion, the analyst should keep in mind that it is necessary that all the actors of the decision process adhere to the comparisons that will be deduced from that model. Criteria (relatively precise, but usually conflicting) are measures, rules and standards that guide decision-making, which also incorporates a model of preferences between the elements of a set of real or fictitious actions (Zavadskas & Turskis, 2010).

In order to create the proper quality evaluation model, we should apply several MCDA principles for creating a suitable model (criteria tree) containing the proper criteria for the comprehensive analysis of the quality of the learning software package.

According to Belton and Stewart (2002), in identifying criteria for the decision analysis, the following considerations are relevant to all multiple criteria decision analysis approaches:

1. **Value Relevance:** Are the decision-makers able to link the concept to their goals, thereby enabling them to specify preferences, which relate directly to the concept?

2. **Understandability:** It is important that decision-makers have a shared understanding of the concepts to be used in an analysis.

3. **Measurability:** All MCDA implies some degree of measurement of the performance of the alternatives against the specified criteria, thus it must be possible to specify this in a consistent manner. According to Belton and Stewart (2002), it is common to decompose criteria to a level of detail which allows this.

4. **Non-Redundancy:** The decision-makers should analyse if there is more than one criterion measuring the same factor. When eliciting ideas often the same concept may arise under different headings. One can easily check for the criteria, which appear to be measuring the same thing by calculating a correlation coefficient if appropriate data is available or carrying out a process of matching as associated with the analysis of repertory grids.

5. **Judgmental Independence:** The decision-makers should keep in mind that the evaluation criteria are not judgementally independent if preferences with respect to a single criterion, or trade-offs between two criteria, depend on the level of another.

6. **Balancing Completeness and Conciseness:** A number of authors note that desirable characteristics of a value tree are that it is complete, i.e., that all important aspects of the problem are captured, and also that it is concise, keeping the level of detail to the minimum required.

7. **Operationality:** The model should be usable with reasonable effort, i.e., the information required does not place excessive demands on the decision-makers. The context in which the model is being used is clearly important in judging the usability of a model.

8. **Simplicity vs. Complexity:** The value tree, or criteria set is itself a simple representation, capturing the essence of a problem, which has been extracted from a complex problem description. The modeller should strive for the simplest tree, which adequately captures the problem for the decision-maker.

3.2.2. Quality Model: Technological Quality Criteria Classification Principle

In the ISO/IEC 9126-1:2001(E) software quality standard, a software product is defined in a broad sense: it encompasses executables, source code, architecture descriptions, and so on. As a result, the notion of user extends to operators as well as to programmers, which are users of components of software libraries.

This standard provides a framework for organisations to define a quality model for a software product. In doing so, however, it leaves up to each organization the task of precisely specifying its own model. This may be done, for example, by specifying target values for quality metrics which evaluate the degree of presence of quality attributes.

These metrics are:

- **Internal Metrics:** Those which do not rely on software execution (static measure]);
- **External Metrics:** Applicable to running software, and
- **Quality In Use Metrics:** Only available when the final product is used in real conditions.

ISO/IEC 9126-1:2001(E) standard is based on a model, which is organised around three types of quality characteristics:

- **Factors (To Specify):** They describe the external view of the software, as viewed by the users.
- **Criteria (To Build):** They describe the internal view of the software, as seen by developers.
- **Metrics (To Control):** They are defined and used to provide a scale and method for measurement.

The software quality model presented in the ISO/IEC 9126-1:2001(E) standard classifies software quality in a structured set of characteristics and sub-characteristics as follows (see Table 1).

Each quality sub-characteristic is further divided into attributes. An attribute is an entity, which can be verified or measured in the software product. Attributes are not defined in the standard, as they vary between different software products.

According to Zavadskas and Turskis (2008), each alternative in the multi-criteria decision making problem can be described by a set of criteria. Criteria can be qualitative and quantitative. Usually they have different units of measurement and a different optimisation direction.

Scientists who have explored the quality of software consider that there exists no simple way to evaluate the functionality characteristics of the internal quality of software. According to Gasperovic and Caplinskas (2006), it is a hard and complicated task that requires relatively high

Table 1. Software quality characteristics

Characteristics	Sub-characteristics
1. **Functionality:** A set of attributes that bear on the existence of a set of functions and their specified properties.	• Suitability • Accuracy • Interoperability • Security • Functionality Compliance
2. **Reliability:** A set of attributes that bear on the capability of software to maintain its level of performance under stated conditions for a stated period of time.	• Maturity • Fault Tolerance • Recoverability • Reliability Compliance
3. **Usability:** A set of attributes that bear on the effort needed for use, and on the individual assessment of such use, by a stated or implied set of users.	• Understandability • Learnability • Operability • Attractiveness • Usability Compliance
4. **Efficiency:** A set of attributes that bear on the relationship between the level of performance of the software and the amount of resources used, under stated conditions.	• Time Behaviour • Resource Utilisation • Efficiency Compliance
5. **Maintainability:** A set of attributes that bear on the effort needed to make specified modifications.	• Analysability • Changeability • Stability • Testability • Maintainability Compliance
6. **Portability:** A set of attributes that bear on the ability of software to be transferred from one environment to another	• Adaptability • Installability • Co-Existence • Replaceability • Portability Compliance

time and labour overheads. From the technological point of view, we can divide the learning software quality criteria into internal quality and quality in use criteria. According to Gasperovic and Caplinskas (2006), internal quality is a descriptive characteristic that describes the quality of software independently from any particular context of its use, while 'quality in use' is evaluative characteristic of software obtained by making a judgment based on the criteria that determine the worthiness of software for a particular project.

According to this technological quality criteria classification principle, any technological quality evaluation model (set of criteria) for the learning software (i.e. LORs) should provide the clear instrumentality for the experts (decision-makers) who (i.e. what kind of experts) should analyse what kind of the software quality criteria in order to select the best software alternative suitable for

their needs. Software engineering experts should analyse internal quality criteria based on the scientific informatics engineering knowledge, and the programmers and users (e.g., teachers) should analyse quality in use criteria based on the users' feedback, design and usability issues, etc.

3.2.3. Quality Evaluation Method: Experts' Additive Utility Function

The main problem in the expert evaluation of the learning software is the application of the suitable models and methods.

There are a number of probably suitable methods for evaluation of the quality of the learning software packages such as LORs that are well known in the optimisation theory, e.g., vector optimisation methods.

One of them is the multiple criteria evaluation method referred here as the experts' additive utility function represented by Formula (1) below including the learning software packages' evaluation criteria, their ratings (values) and weights. This method is well known in the theory of optimisation and is named "scalarisation method." According to this method, a possible decision can be to transform a multiple criteria task into a one-criterion task by adding all the quality criteria multiplied by their weights. This is valid from the optimisation point of view, and a special theorem exists for this case.

Therefore, here we have the experts' additive utility function:

$$f(X) = \sum_{i=1}^{m} a_i f_i(X) \qquad (1)$$

where $f_i(X_j)$ is the rating (i.e., non-fuzzy value) of the criterion i for the each of the examined LOs alternatives X_j.

The weight a_i of the evaluation criterion reflects the expert's opinion on the criterion's importance level in comparison with the other criteria for the particular needs (e.g., different projects or users).

The following normalisation requirement exists for choosing the weights of the evaluation criteria in Formula (1):

$$\sum_{i=1}^{m} a_i = 1, \qquad (2)$$

According to Zavadskas and Turskis (2010), the normalisation aims at obtaining comparable scales of criteria values.

The major is the meaning of the utility function (1) the better the learning software package meets the quality requirements in comparison with the ideal (100%) quality (Kurilovas, 2009a, 2009b, 2009d; Kurilovas, Bireniene, & Serikoviene, 2011). The biggest value of the function (1) is the best, and the least one is the worst (Zavadskas & Turskis, 2010).

3.2.4. Quality Evaluation Method: Ratings and Weights of the Quality Criteria

3.2.4.1. Ratings of the Quality Criteria

According to Ounaies et al. (2009), the widely used measurement criteria of the decision attributes quality are mainly qualitative and subjective. In this context, decisions are often expressed in natural language, and evaluators are unable to assign exact numerical values to different criteria.

Assessment can be often performed by the linguistic variables such as 'bad,' 'poor,' 'fair,' 'good,' and 'excellent.' Several methods such as Qualitative Weight and Sum (QWS) approach presented by Graf and List (2005) apply the symbols E, *, #, +, |, and 0 to express the values of the evaluated quality. The problem is that all these values are imprecise and uncertain: they are commonly called fuzzy values. Integrating these different judgments to obtain a final evaluation is not evident.

In order to solve this problem Ounaies et al. (2009) suggest using the fuzzy group decision-making theory to obtain final assessment measures. According to their proposal, first, linguistic variable values should be mapped into, e.g., Triangular Fuzzy Numbers—TFNs (l, m, u) (see Table 2).

After the 'defuzzification' procedure that converts the global fuzzy evaluation results, expressed by a TFN (l, m, u), to a non-fuzzy value E, the following equation has been adopted by Ounaies et al. (2009):

Table 2. Conversion of linguistic variables into triangular fuzzy numbers

Linguistic variables	Triangular fuzzy numbers
Excellent	(0.700, 0.850, 1.000)
Good	(0.525, 0.675, 0.825)
Fair	(0.350, 0.500, 0.650)
Poor	(0.175, 0.325, 0.475)
Bad	(0.000, 0.150, 0.300)

$$E = [(u - 1) + (m - 1)] / 3 + 1, \qquad (3)$$

Finally, the non-fuzzy values E for all the aforementioned linguistic variables and symbols are calculated according to the Equation (3).

The conversion of the linguistic variables and symbols into non-fuzzy values E is shown in Table 3.

Now we have obtained digital non-fuzzy values (ratings) to evaluate learning software quality criteria.

3.2.4.2. Weights of the Quality Criteria

According to Saaty (1990), Analytic Hierarchy Process (AHP) is a useful method for solving complex decision-making problems involving subjective judgment.

In AHP, the multi-attribute weight measurement is calculated via pair-wise comparison of the relative importance of two factors (Lin, 2010). The design of the questionnaire incorporates pair-wise comparisons of decision elements within the hierarchical framework. Each evaluator is asked to express relative importance of two criteria in the same level by a nine-point rating scale. After that, we have to collect the scores of pair-wise comparison and form pair-wise comparison matrices for each of the evaluators.

According to Saaty (2008), the fundamental scale of absolute numbers is as follows.

After that, we have to construct a set of pair-wise comparison matrices (size n x n) for each of the lower levels with one matrix for each element in the level immediately above by using the relative scale measurement shown in Table 4.

The pair-wise comparisons are done in terms of which element dominates the other. There are *n(n-1)/2* judgments required to develop the set of matrices in this step. Reciprocals are automatically assigned in each pair-wise comparison.

Then hierarchical synthesis is used to weight the eigenvectors by the weights of the criteria and the sum is taken over all weighted eigenvector entries corresponding to those in the next lower level of the hierarchy.

Table 3. Conversion of linguistic variables and QWS symbols into triangular non-fuzzy values

Linguistic variables	Non-fuzzy values
Excellent (*)	0.850
Good (#)	0.675
Fair (+)	0.500
Poor (|)	0.325
Bad (0)	0.150

Table 4. Pair-wise comparison scale for AHP preferences

Numerical rating	Verbal judgements of preferences
9	Extremely preferred
8	Very strongly to extremely
7	Very strongly preferred
6	Strongly to very strongly
5	Strongly preferred
4	Moderately to strongly
3	Moderately preferred
2	Equally to moderately
1	Equally preferred

4. COMPREHENSIVE LEARNING REPOSITORIES EVALUATION MODEL

4.1. Technological Quality Criteria for Learning Repositories

A general technological quality model for learning repositories was presented in Kurilovas and Dagiene (2011).

To create their model, they analysed several well-known sets of technological quality criteria developed while implementing large-scale R&D projects, namely:

1. The SWITCH project tool (SWITCH Collection, 2008) developed while evaluating DSpace (2009) and Fedora (2009) LORs in 2008;

2. A tool developed by Catalyst IT while evaluating DSpace (2009), EPrints (2009), and Fedora (2009) LORs in the "Technical Evaluation of Selected Open Source Repository Solutions" presented by Wyles et al. (2006);

3. A tool "Software Repository Evaluation Criteria and Dissemination" developed in the Open Middleware Infrastructure Institute (OMII) presented in Newhouse (2005).

The technological quality criteria arrangement *principle* presented in Section 3.2.2 claims that there exist both internal quality and quality in use evaluation criteria of the software packages (such as LORs).

Kurilovas and Dagiene's (2011) analysis shows that none of the aforementioned tools clearly divides the LORs quality evaluation criteria into two separate groups: LORs internal quality evaluation criteria and quality in use criteria. Therefore, it is difficult to understand which criteria reflect the basic LORs quality aspects suitable for all software package alternatives, and which are suitable only for a particular project or user, and therefore depend on the user's feedback.

While analysing the LOR quality evaluation criteria, presented previously, Kurilovas and Dagiene (2011) noticed that several tools pay more attention to the general software 'internal quality' evaluation criteria (such as the 'Architecture' group criteria) and some of them to the 'customizable' 'quality in use' evaluation criteria groups suitable for a particular project or user: 'Metadata,' 'Storage,' 'Graphical User Interface,' and 'Other.'

According to the aforementioned quality criteria arrangement *principle*, the comprehensive LOR quality evaluation tool should include both the general software internal quality criteria and the quality in use criteria suitable for a particular project or user.

This LOR quality tool is presented in Table 5.

This tool is similar to the SWITCH tool but also includes criteria from other aforementioned tools as well as the author's own research.

The main ideas for the constitution of this tool are to clearly divide LORs quality evaluation criteria in conformity with the aforementioned criteria arrangement *principle* as well as to ensure the comprehensiveness of the tool and to avoid the criteria overlap.

The advantage of the tool proposed is its comprehensiveness and the clear division of the criteria: 'internal quality' criteria are mainly the area of interest of software engineers, and 'quality in use' criteria are mostly to be analysed by programmers, taking into account the users' feedback on the usability of software.

Two of the criteria in Table 5 could be interpreted from different perspectives: 'Accessibility, design for all' could be included into the 'Architecture' group, but as it requires users' evaluation, it has been included in the 'Quality in use' criteria group. Also, 'Property and metadata inheritance' could also be included in the 'Metadata' group, although it deals with 'Storage' issues as well.

We have 34 different evaluation criteria in this model (set of criteria), from which 11 criteria deal with 'Internal quality' (or 'Architecture'), and 23 criteria deal with 'Quality in use.' The twenty-three 'Quality in Use' criteria are further divided into four groups to increase the precision and convenience in practical evaluation. Different experts (programmers and users) could be used for different groups of the 'Quality in Use' criteria. Indeed, 'Metadata,' 'Storage,' and 'Graphical User Interface' criteria need different kinds of evaluators' expertise.

4.2. Quality of User Interface of Learning Repositories

EdReNe (2011) project partners identified a number of quality criteria for evaluation of LORs user interface. The main question here was how to engage users to use LORs.

Table 5. LORs general technological quality evaluation criteria

Internal quality evaluation criteria	Architecture	1. Flexibility and modularity of the LOR system
		2. Possibility to use LOR system as part of a federation
		3. Performance and scalability
		4. Security
		5. Interoperability
		6. Stability
		7. Ease of deployment
		8. API for storage engine, user access rights and federation functions
		9. Coding: an inspection of the code within the software
		10. Full-text search
		11. Internationalization
Quality in use evaluation criteria	Metadata	12. Minimal metadata schema
		13. Predefined sets of metadata
		14. Customizable metadata schema
		15. Metadata mapping for metadata search
		16. Unicode support
		17. Social tagging
	Storage	18. Object can be of any format
		19. Access rights
		20. Hierarchical organization
		21. Property and metadata inheritance
		22. Large objects
	Graphical user interface	23. Complete standard UI
		24. Customizable and extensible standard UI
		25. Multiple standard UIs
		26. Direct distribution
	Other	27. Strength of development community
		28. Strength of users community
		29. LOs retrieval quality: user able to retrieve LOs in different ways
		30. Ease of installation
		31. Accessibility, design for all
		32. Sustainability
		33. System administration: ability to customize look and feel
		34. Documentation quality

Table 6 presents LOR user interface quality criteria.

Table 6 is the result of the author's analysis and aggregation of the criteria identified by EdReNe experts.

4.3. How to Apply the MCEQLS Approach for Evaluating the Quality of Learning Repositories

In order to evaluate quality of the learning repositories alternative, the experts-evaluators should use several steps:

1. Use the evaluation model for LOR constructed with the help of the MCDA principles for the identification of quality evaluation criteria as well as technological quality criteria classification principle. These principles are suitable both for the general LOR technological quality model presented in Table 5 as well as LOR user interface quality model presented in Table 6.
2. Evaluate all the quality criteria using, e.g., triangular non-fuzzy values (ratings) (see Table 3).
3. Establish all the weights of the evaluation criteria using normalisation requirement for the weights of the evaluation criteria (see Formula [2]). The aforementioned Analytic Hierarchy Process (AHP) method is convenient in this case.
4. Calculate the numerical value of the quality of the particular LOR alternative using the obtained numerical values (ratings) and the weights of the evaluation criteria with the help of the experts additive utility (scalarisation) function expressed by the Formula (1).

The higher the numerical value of the quality of the particular LOR alternative, the higher is the quality of this alternative in comparison with the other evaluated alternatives, and the educational institutions should decide on purchase or create this alternative for their educational needs.

5. FUTURE RESEARCH TRENDS

The application of the MCEQLS (Multiple Criteria Evaluation of Quality of the Learning Software) approach, being useful and convenient for the stakeholders (Kurilovas, Vinogradova, & Serikoviene, 2011), does not solve all the problems of the expert evaluation of learning software such as LORs.

There are a number of trends for future research. Some of them are as follows.

5.1 Minimisation of the Experts' Subjectivity

An additional very complicated problem for such multiple criteria evaluation and optimisation tasks is the minimisation of the experts' (decision-makers') subjectivity. The experts' subjectivity can influence the quality criteria ratings (values) and their weights.

According to Kendall (1979), in general, the experts' influence is of different importance, and therefore this importance should be assessed, using the appropriate methodology. It is important to form the expert group purely in line with their competence. Furthermore, according to Kendall (1979), one should eliminate the extreme experts' assessments of the ratings and weights.

There are some scientific approaches regarding this item. One of them has been presented by Kurilovas and Serikoviene (2010). Additional research is necessary to apply these approaches for evaluating the quality of LORs.

Table 6. Quality criteria of the user interface of learning repositories

Criteria	Description
1. Navigation	The criterion describes multiple ways that support users navigating a repository in order to find resources. Users navigate in many ways and if any key navigation tools are missing or hard to find, the Web site will be regarded as hard to use. The major forms of navigating repositories generally consist of searching and browsing. Most sites contain both a simple search form, typically linked to an advanced search form (or an expandable search area) giving more fine-grained control over search parameters and filtering of results. A common element of the basic navigation is the page listing the search results including the special version of it where no results are found. In the general case consideration to what level of detail should be shown (can the user choose between different formats), what sorting and filtering options should be available, and what actions related to a specific LO can be initiated from a list of search results (rating, adding to favourites, sharing, commenting, etc.) are necessary considerations. When browsing LOs the different possibilities of navigation are closely linked to the amount of structured descriptive metadata available for the individual LOs. Often the most hierarchical structures are represented by links to the relevant curriculum or use of library classification system or thesauri. When navigating hierarchies the subcategories often have a prominent place in the centre of the page. Other descriptive metadata is typically relevant only for filtering purposes. Using tags (often in the form of tag clouds, but also just as traditional clickable keywords) as a means of navigation is also beginning to occur at a number of repositories.
2. Collecting and sharing LOs	When browsing or searching a repository, users would need to collect interesting LOs they find for example to review later, share with others, discuss, or collaborate around. Having users build personal collections and allowing them to share these both through the repository itself, but also to other communities they participate in, is an important aspect of community building—for example allowing the connection of people that share interests, attracting new users from other communities and recommending other LOs. Linked to this functionality is also the possibility to save searches, keep track of a search history and being updated about new relevant content.
3. Metadata page	The metadata page is the page that describes a single LO that users have found either through searching or by browsing. The central goal of the page is to provide an easy overview of information about the LO, and present possibilities to use / interact with the LO. This is also where most possibilities for interaction with a LO are provided—including those not available from a list of search results. Apart from interactions (including rating, tagging, commenting, previewing, downloading, adding to favourites / collections, sharing etc.) this is also where a site typically makes use of other user generated metadata / attention metadata to for example recommend other relevant content.
4. Repository homepage	A homepage must satisfy the needs of all potential and current users by identifying the organisation and at the same time providing multiple ways to navigate. The clear trend in front pages of repositories is that they should provide: (1) potential users with a clear idea of why they should join (up-front value proposition); (2) existing users (logged in) with personalized news and activity since their latest visit to the site. If more community features are built into repositories this will add to the possibilities of a user tailored front page. Especially for national repositories, these are often part of a larger educational portal and personalization of the front page will typically be done for the entire portal instead of just the repository.
5. Keeping users updated	Maintaining contact with users is a central goal of all websites. Users may have a need to stay updated within a specific topic area covered by the LOR. A central way to establish a lasting relationship with users is providing services, which keep users informed of new and interesting content. Often educational repositories are not in use every day by their primary target group of users. This makes it important to LOR owners to provide possibilities for users to be updated when activity relevant to them occurs. A number of LORs provide email newsletters, which can often be customized to information relating to, e.g., specific teaching subjects or other areas of interest. Other examples include email alerts, feed subscriptions to user defined searches and providing widgets to be embedded in, e.g., Learning Management Systems (LMSs).
6. Personal settings on the profile page	Registered users need to see and manage the information that a LOR keeps about them. A repository that lets certain users register LOs, needs a way to let these users manage personal information, and manage LOs they have registered. Users that have logged in can be offered additional functionality such as default values for searches, rating / reviewing LOs, statistics on the use of LOs they have provided. LORs are beginning to include elements found on other social networks including: profile pages, personal settings / options, list of favourites / personal collections, accounts of recent activity, personal messages, possibility to follow users, sharing, inviting, etc.

continued on following page

Table 6. Continued

Criteria	Description
7. Metadata editors	Content providers need to be able to register their LOs in a way that makes the LOs findable for end-users and includes enough information for the end-user to decide whether the material is relevant. An important aspect is for example linking the LOs to the relevant curriculum. The registration process needs to be as simple and quick as possible to encourage content providers to submit their LOs and to avoid mistakes in the metadata that might confuse the end-user.
8. Implementation of user generated metadata	The strategies for implementing user-generated metadata such as ratings, comments and tagging vary considerably across the learning repositories. For most repositories, the major problem with this is not the choice between "thumb up" or "one to five stars" but rather to ensure an engaged community actually willing to tag, rate and comment.
9. Adding descriptive metadata	When users deposit content, they are required to provide descriptive metadata for their LOs. The pages / tools for doing this currently range from very simple forms, to use of complex stand-alone tagging tools. As describing a LO presumably is one of the most difficult tasks for users to perform, and often cited as a perceived barrier, this could qualify it as a particularly important area to optimize design of. Most fields in the entry forms on a LOR depositing page would correspond to other familiar forms. Of particular interest in relation to LORs would be how LOs are linked to the curriculum, and for user generated content also how licensing scheme / user rights are specified in an easy comprehensible manner.
10. Remixing content	Building your own content from other repository LOs is something not yet easily feasible in most LORs. Workflows as simple as "Build a book" in Wikipedia are presumably required in order to be successful. The question is also whether the combination of LOs should really take place in LORs. With the dramatic increase in use of LMSs, they might be more suitable environments for combining content—underlining the need for good integration between such systems (open or closed) and content repositories.

5.2 More Comprehensive Analysis of Quality Models

In this chapter, the author analysed only several well-known models for the multiple criteria evaluation of the learning software such as LOR.

Future research trends should include the analysis of more models for evaluating the quality of learning repositories with a view to create more comprehensive sets of LOR quality criteria.

Furthermore, additional research is also needed to avoid the overlap of the LOR quality criteria. This research should additionally analyse and take into account the ISO/IEC 9126-1:2001(E) characteristics and framework.

Finally, the problems of personalisation and adaptation of LORs should be analysed in more detail in the future.

5.3 More Comprehensive Analysis of Quality Evaluation Methods

The author analysed the application of the only MCEQLS approach based on the experts' additive utility function, in the multiple criteria evaluation of the learning software. This method is often used in MCDA approaches.

There is a number of different methods probably suitable for the expert evaluation of the learning software. According to Zavadskas *et al.* (2008), there is a wide range of methods, based on the multi-criteria utility theory, e.g., SAW—Simple Additive Weighting (Ginevicius, et al., 2008; Sivilevicius, et al., 2008); MOORA—Multi-Objective Optimization on the Basis of Ratio Analysis (Brauers & Zavadskas, 2006; Brauers, et al., 2008; Kalibatas & Turskis, 2008); TOPSIS—Technique for Order Preference by Similarity to Ideal Solution (Hwang & Yoon, 1981; Zavadskas, et al., 2006); VIKOR—a compromise ranking method (Zavadskas & Antucheviciene, 2007); COPRAS—Complex Proportional Assessment

(Zavadskas, et al., 2007); games theory methods (Peldschus & Zavadskas, 2005; Antucheviciene, et al., 2006), and other approaches (Turskis, 2008).

Therefore, other MCDA-based methods should be used in the future research, and their efficiency should be compared with the MCEQLS approach.

5.4 Validation

Finally, all models and methods need a large-scale validation.

In the future, large-scale validation is needed to further analyse and improve the proposed LOR quality models and methods for the expert evaluation of LOR alternatives. In particular, the most popular LORs packages should be practically evaluated by the experts in the field using the MCEQLS approach.

6. CONCLUSION

In this chapter, the author proposed the MCEQLS (Multiple Criteria Evaluation of Quality of the Learning Software) scientific approach in the evaluation of quality of learning repositories.

The author proposed the general LOR technological quality model (see Table 5) and LOR user interface quality model (see Table 6).

The author found that the application of the MCEQLS approach could significantly improve the quality of the expert evaluation of the learning repositories and reduce the expert evaluation subjectivity level in comparison with other existing approaches.

The proposed MCEQLS approach provides the experts (decision-makers) with clear principles for constructing the quality model (criteria system) for evaluating LOR alternatives.

Moreover, the proposed MCEQLS approach provides the experts with a clear instrumentality who (i.e. what kind of experts) should analyse which kind of the software quality criteria in order to select the best software suitable for their

needs. According to the proposed technological quality criteria classification principle, the internal quality criteria should be mainly the interest for software designers, and the quality in use criteria should be mostly analysed by programmers and users, taking into account the users' feedback on the usability of the learning software.

Finally, the proposed MCEQLS approach provides the experts with a clear method for a comparative analysis and choosing the alternatives represented by the experts' additive utility function, using the numerical ratings (values) of quality evaluation criteria and the normalisation requirement to criteria weights. For example, triangular fuzzy method is suitable for establishment of the values of quality criteria, and the Analytic Hierarchy Process (AHP) method is suitable to establish the weights of quality criteria.

The research results have also shown that the MCEQLS approach proposed for evaluating quality of the learning software such as LOR is easy to use by the experts and practitioners in real-life situations.

REFERENCES

Antucheviciene, J., Turskis, Z., & Zavadskas, E. K. (2006). Modelling renewal of construction objects applying methods of the game theory. *Technological and Economic Development of Economy, 12*(4), 263–268.

Ardito, C., Costabile, M. F., De Marsico, M., Lanzilotti, R., Levialdi, S., Roselli, T., & Rossano, V. (2006). An approach to usability evaluation of e-learning applications. *Universal Access in the Information Society, 4*, 270–283. doi:10.1007/s10209-005-0008-6

ASPECT. (2011). *EU eContentplus programme's ASPECT (adopting standards and specifications for educational content) best practice network (2008 – 2011) web site.* Retrieved from http://aspect-project.org/

Belton, V., & Stewart, T. J. (2002). *Multiple criteria decision analysis: An integrated approach.* Dordrecht, The Netherlands: Kluwer Academic Publishers.

Bourret, R. (2005). *XML and databases.* Retrieved from http://www.rpbourret.com/xml/XMLAnd-Databases.htm#isxmladatabase

Bouysou, D. (1990). Building criteria: A perquisite for MCDA. In C. A. Bana a Costa (Ed.), *Readings in Multiple Criteria Decision Aid,* (pp. 319-334). Berlin, Germany: Springer-Verlag.

Brauers, W. K., & Zavadskas, E. K. (2006). The MOORA method and its application to privatization in a transition economy. *Control and Cybernetics, 35*(2), 443–468.

Brauers, W. K., Zavadskas, E. K., Peldschus, F., & Turskis, Z. (2008). Multi-objective decision-making for road design. *Transport, 23*(3), 183–193. doi:10.3846/1648-4142.2008.23.183-193

Calibrate. (2011). *EU FP6 IST calibrate (calibrating elearning in schools) project (2005 – 2008) web site.* Retrieved from http://calibrate.eun.org

Chua, B. B., & Dyson, L. E. (2004). Applying the ISO9126 model to the evaluation of an elearning system. In R. Atkinson, C. McBeath, D. Jonas-Dwyer, & R. Phillips (Eds.), *Beyond the Comfort Zone: Proceedings of the 21st ASCILITE Conference,* (pp. 184-190). Perth, Australia: ASCILITE.

Collection, S. W. I. T. C. H. (2008). *The national learning object repository project website.* Retrieved from http://www.switch.ch/it/els/collection/evaluation.html

Dallas, L. (2008). *XML repositories – If you can't beat 'em – Open source 'em.* Retrieved from http://bigmenoncontent.com/2008/03/26/xml-repositories-if-you-cant-beat-em-open-source-em/

DSpace. (2009). *DSpace repository software website.* Retrieved from http://www.dspace.org/

Dzemyda, G., & Saltenis, V. (1994). Multiple criteria decision support system: Methods, user's interface and applications. *Informatica, 5*(1-2), 31–42.

EdReNe. (2011). *EU eContentplus programme's educational repositories network project web site.* Retrieved from http://edrene.org/

EPrints. (2009). *EPrints repository website.* Retrieved from http://www.eprints.org/

Fedora. (2009). *Fedora repository website.* Retrieved from http://fedoraproject.org/

Gasperovic, J., & Caplinskas, A. (2006). Methodology to evaluate the functionality of specification languages. *Informatica, 17*(3), 325–346.

Ginevicius, R., Podvezko, V., & Bruzge, S. (2008). Evaluating the effect of state aid to business by multicriteria methods. *Journal of Business Economics and Management, 9*(3), 167–180. doi:10.3846/1611-1699.2008.9.167-180

Graf, S., & List, B. (2005). An evaluation of open source e-learning platforms stressing adaptation issues. In *Proceedings of ICALT 2005.* ICALT.

Hwang, C. L., & Yoon, K. S. (1981). *Multiple attribute decision-making / methods and applications.* Berlin, Germany: Springer-Verlag. doi:10.1007/978-3-642-48318-9

International Standard ISO. IEC 14598-1:1999. (1999). *Information technology – Software product evaluation – Part 1: General overview*. Retrieved from http://www.itu.int

International Standard ISO. IEC 9126-1:2001(E). (2001). *Software engineering – Product quality – Part 1: Quality model. 2001*. Retrieved from http://www.itu.int

Kalibatas, D., & Turskis, Z. (2008). Multicriteria evaluation of inner climate by using MOORA method. *Information Technology and Control, 37*(1), 79–83.

Kellokoski, K. (1999). *XML repositories*. Retrieved from http://www.tml.tkk.fi/Opinnot/Tik-111.590/2000/Papers/XML_Repositories.pdf

Kendall, M. (1979). *Rank correlation methods*. London, UK: Griffin and Co.

Kurilovas, E. (2009a). Interoperability, standards and metadata for e-learning. In Papadopoulos, G. A., & Badica, C. (Eds.), *Intelligent Distributed Computing III: Studies in Computational Intelligence* (pp. 121–130). Berlin, Germany: Springer-Verlag. doi:10.1007/978-3-642-03214-1_12

Kurilovas, E. (2009b). Learning content repositories and learning management systems based on customization and metadata. In *Proceedings of the 1st International Conference on Creative Content Technologies (CONTENT 2009)*, (pp. 632-637). Athens, Greece: CONTENT.

Kurilovas, E. (2009c). Evaluation and optimisation of e-learning software packages: Learning object repositories. In *Proceedings of the 4th International Conference on Software Engineering Advances (ICSEA 2009)*. Porto, Portugal: ICSEA.

Kurilovas, E. (2009d). Learning objects reusability and their adaptation for blended learning. In *Proceedings of the 5th International Conference on Networking and Services (ICNS 2009)*, (pp. 542-547). Valencia, Spain: ICNS.

Kurilovas, E. (2012). European learning resource exchange – A platform for collaboration of researchers, policy makers, practitioners, and publishers to share digital learning resources and new e-learning practices. In Cakir, A., & Ordóñez de Pablos, P. (Eds.), *Social Development and High Technology Industries: Strategies and Applications* (pp. 200–243). Hershey, PA: IGI Global.

Kurilovas, E., Bireniene, V., & Serikoviene, S. (2011). Methodology for evaluating quality and reusability of learning objects. *Electronic Journal of e-Learning, 9*(1), 39–51.

Kurilovas, E., & Dagienė, V. (2009a). Multiple criteria comparative evaluation of e-learning systems and components. *Informatica, 20*(4), 499–518.

Kurilovas, E., & Dagiene, V. (2009b). Learning objects and virtual learning environments technical evaluation criteria. *Electronic Journal of e-Learning, 7*(2), 127–136.

Kurilovas, E., & Dagiene, V. (2010a). Multiple criteria evaluation of quality and optimisation of e-learning system components. *Electronic Journal of e-Learning, 8*(2), 141–150.

Kurilovas, E., & Dagiene, V. (2010b). *Evaluation of quality of the learning software: Basics, concepts, methods. monograph*. Saarbrücken, Germany: LAP LAMBERT Academic Publishing.

Kurilovas, E., & Dagiene, V. (2011). Technological evaluation and optimisation of e-learning systems components. In Magoulas, G. D. (Ed.), *E-Infrastructures and Technologies for Lifelong Learning: Next Generation Environments* (pp. 150–173). Hershey, PA: IGI Global.

Kurilovas, E., & Serikoviene, S. (2010). Learning content and software evaluation and personalisation problems. *Informatics in Education, 9*(1), 91–114.

Kurilovas, E., Vinogradova, I., & Serikoviene, S. (2011). Application of multiple criteria decision analysis and optimisation methods in evaluation of quality of learning objects. *International Journal of Online Pedagogy and Course Design, 1*(4), 62–76. doi:10.4018/ijopcd.2011100105

Lin, H.-F. (2010). An application of fuzzy AHP for evaluating course website quality. *Computers & Education, 54*, 877–888. doi:10.1016/j.compedu.2009.09.017

LRE. (2011). *European learning resource exchange service for schools web site*. Retrieved from http://lreforschools.eun.org/

MCDM. (2011). *International society on multiple criteria decision making web site*. Retrieved from http://www.mcdmsociety.org/

Newhouse, S. (2005). *Software repository - Evaluation criteria and dissemination*. Retrieved from http://www.omii.ac.uk/dissemination/Evaluation-Criteria.pdf

Oliver, M. (2000). An introduction to the evaluation of learning technology. *Journal of Educational Technology & Society, 3*(4), 20–30.

Ounaies, H. Z., Jamoussi, Y., & Ben Ghezala, H. H. (2009). Evaluation framework based on fuzzy measured method in adaptive learning system. *Themes in Science and Technology Education, 1*(1), 49–58.

Peldschus, F., & Zavadskas, E. K. (2005). Fuzzy matrix games multi-criteria model for decision-making in engineering. *Informatica, 16*(1), 107–120.

Saaty, T. L. (1990). How to make a decision: The analytic hierarchy process. *European Journal of Operational Research, 48*(1), 9–26. doi:10.1016/0377-2217(90)90057-I

Saaty, T. L. (2008). Relative measurement and its generalization in decision making: Why pairwise comparisons are central in mathematics for the measurement of intangible factors – The analytic hierarchy/network process. *Review of the Royal Spanish Academy of Sciences, Series A. Mathematics, 102*(2), 251–318.

Shaffner, B. (2001). *Managing hierarchical data: A look at XML repositories*. Retrieved from http://www.techrepublic.com/article/managing-hierarchical-data-a-look-at-xml-repositories/1045074

Sivilevicius, H., Zavadskas, E. K., & Turskis, Z. (2008). Quality attributes and complex assessment methodology of the asphalt mixing plant. *Baltic Journal of Road and Bridge Engineering, 3*(3), 161–166. doi:10.3846/1822-427X.2008.3.161-166

Turskis, Z. (2008). Multi-attribute contractors ranking method by applying ordering of feasible alternatives of solutions in terms of preferability technique. *Technological and Economic Development of Economy, 14*(2), 224–239. doi:10.3846/1392-8619.2008.14.224-239

Turskis, Z., Zavadskas, E. K., & Peldschus, F. (2009). Multi-criteria optimization system for decision making in construction design and management. *Inzinerine Ekonomika – Engineering Economics, 1*, 7–17.

Wiley, D. A. (2000). Connecting learning objects to instructional design theory: A definition, a metaphor, and a taxonomy. *Utah State University*. Retrieved from http://www.reusability.org/read/

Wyles, R., et al. (2006). *Technical evaluation of selected open source repository solutions*. Retrieved from http://www.eprints.org/community/blog/index.php?/archives/118-Technical-Evaluation-of-selected-Open-Source-Repository-Solutions.html

Zavadskas, E. K., & Antucheviciene, J. (2007). Multiple criteria evaluation of rural building's regeneration alternatives. *Building and Environment, 42*(1), 436–451. doi:10.1016/j.buildenv.2005.08.001

Zavadskas, E. K., Kaklauskas, A., Peldschus, F., & Turskis, Z. (2007). Multi-attribute assessment of road design solutions by using the COPRAS method. *The Baltic Journal of Road and Bridge Engineering, 2*(4), 195–203.

Zavadskas, E. K., & Turskis, Z. (2008). A new logarithmic normalization method in games theory. *Informatica, 19*(2), 303–314.

Zavadskas, E. K., & Turskis, Z. (2010). A new additive ratio assessment (ARAS) method in multicriteria decision-making. *Technological and Economic Development of Economy, 16*(2), 159–172. doi:10.3846/tede.2010.10

Zavadskas, E. K., Turskis, Z., Tamosaitiene, J., & Marina, V. (2008). Multicriteria selection of project managers by applying grey criteria. *Technological and Economic Development of Economy, 14*(4), 462–477. doi:10.3846/1392-8619.2008.14.462-477

Zavadskas, E. K., Zakarevicius, A., & Antuchev-iciene, J. (2006). Evaluation of ranking accuracy in multicriteria decisions. *Informatica, 17*(4), 601–618.

Zeleny, M. (1982). *Multiple criteria decision making*. New York, NY: McGraw-Hill.

Chapter 7
Using Device Detection Techniques in M–Learning Scenarios

Ricardo Queirós
CRACS and ESEIG/IPP, Porto, Portugal

Mário Pinto
ESEIG/IPP, Porto, Portugal

ABSTRACT

Recent studies of mobile Web trends show the continued explosion of mobile-friend content. However, the wide number and heterogeneity of mobile devices poses several challenges for Web programmers, who want automatic delivery of context and adaptation of the content to mobile devices. Hence, the device detection phase assumes an important role in this process. In this chapter, the authors compare the most used approaches for mobile device detection. Based on this study, they present an architecture for detecting and delivering uniform m-Learning content to students in a Higher School. The authors focus mainly on the XML device capabilities repository and on the REST API Web Service for dealing with device data. In the former, the authors detail the respective capabilities schema and present a new caching approach. In the latter, they present an extension of the current API for dealing with it. Finally, the authors validate their approach by presenting the overall data and statistics collected through the Google Analytics service, in order to better understand the adherence to the mobile Web interface, its evolution over time, and the main weaknesses.

DOI: 10.4018/978-1-4666-2669-0.ch007

INTRODUCTION

In ESEIG (Escola Superior de Estudos Industriais e de Gestão) of the Polytechnic Institute of Porto, we use a Learning Management System (LMS) to provide access to the learning resources and activities. In a recent survey (see section 3), we verify that a large number of students use mobile devices. They are already experienced with mobile technology and are eager to use their devices in e-Learning scenarios. Another argument for the use of mobile devices came from the students' profile since most of them are already employed while studying part-time. This situation decreases the chance to attend virtual events synchronously. Moreover, we also noticed that the students present different mobile devices with different characteristics that difficult the user experience regarding the access to mobile content. Based on these facts, we argue the need to automatically deliver uniform educational content on particular devices, normally referred to as content adaptation.

In this chapter, we explore the use of open source technologies to provide a better design experience regarding mobile learning (m-Learning) content adaptation and promoting the "write once run anywhere" concept.

To understand the needs of our students we based on a survey conducted by a group of teachers at ESEIG. The aim of this study was to characterize the mobile devices usage, namely, the diversity of mobile technologies and services used by students and teachers, and analyze the future expectations concerning the usage of m-Learning platforms.

Based on this survey we obtained the basis for the ESEIG-Mobile system architecture. The ultimate goal of ESEIG-Mobile is to standardize the delivery of e-learning content to the mobile devices of our students. This system uses a three-tier model on a client–server architecture in which the user interface, functional process logic and data access are developed and maintained as independent modules. For each module, our concern was to use emergent and open-source solutions to lever-

age the potential of this new e-Learning paradigm where the characteristics of the mobile device of the student represents an important role and, at the same time, a huge issue. The large number and variety of Web-enabled devices poses challenges for Web content creators who want to automatic get the delivery context and adapt the content to mobile devices. This requires a thorough analysis of the available technologies and knowing good practices to help addressing this issue.

The remainder of this chapter is organized as follows: Section 2 defines context delivery and enumerates several initiatives working on this subject. In the following section, we present a survey made in our School regarding mobile devices. Then, we introduce the architecture of ESEIG Mobile and the design of its internal components. In the next section, we validate the ESEIG-Mobile prototype system based on the students' access statistics. Finally, we conclude with a summary of the main contributions of this work and a perspective of future research.

MOBILE CONTENT ADAPTATION

Mobile learning (m-learning) applications extend the electronic learning (e-learning) experience into the mobile context (Chang & Sheu, 2002; Chen, et al., 2002; Liu, et al., 2002). M-learning uses mobile devices to enhance the teaching-learning process. However, it should not be seen as just another e-Learning channel for delivering the same content. In fact quality M-learning can only be delivered with an awareness of the special limitations and benefits of mobile devices (Parsons & Hyu, 2007). Due to those constraints, the learning content must be adapted to suit the mobile device characteristics. Adaptation means a process of selection, generation or modification of content (text, images, audio, and video) to suit the user's computing environment and usage context (Parupalli, 2009). The concept of Content Adaptation is commonly related to mobile devices. Due to the variety of types and technologies supported they require special handling through a series of content transformations, in the deliver process, made by the content provider (server) (Zhang, 2007). Instead of authors having to create specialised pages for each kind of device, content adaptation automatically transforms an author's content to match the device characteristics. Some examples of such features are related with their limited computational power, small screen size, constrained keyboard functionality, and media content type supported. The W3C Device Independence Working Group described many of the issues (Lewis, 2003) that authors must face in an environment in which there is an increasingly diverse set of devices used to access Web sites.

One approach is to use the common capabilities of the mobile devices and ignore the rest. Finding the Lowest Common Denominator (LCD) of the capabilities of target devices, will allow to you design a site that will work reasonably well in all devices. In order to allow content providers to share a consistent view of a default mobile experience the Best Practice WG has defined the Default Delivery Context (DDC) as a universal LCD (Rabin, 2008). This purpose is commonly adopted; however, it limits the devices with better capabilities than LCD and decreases the use of a wider and heterogeneous mobile audience.

There are different adaptation points in the delivery of content to the device: server-side, in-network, and client-side. The former needs to negotiate which version of a document should be delivered to a user in order to define the delivery context. One of the most widely used delivery context information is through the HTTP accept headers. These headers can be used to obtain the capabilities of a requesting device, such as, MIME types, character sets, preferred reply encoding, and natural languages. In addition to the accept headers, the User-Agent header includes not standard information about the device and the browser being used. This lack of standardisation increases the difficult to interpret and extend this data (Gimson, 2006).

To overcome these difficulties emerged in recent years the device-profiling concept—a repository of device capabilities, where a user agent (client) can supply the profile to the content provider (server), which can then adapt the content to suit the client device capabilities. The definition of the structure of the profile data is being covered by several standards, such as CC/PP (Kiss, 2010), User Agent PROFile (UAProf) (WAP, 2001), and Wireless Universal Resource FiLe (WURFL) (Passani, 2007).

The W3C CC/PP specification defines how client devices express their capabilities and preferences (the user agent profile) to the server that originates content (the origin server). The origin server uses the user agent profile to produce and deliver content appropriated to the client device. Using this specification, Web mobile content creators and user agents can easily define precise profiles for their products (e.g. Web servers use these profiles to adapt, through fine-tuned content selection or transformation, the content they serve to the needs of the Web device).

The UAProf (User agent profile) is a standard created by the Open Mobile Alliance (formerly the WAP Forum) to represent a concrete CC/PP vocabulary for mobile phones and defines an effective transmission of the CC/PP descriptions over wireless networks. Mobile phones that are conformant with the UAProf specification provide CC/PP descriptions for their capabilities to servers that use this information to optimize the content, where the information is communicated using XML containing several attributes (e.g. screen size, colour and audio capability, operating system and browser info, encoding).

The WURFL (Wireless Universal Resource File) is an XML configuration file, which contains information about device capabilities and features for a variety of mobile devices. Developers around the world contribute with device information and the WURFL repository is often updated reflecting new wireless devices coming on the market. In short, WURFL is a repository of wireless device capabilities describing the capabilities of common wireless devices worldwide and providing an API to programmatically query the capability repository.

Recently, to overcome the UAProf issues, the W3C MWI (Mobile Web Initiative) have outlined specifications for a Device Description Repository. These specifications include a formal vocabulary of core device properties and an Application Programming Interface (API). The consortium also published a working draft for a new independent language specification named W3C's DIAL (Device Independent Authoring Language). This specification is a language profile based on XHTML 2 and XForms, and uses the DISelect vocabulary to overcome the authoring for multiple delivery contexts. One known implementation is the XDIME language.

Others specifications arises recently to address the mobile content adaptation issues. It is the case of WNG (Passani, 2010) and WURFL. The Wireless Abstraction Library New Generation (WNG) is a Java tag-library that supports the use of universal mark-up for wireless devices. WNG allows the developer to write a Web application once and have optimized content delivered to a variety of devices. It works on combination with the WURFL repository already detailed in this section.

Targeting e-Learning, several extensions appears recently to expose the LMS (e.g. Moodle) in mobile devices. One such case is the Mobile Moodle (MOMO).

All these standards and specifications help to formalize the design and implementation of mobile frameworks (Parsons, 2007; Paes & Moreira, 2008; Myers, 2004).

MOBILE EXPERIENCE SURVEY

An exploratory study concerning mobile devices usage was made at our Institution. The aim of this study was characterizing the mobile devices usage, namely the diversity of mobile technolo-gies and services used by students and professors, and analyzing future expectations concerning the usage of m-Learning platforms (Queirós & Pinto, 2010; Seung-Won, 2005).

Research Methodology

The survey was made using a questionnaire, sent to the Institution community, which includes almost a thousand and two hundred students, and eighty teachers. The questionnaire was sent by e-mail to all teachers, and the students were invited to answer the questionnaire through the Moodle e-Learning platform. The questionnaire was accomplished with a brief description of the study and their objectives, and it was structured in three main sections:

- **Inquired Profile:** Student or teacher;
- **Services and Technological Characteristics:** It comprises the identification of the main mobile services used and technological issues concerned with mobile devices;
- **Educational Mobile Contents:** It comprises the expectations about the usage of m-Learning platforms, the main services that they would like to use and the m-Learning constraints.

Results and Discussion

We received one hundred and fifty valid questionnaires answers. From these ones, thirty-two were from teachers and one hundred and eighteen were from students. Only two students answered that they have not mobile devices. Regarding those who have mobile devices, we analyze that the majority of them owns a mobile device with Internet connection as shown in Figure 1.

In fact, according to the survey results, eighty two percent of inquired persons have mobile devices with Internet connectivity; from these ones, eighty six percent use Internet connectivity

Figure 1. Internet connectivity

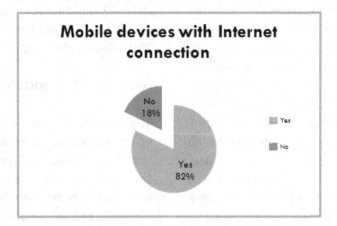

based on GPRS (General Packed Radio Service) or WAP (Wireless Application protocol) technology, and only twelve percent of mobile devices support WiFi (Wireless LAN) technology.

One question addressed in the survey was about the main mobile services generally used by inquired persons. Figure 2 summarizes the achieved results.

Another issue addressed in the study was the potential role and expectations about educational mobile contents and services. Figure 3 summarizes the most relevant educational mobile services, according the survey answers.

On the other hand, Figure 4 presents the main m-Learning constraints identified through the survey. The cost of the Internet provider, the screen dimensions, and resolution are some of the students' complaints regarding the use of mobile devices.

The survey also includes two questions to analyse the expectations about the value added that m-Learning can bring to the students learning process. These questions are based on a Likert scale of five degrees (Jamieson, 2004), from nothing important (level one) to very important (level five).

Figure 2. Mobile services used

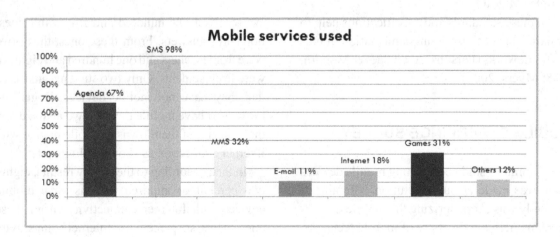

Figure 3. Educational mobile services desired

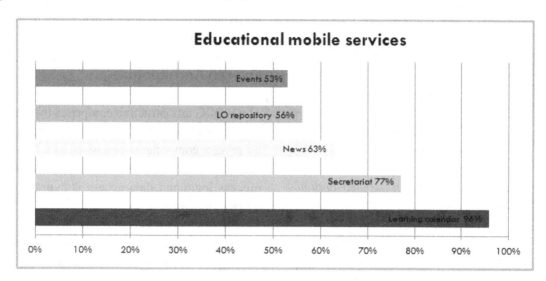

Figure 4. Main constrains for the use of mobile devices

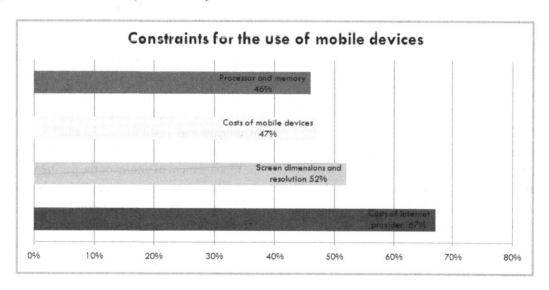

One of them if about the potential role of m-Learning in the learning student's process: eighty six percent on inquired persons answered from important to very important, like shows Table 1.

Another question is about the potential role of m-Learning in the distribution/access to learning contents: eighty five percent answered that m-Learning could perform an important or very important role in this field as shown in Table 2.

According the survey results it is possible to present some considerations:

• Almost all students and teachers use mobile devices with Internet connectivity, however these devices present different characteristics and support different technologies;

Table 1. Role of m-learning in the learning students process

Likert scale	Answers (%)
Nothing important	3%
Some significance	13%
Important	39%
Significant	34%
Very important	13%

Table 2. Role of m-learning in the distribution/ access to learning contents

Likert scale	Answers (%)
Nothing important	4%
Some significance	11%
Important	38%
Significant	42%
Very important	5%

- There are a set of educational mobile contents and services, identified by inquired persons, that they would like to use in a m-Learning platform;
- A large percentage of students and teachers recognize the potential contribute of m-Learning in supporting educational contents and services, bringing added value to the learning students' process.

ARCHITECTURE

Based on the previous survey, we decided to design an open system, called ESEIG-Mobile. The ultimate goal of ESEIG-Mobile is to standardize the delivery of learning content produced at our School (ESEIG) to the diversity of mobile devices used by our students.

In the following subsections, we present the overall architecture of the ESEIG learning systems and the concrete architecture of the ESEIG-Mobile system that will be integrated in the former. An evaluation of the ongoing development is also presented in the last subsection in order to validate our development strategy.

Overall Architecture

The ESEIG infrastructure comprises two servers as depicted in Figure 5. Each server is composed by several components organized as a three-tier model in which the users interface, functional process logic and data access is maintained as independent modules.

The first server (1) stores the Learning Management System (LMS) and the Content Management System (CMS). The former is used for the administration, documentation, tracking, reporting of training programs, classroom and online events, and training content. The later is used for publishing and managing content on the World Wide Web and intranets.

The second server (2) stores the Academic Management System (AMS). An AMS aggregates all the information regarding administrative, financial, technical, or scientific processes usual in educational institutions. Examples of these processes are the enrolment of students in courses, the management of grades or the payment of fees.

Both servers interact through Web services using SOAP. A typical scenario is the LMS importing data on students, courses, and student enrolment in courses from the AMS to avoid the burden of entering this data manually.

The first server includes the ESEIG-Mobile system, and for this reason, we will give more importance in our study. In this server, the installation of the components relied on XAMPP—a free and open source cross-platform Web server solution package that includes the Apache HTTP Server, the MySQL database and a set of interpreters for scripts written in the PHP and Perl programming languages. In this server, we installed a LMS and a CMS. The selection of the LMS was based on the open source LMS systems available (e.g. Moodle, Sakai, LRN, or Dokeos) and in the significant

Figure 5. Overall architecture

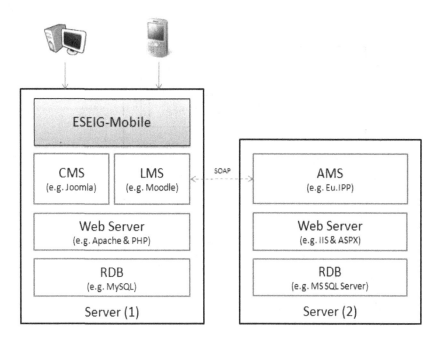

share on the LMS market (Davis, Carmean, & Wagner, 2009). Based on these criteria we choose Moodle as our LMS. Moodle is a free and open-source LMS written in PHP and created by Martin Dougiamas. Its name is an acronym for Modular Object-Oriented Dynamic Learning Environment. In early January of 2010, Moodle had a user-base of 46,624 registered sites with 32,464,992 users in 3,161,291 courses in 209 countries and in more than 75 languages (Cole & Foster, 2007). The most common functions of Moodle are the course information and documentation, documents repository, announcements, synchronous and a synchronous communication (email, chat room, discussion forum) and assignments. The selection of the CMS was based on the available open source CMS (e.g. Joomla!, Drupal, Wordpress). From this list, we choose Joomla! as our CMS. The Joomla! CMS is also written in PHP and stores data in a MySQL database. The most important features are a rich back-office to manage content in real time, page caching, RSS feeds, blogs, polls, search engine, and support for language internationalization.

ESEIG-Mobile Architecture

The architecture of the ESEIG-Mobile system is described by the component diagram shown in Figure 6.

The diagram includes the following components:

- The Repository component includes a repository with device capabilities and a patch to handle new updates. This component communicates with a public repository fed by a worldwide community;
- The Detector component receives HTTP requests and detects its origin by querying a special database formatted as an XML configuration file—the device repository;
- The Adapter component adapts the content based on the capabilities of the device. The adaptation process uses the Connector subcomponent to deal with the selection of resources based on the request of the Adapter component.

Figure 6. Component diagram of the ESEIG-mobile system

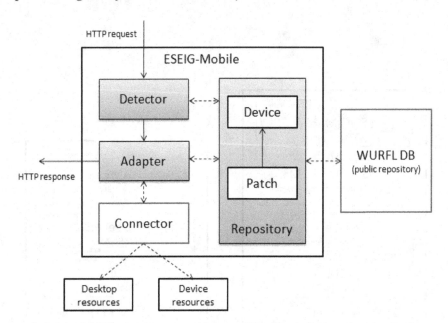

In the following sub-subsections these components are explained in more detail.

The Repository Component

The Repository component contains a file with a large list of device features based on WURFL. The WURFL is an open source database (based on a file called wurfl.xml) of wireless device capabilities. The WURFL repository can synchronize with a public repository of the WURFL DB where the developer community can make new additions to the WURFL DB. The Patch repository is a small XML file called wurfl_patch.xml that can enrich WURFL data dynamically. This file stores modified/enhanced groups and capability lists for new or existing WURFL devices. When the WURFL is parsed, the patch file is also imported to build a modified version of the device database.

The WURFL structure is formalize in a Document Type Definition (DTD) file. The DTD was the language inherited from Standard Generalized Markup Language (SGML) to define types of documents in XML. Its many limitations (e.g.

insufficient data type support, lack of namespace awareness) (Harold, 2004) lead to an official W3C recommendation for a schema language called XML Schema Definition language (XSD) (Fallside, 2004) in 2001. XML Schemas are richer and more powerful than DTDs (Song & Zhang, 2004) and are written in XML. This new language overcame DTD limitations and provided several advanced features, such as the ability to build new types derived from basic ones (Biron, 2004), manage relationships between elements (similar to relational databases) and combine elements from several schemata (Queirós & Leal, 2009). Based on these facts, we convert the WURFL DTD file[1] in a XML Schema file.

Figure 7 shows an overall view of the WURFL XML Schema.

The schema has two top-level elements: the version and the devices elements. The version element is composed by a set of sub-elements:

- **Ver:** The version of the WURFL database;
- **Last_Update**: The date of the last update of the database;

Figure 7. The WURFL schema

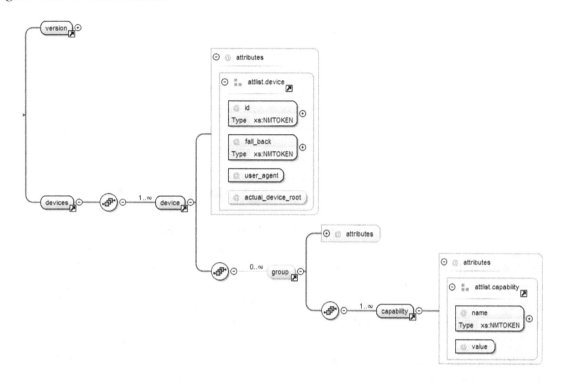

- **Maintainers:** A set of maintainer elements related with the person(s) responsible by maintaining the database;
- **Authors:** A set of author elements related with the person(s) responsible by creating the database.

The devices element contains one or more device sub-elements that model a certain device. This element contains the user_agent attribute, the device id attribute (created by the WURFL maintainer), the fall_back attribute (gives a way to infer more information about the device) and the actual_device_root attribute signals that the current device element may be chosen as the representative for all devices by the same brand and model name.

In addition to this data, a device element may carry information about device features commonly referred to as capabilities. A device capability is an XML fragment, which contains information about a specific feature of a given device. The device capabilities are organized in groups. Groups are used to improve the readability of the WURFL XML database by humans.

For instance, Nokia phones support tables because fall_back is defined as generic (WURFL default) as described in Algorithm 1.

The WURFL is based on the concept of family of devices. All devices are descendent of a generic device, but they may also descend of more specialized families. This mechanism, called 'fall_back,' lets programmers derive the capabilities of a given phone by looking at the capabilities of its family, unless a certain feature is specifically different for that phone (Passani, 2007).

Algorithm 1. Tables

```
<device user_agent="Nokia" fall_back="generic" id="nokia_generic">
 <group id="ui">
  <capability
      name="break_list_of_links_with_br_element_recommended"
      value="false" />
 </group>
</device>
```

The Detector Component

The Detector component receives HTTP requests and detects its origin by querying the WURFL device repository. A Web browser, when requesting a Web page, sends a set of HTTP headers, which is included the user-agent header. In PHP it's easy to obtain the value of this header by using the global variable $_SERVER['HTTP_USER_AGENT']. Using WURFL we can verify if the request was made either by a desktop computer browser or a mobile device browser. Algorithm 2 presents a simple way to obtain the origin of an HTTP request.

Algorithm 2 uses the getDeviceCapability method. This method expects a capability name as a parameter and returns the respective capability value in return. For testing purposes there is a Firefox extension called "User Agent Switcher" that allows the manual edition of the user-agent.

The Adapter Component

The Adapter component is the responsible for the content adaptation of the requests from the client mobile devices. This adaptation will be ensured, in a near future, by the use of WNG (Passani, 2010). WNG is a JSP tag library that abstracts the markup differences in all known wireless devices and allows the page creation similar to HTML, while delivering WML, C-HTML, and XHTML Mobile Profile to the client device. Device capabilities are queried dynamically using the WURFL API. The connector component handles the connection with Web resources and deals with the information querying and merging from the specific resources.

At this moment, ESEIG-Mobile is in early development as we are only detecting if the HTTP request is made from a mobile device. We use the WURFL API to query the repository based on the User Agent header of the request and present a resource suitable to the respective device capabili-

Algorithm 2. A simple way to obtain the origin of an http request

```php
<?php
    require_once('/myDirectory/wurfl_config.php');
    require_once(WURFL_CLASS_FILE);
    $wurflObj = new wurfl_class();
    $wurflObj->GetDeviceCapabilitiesFromAgent($_SERVER["HTTP_USER_AGENT"]);
    if ($wurflObj->getDeviceCapability('is_wireless_device')) {
    header("Location: http://mobile.eseig.ipp.pt ");}
    else { header("Location: http://eseig.ipp.pt"); }
?>
```

ties. Algorithm 3 demonstrates how the detection is performed and how we can query a particular device capability (e.g. maximum number of color supported).

Algorithm 3 returns the maximum number of colors supported by the device. Based on this value the connector will serve the suitable Web resource according with the requester device capabilities as shown in Figure 8.

USAGE STATISTICS

In order to characterize the levels of access and usage of the ESEIG-Mobile Web interface, a data set was collected through the Google Analytics service. This service is connected to the ESEIG-Mobile system, gathering a comprehensive set of data and statistics related with hit counters, rejected requests, new visitors, traffic, and mobile operating systems used to access the ESEIG-Mobile interface.

The data was collected since November 2010, and in this chapter we analyze the last four months, i.e., to February 2011.

In the following subsections, we present the overall data and statistics collected through the Google Analytics service, in order to better understand the adherence to the mobile Web interface, its evolution over time and the main weaknesses. These results are important to better understand the difficulties or constraints on the usage of

ESEIG-Mobile system by ESEIG students and also to monitor the interest to use the mobile services offered through this system.

Data Analysis

According to Figure 9, the access number (hit number) has risen hardly in the last few months. In fact, in November 2010 we had only eighteen system accesses; on the other hand, in February 2011 the hits number was three hundred and seven. Despite this strong grow, the number of new visitors has fixed around 60% of total accesses. These data clearly indicates that there are a large number of users who are still making the first contact with de ESEIG-Mobile services.

Other interesting data that were collected refer to mobile operating systems and platforms used to access the ESEIG-Mobile Web interface, depicted in Figure 10. Based on this data, it is possible to relate each of the mobile access platforms used by students with the service rejection rate and also the number of hits.

This in a relevant information, since it allows us to understand which are the mobile platforms most commonly used, and which ones have a higher rate of access rejection. That information is an important feedback regarding the efficiency and effectiveness of the Repository, Detector, and Adaptor components included in the ESEIG-Mobile system.

Algorithm 3. How the detection is performed

```
...
require_once('./wurfl_config.php');
require_once(WURFL_CLASS_FILE);
$userAgent = $_SERVER['HTTP_USER_AGENT'];
$wObj = new wurfl_class();
$wObj->GetDeviceCapabilitiesFromAgent($userAgent);
$max_colors = $wObj->getDeviceCapability('colors');
...
```

Figure 8. An ESEIG-mobile resource

ESEIG MOBILE

Ciências e Tecnologias da Documentação e Informação

Cursos | Descrição | 1.º Ano | 2.º Ano | 3.º Ano

⇨ **Objectivos**

Este curso forma técnico de nível superior qualificados em Biblioteconomia, Arquivo, Documentação e Informação.

Forma quadros com competências técnicas de elevado nível, incluindo a capacidade de gerir documen...

In fact, Symbian and Android are the main platforms used to access the ESEIG-Mobile interface, followed by iPhone, iPad and iPod. A surprising fact is the lower number of devices with the Windows Mobile operating system.

Moreover, the rejection rate in accessing the ESEIG-Mobile services is very low when using mobile devices with Windows Mobile or Samsung platforms. With iPhone and Android platforms the rejection rate is near to 50%; with other systems, the tendency is for higher rates of rejection. In order to obtain lower rates of rejection it is crucial to continue:

- To improve the Graphical User Web Interface (GUI) of the ESEIG-Mobile and its usability;
- To improve the Detector and Adaptor components of ESEIG-Mobile system.

Another important issue is to compare and monitoring the traffics evolution of both ESEIG-Mobile Web interface and the traditional ESEIG Web interface, accessible from any desktop or laptop. Table 3 illustrates the hit numbers from both platforms over the last four months.

In fact, there are differences in the number of hits between the two platforms. However, both platforms increased the number of requests over time. The ESEIG-Mobile Web interface has recorded higher growth rates, according data in Table 3. This fact is due to the new trends on the learning paradigm where the mobile learning occupy a main role and to the evolution and dissemination of the mobile devices.

Figure 9. ESEIG-mobile usage: hits and new visitors

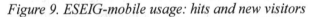

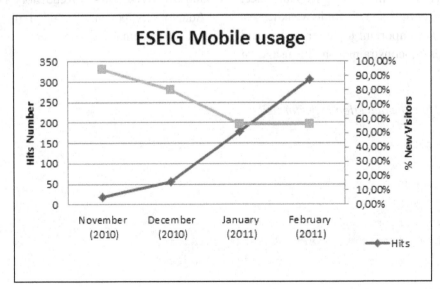

Figure 10. Mobile devices operating systems

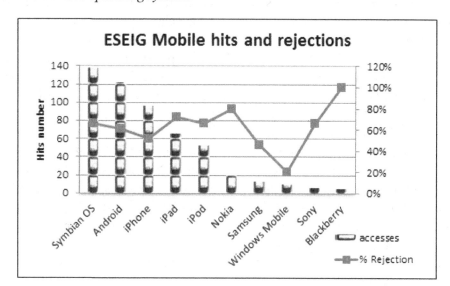

Table 3. ESEIG traffic data

Months	FSEIG-Mobile hits	ESEIG Desktop hits
November 2010	18	21.351
December 2010	55	16.388
January 2011	179	29.085
February 2011	307	31.417

Data Discussion

The results presented in the above subsection illustrate the current status on the usage of ESEIG-Mobile Web interface. The analysis of this data could help us to better understand the strengths and weaknesses in the access and usage of the ESEIG-Mobile Web interface.

Regarding the access rate, one can consider that although the access rate is relatively low, it has increased significantly. The amounts collected can result from the fact that the platform is very recent, and therefore still unknown by most students. Moreover, the high rates of new visitors may indicate that the ESEIG-Mobile Web interface starts to be increasingly popular.

Another important issue that arises from the data analysis is the diversity and heterogeneity of the client devices. Symbian, Android, iPhone and iPad are the leading mobile devices, but there are a large number of other devices that ESEIG-Mobile system should respond. This fact proves the need to find an approach to deliver uniform content to address the heterogeneity of mobile devices existent nowadays.

It is also important to understand the reasons for the high rejection rates observed in some mobile devices. This will be, certainly, a critical success factor for ESEIG-Mobile interface. We anticipate two possible causes for these rejection rates:

1. **Incomplete Representation of the Device Characteristics:** The Repository component included in the ESEIG-Mobile system contains a file with a large list of device features based on WURFL. This list could need to be

complemented with a more comprehensive set of device features.

2. **Performance Issues:** Each request is detected and validated using the WURFL database. A cache-aware approach could increase the ESEIG-Mobile responsiveness. The Tera-WURFL project is a good candidate to fulfill this requirement since it uses a MySQL database backend to store the WURFL data and caches the results of device detections. The project also supports implementations of WALL such as WALL4PHP to create Websites in an abstract language which is delivered to the visiting user in several formats (e.g. CHTML, XHTML, XHTML-MP) based on the mobile browser's support.

CONCLUSION

In this chapter, we present several approaches for defining delivery context and also a survey targeted to ESEIG students and teachers that base our work. The survey shows the real perspectives and expectations of the students and teachers' community on this emergent field of educational mobile contents. The mobile devices advent could enable a more useful proximity between students and teachers, facilitating and promoting the learning process.

In order to address the main issues regarding the heterogeneity of mobile devices found in our community we also present the design and the prototype implementation of an open system for the delivery of suitable and uniform e-Learning content to the mobile devices of our students.

To validate our approach we present the usage statistics of the ESEIG-Mobile project based on the Google Analytics data. The analysis of this data is very important since it helps us to confirm and understand the heterogeneity of the students' mobile devices and their usage habits and prefer-

ences. It also helps to identify and find the best approaches to improve the ESEIG-Mobile system.

At this moment, ESEIG-Mobile is in early development as we are only detecting if the HTTP request is made from a mobile device and query some device capabilities from the WURFL device repository. We expect some challenges in the prototype implementation process regarding, for instance, the transformation of the Web resources in the WNG format. For this task we are considering using Extensible Stylesheet Language for Transformation (XSLT) to formally describe the transformations. Other ongoing work is related with increasing the device repository performance migrating from the WURFL XML database to a relational database (e.g. MySQL) using, for instance, the Tera-WURFL project.

REFERENCES

Biron, P. V., & Malhotra, A. (2004). *XML schema part 2: Datatypes* (2nd ed). Retrieved from http://www.w3.org

Chang, C., & Sheu, J. (2004). Design and implementation of ad hoc classroom and eschoolbag systems for ubiquitous learning. In *Proceedings of the IEEE International Workshop Wireless and Mobile Technologies in Education*. IEEE Press.

Chen, Y., et al. (2002). A mobile scaffolding-aid-based bird-watching learning systems. In *Proceedings of the IEEE International Workshop Wireless and Mobile Technologies in Education*. IEEE Press.

Cole, J., & Foster, H. (2007). *Using Moodle - Teaching with the popular open source cours management system*. New York, NY: O'Reilly.

Davis, B., Carmean, C., & Wagner, E. D. (2009). *The evolution of the LMS: From management to learning - Deep analysis of trends shaping the future of elearning*. Thousand Oaks, CA: Sage Road Solutions, LLC.

Fallside, D. C. (2004). *XML schema part 0: Primer* (2nd ed). Retrieved from http://www.w3.org

Gimson, R., Lewis, R., & Sathish, S. (2006). *Delivery context overview for device independence - W3C working group note*. Retrieved from http://www.w3.org/TR/di-dco

Harold, E. R. (2204). *The XML bible* (3rd ed). New York, NY: Hungry Minds.

Jamieson, S. (2004). *Likert scales, how to (ab) use them*. Oxford, UK: Blackwell Publishing. doi:10.1111/j.1365-2929.2004.02012.x

Kiss, C. (2010). *Composite capability/preference profiles (CC/PP): Structure and vocabularies 2.0 - W3C working group note*. Retrieved from http://www.w3.org/TR/CCPP-struct-vocab2/

Lewis, R. (2003). *Authoring challenges for device independence*. Retrieved from http://www.w3.org/TR/acdi/

Liu, T., et al. (2002). Applying wireless technologies to build a highly interactive learning environment. In *Proceedings of the IEEE International Workshop Wireless and Mobile Technologies in Education*. IEEE Press.

Myers, A., Nichols, J., & Miller, R. (2004). Taking handheld devices to the next level. *IEEE Computer Society*. Retrieved from http://www.cs.cmu.edu/~pebbles/papers/pebblesControlIEEE.pdf

Paes, C., & Moreira, F. (2008). Aprendizagem com dispositivos móveis: aspectos técnicos e pedagógicos a serem considerados num sistema de educação. In *Proceedings of the V Conferência Internacional de Tecnologias de Informação e Comunicação na Educação*. IEEE.

Parsons, D., & Ryu, H. (2007). Software architectures for mobile learning. In Parsons, D., & Ryu, H. (Eds.), *Mobile Learning Technologies and Applications*. Wellington, New Zealand: Massey University.

Parsons, D., Ryu, H., & Cranshaw, M. (2007). A design requirements framework for mobile learning environments. *Journal of Computers, 2*(4). doi:10.4304/jcp.2.4.1-8

Parupalli, R. (2009). Dynamic content adaptation to mobile devices. In *Proceedings of the 3rd National Seminar on e-Learning and e-Learning Technologies*. IEEE.

Passani, L. (2010). *Introducing WALL: A library to multiserve applications on the wireless*. Retrieved from http://wurfl.sourceforge.net/java/tutorial.php

Passani, L. (2012). *Wireless universal resource file (WURFL)*. Retrieved from http://wurfl.sourceforge.net/

Queirós, R., & Leal, J. P. (2009). *Schem@Doc: A web-based XML schema visualize*. Paper presented at Inforum - Simpósio de Informática - 7th edition of XML: Aplicações e Tecnologias Associadas. Lisboa, Portugal.

Queirós, R., & Pinto, M. (2010). ESEIG mobile: An m-learning approach in a superior school. In *Proceedings of the Enterprise Information Systems International Conference,* (vol. 110, pp. 355-363). Viana do Castelo, Portugal. IEEE.

Rabin, J., & McCathieNevile, C. (2008). *Mobile web best practices 1.0 – Basic guidelines*. Retrieved from http://www.w3.org/TR/mobile-bp/#ddc

Seung-Won, N. (2005). Design and implementation of resource sharing system for creation of multiple instructions in mobile internet environment. *Advances in Intelligent and Soft Computing, 29,* 797–807. doi:10.1007/3-540-32391-0_84

Song, G., & Zhang, K. (2004). Visual XML schemas based on reserved graph grammars. In *Proceedings of the International Conference on Information Technology: Coding and Computing (ITCC 2004)*, (Vol. 1). ITCC.

Wireless Application Protocol Forum, Ltd. (2012). *User agent profile (UAProf)*. Retrieved from http://www.openmobilealliance.org/tech/affiliates/wap/wap-248-uaprof-20011020-a.pdf

Zhang, W., Kunz, T., & Hansen, K. M. (2007). Product line enabled intelligent mobile middleware. In *Proceedings of the 12th IEEE Interational Conference on Engineering of Complex Computer Systems*, (pp. 148-157). Auckland, New Zealand: IEEE Press.

ENDNOTES

[1] Available at http://wurfl.sourceforge.net/wurfl.dtd

Section 3
Databases and Repositories

Chapter 8
Preservation of Data Warehouses:
Extending the SIARD System with DWXML Language and Tools

Carlos Aldeias
University of Porto, Portugal

Gabriel David
University of Porto, Portugal

Cristina Ribeiro
University of Porto, Portugal

ABSTRACT

Data warehouses are used in many application domains, and there is no established method for their preservation. A data warehouse can be implemented in multidimensional structures or in relational databases that represent the dimensional model concepts in the relational model. The focus of this work is on describing the dimensional model of a data warehouse and migrating it to an XML model, in order to achieve a long-term preservation format. This chapter presents the definition of the XML structure that extends the SIARD format used for the description and archive of relational databases, enriching it with a layer of metadata for the data warehouse components. Data Warehouse Extensible Markup Language (DWXML) is the XML language proposed to describe the data warehouse. An application that combines the SIARD format and the DWXML metadata layer supports the XML language and helps to acquire the relevant metadata for the warehouse and to build the archival format.

DOI: 10.4018/978-1-4666-2669-0.ch008

INTRODUCTION

The technological generation in which we live has gradually modified the method to create, process, and store information, using digital means for this purpose. The institutions, enterprises, and governments rely more and more on information systems that increase the availability and accessibility of information. These information systems typically require relational databases, which become valuable assets for those entities.

However, rapid technological changes degenerate into rapid obsolescence of applications, file formats, media storage, and even databases management systems (DBMS) (Date, 2004). If nothing is done, access to large chunks of stored information may become impossible and it will eventually be lost. So, it is important that entities which have major responsibilities in preserving information in digital form become aware of this problem and join initiatives all over the world, seeking for the best methodology for long-term digital preservation, and in particular for database preservation.

The work presented here has been developed in the context of DBPreserve, a research project funded by the Portuguese Foundation for Science and Technology (FCT), in collaboration with INESC Porto, University of Minho, and the Portuguese National Archives (DGARQ). The project goal is to study the feasibility of data warehousing technologies to preserve complex electronic records, such as those constituting databases. The DBPreserve project approaches the long-term preservation of relational databases issue with a new concept, a two-step migration:

- A model migration from the relational model to the dimensional model, using data warehouse concepts to simplify the model simplification and increase efficiency (Rahman, David, & Ribeiro, 2010);

- An XML migration from the dimensional model to an XML (Consortium, 2008) format that represents the data warehouse, to ensure a long-term preservation format.

A data warehouse is structured by star or snowflake representations. A star is made up of a fact table that stores the facts, and dimensional tables that contextualize the facts. There are also bridge tables used to resolve a many to many relationship between a fact table and a dimension table, or to flatten out a hierarchy in a dimension table. A snowflake is similar to a star but the dimension tables have been subject to a partial normalization, resulting in subdimensions. Data marts are subsets of a data warehouse.

We propose the Data Warehouse Extensible Markup Language (DWXML), an XML dialect for describing a Data Warehouse (DW) (Inmon, 2002; Kimball & Ross, 2002; Date, 2004). It has been defined and refined according to data warehouse's properties and tested using a case study of SiFEUP[1]. It is used in the project as a complement to the SIARD format (Archives, 2008) used for the description and archive of relational databases. This enrichment leverages past efforts to define an archive format suitable for data tables from databases and adds a layer of metadata for the data warehouse components.

BACKGROUND

Digital preservation concerns sustainable and efficient strategies for the long-term preservation of digital objects (Ferreira, 2006). However, databases and data warehouses are different from conventional digital objects as they have an internal structure, and include schemas and integrity constraints, which are vital for interpreting data.

Digital Preservation Projects

There are already many efforts and projects developed under the digital preservation scope. Projects such as CAMiLEON (Hedstrom & Lampe, 2001), InterPARES (Force, 2002), FEDORA (Lagoze, Payette, Shin, & Wilper, 2006), or PLANETS (Hoeven, 2007; Zierau & Wijk, 2008; Sinclair, 2010) contributed to the study of requirements, strategies, and proposals for preserving digital objects and ensure their authenticity.

Regarding complex digital objects, such as databases, projects like SIARD (Archives, 2008), Chronos (Brandl & Keller-Marxer, 2007), or RODA (Ramalho, Ferreira, Faria, & Castro, 2007), analyzed in detail the preservation of relational databases. The PLANETS project built a framework that deals with Access, MS SQL Server and Oracle databases, as well as the SIARD format (PLANETS, 2009), a preservation format for relational databases.

The PresDB 2007 workshop report states that *"existing preservation techniques for fixed digital objects are not suited for databases, thus some of our most critical digital assets are endangered—both economically and technically—in the long term"* (Christophides & Buneman, 2007).

This section introduces the concepts, requirements, and strategies for digital preservation in the long term. *"Long term is long enough to be concerned with the impacts of changing technologies, including support for new media and data formats, or with a changing user community. Long term may extend indefinitely"* (CCSDS, 2002).

Thibodeau's organization of digital preservation strategies relates them to their applicability and objective (Thibodeau, 2002). Figure 1 shows a simplified version of this bidimensional mapping, according to Ferreira' perspective (Ferreira, 2006), that is sufficiently clear and synthesized for our purposes. As Thibodeau's organization, this viewpoint arranges on the left the strategies focusing on preservation of the physical/logical object, and on the right side, the strategies focused on preserving the conceptual object.

Among all these strategies, the one that has been considered most feasible for database preservation is data migration to a standard XML format. XML stands for eXtensible Markup Language and is an open standard defined by the World Wide Web Consortium (W3C). It is a very flexible text format derived from SGML (ISO8879) (Sperberg-McQueen & Burnard, 1994), and it is widely used to structure, exchange, and store data

Figure 1. Digital preservation methods (Ferreira, 2006)

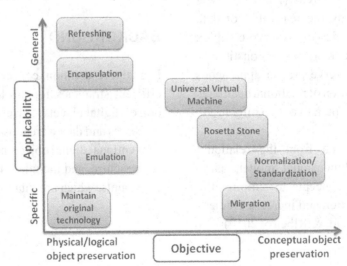

(Consortium, 2008). XML is platform and application independent, has a simple text format and is human readable, and is therefore an effective technology for the long-term preservation of relational databases.

The Open Archival Information System (OAIS) Reference Model (CCSDS, 2002), approved as an ISO standard in 2003, introduces, in the context of long-term preservation, the terminology for communication between the concerned parties in the preservation of digital objects, and defines the functional components necessary to implement a digital archive. An Open Archival Information System is *"an organization of people and systems that has accepted the responsibility to preserve information and make it available for a designated community"* (CCSDS, 2002). The term 'Open' emphasizes the fact that it has been developed in an open public forum, in which any interested party was encouraged to participate.

Data Warehouse Metadata

The research produced around digital preservation of databases does not account for the concepts of the dimensional model. Concepts like facts, dimensions, bridges, hierarchies, levels, data marts, star schemas, or snowflake schemas are essential for the full description of a data warehouse.

Data warehouses are often implemented using relational database technology, and thus they are made up of tables that store data. A deeper inspection leads to the finding of facts, dimensions, bridges tables, indexes, level keys, and views. However, there are some important differences between a database used in an operational system and in a data warehouse.

W. H. Inmon defined a data warehouse as *"a subject-oriented, integrated, nonvolatile, time variant collection of data in support of management's decisions"* (Inmon, 1992). Data warehouses fulfill two major purposes: provide a single, clean, and consistent source of data for

decision support and unlink the decision platform from the operational system (Date, 2004).

In a data warehouse the tables and joins are simple and de-normalized, in order to reduce the response time for analytical queries. For the characterization of a data warehouse, additional metadata is required that defines the dimensional model and allows data interpretation across different perspectives. The structure of a data warehouse is referred to as a dimensional schema, where dimensional tables, forming star schemas, surround the fact tables. A fact table is often located at the center of a star schema and consists of facts of a business process (e.g., measurements, transaction values).

To understand the facts it is necessary to introduce the context and meaning of the dimensional model, captured in the dimensions, representing the relevant vectors of analysis of the business process facts. The dimensions allow us to identify the how, what, who, when, where and why of the data. Dimensions are usually represented by one or more dimensional tables. A dimensional table contains attributes to define and group the data for data warehouse querying.

The dimensions are characterized by a set of levels with defined hierarchies. Hierarchies are logical structures that use levels to organize and aggregate data, define navigation paths or establish a family structure (Inmon, 1992; Kimball & Ross, 2002). A common example is a time dimension, where the hierarchy might aggregate data from the day level to the week, month, and quarter or year levels.

Figure 2 shows an example of a star schema in a real-world case study used in the project, a *"Course Evaluation"* information system where statistics about user satisfaction (anonymous students) are collected in an academic environment, specifically on professor and class evaluation.

In the center, a fact table contains the submitted answers (IPDW_ANSWERS). As dimensional tables, there are the question table (IPDW_QUESTION), the quiz table (IPDW_QUIZ), also

Figure 2. Star schema example

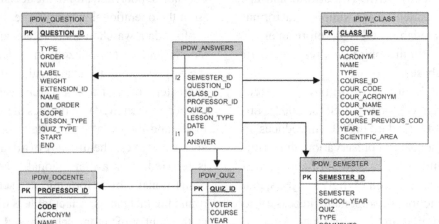

the semester table (IPDW_SEMESTER), the class table (IPDW_CLASS), and the professor table (IPDW_PROFESSOR). Because the answers are anonymous, there is no relationship with the students who actually answered the questionnaires. An important step in the data warehouse building process is to declare the dimensions. The following sample code shows the declaration of a dimension with the CREATE DIMENSION SQL statement (Oracle, 2011) using Oracle (see Algorithm 1).

Algorithm 1 defines a dimension (class_dim) with a hierarchy (class_rollup) of two levels: the level course with COURSE_ID as the level key, and a child level class with CLASS_ID as the level key. This dimension uses the data from the table IPDW_CLASS. The ATTRIBUTE clause specifies the attributes that are uniquely determined by a hierarchy level. Thus, it is possible to analyze the data in a more global perspective, through the course level, or get a more detailed view using the class level.

Another data warehouse concept is a bridge table. A bridge table is used to resolve a many to many relationship between a fact table and a dimension table and is also used to flatten out a hierarchy in a dimension table (Kimball & Ross, 2002).

Storing snowflake schemas and data marts is also needed. The snowflake schema is similar to the star schema, but dimensions are normalized into multiple related tables. A data mart is a subset of a data warehouse (Kimball & Ross, 2002; Hackney, 1997).

Algorithm 1. Example of a dimension declaration

```
CREATE DIMENSION class_dim
  LEVEL class IS (IPDW_CLASS.CLASS_ID)
  LEVEL course IS (IPDW_CLASS.COURSE_ID)
  HIERARCHY class_rollup(
    class CHILD OF
    course)
  ATTRIBUTE class DETERMINES
    (IPDW_CLASS.CODE, IPDW_CLASS.ACRONYM,
    IPDW_CLASS.NAME, IPDW_CLASS.TYPE)
  ATTRIBUTE course DETERMINES
(IPDW_CLASS.COUR_CODE, IPDW_CLASS.COUR_ACRONYM,
    IPDW_CLASS.COUR_NAME, IPDW_CLASS.COUR_TYPE,
    IPDW_CLASS.COURSE_PREVIOUS_COD);
```

A DATA WAREHOUSE PRESERVATION FORMAT

The main goal of this proposal is to provide a preservation format that suits the characteristics of a generic data warehouse. This format should allow the definition of the relevant metadata from the data warehouse perspective and archive the metadata as well as the data from the tables in a format that would guarantee long-term preservation. The use of XML to satisfy these requirements appeared as an obvious option.

The study of the work already produced around the preservation of databases (Brandl & Keller-Marxer, 2007; SFA, 2008; Sinclair, 2010), including the model migration approach developed in the DBPreserve project (Rahman, David, & Ribeiro, 2010), and on XML representation of a data warehouse (Pokorny, 2002; Hummer, Bauer, & Harde, 2003), resulted in the decision to adopt and complement the SIARD format, an XML based format for the archival of relational databases, in order to adapt it to the characteristics of the dimensional model used in data warehouses.

The SIARD format proved to be the most appropriate starting point for this representation given the inherent modularity of data warehouses, with independent stars sharing some dimensions. SIARD has a segmented structure of directories and files, unlike the DBML (Database Markup Language) used in RODA (Ramalho, Ferreira, Faria, & Castro, 2007), which represents everything in a single file, making data handling harder.

Thus, reusing the archival format that stores the definition of the tables and their data, we propose to add a metadata layer for data interpretation according to the data warehouse perspective. Given the simplicity of the dimensional model in terms of relationships between tables, it becomes possible to analyze the archived data with greater efficiency through simplified queries applied directly to the XML files using XQuery[2] and XPath[3].

Relational Database Preservation with SIARD

The Swiss Federal Archives (SFA) have developed an open storage format for relational databases called SIARD (Software Independent Archiving of Relational Databases), as well as a set of conversion tools named the SIARD Suite (Thomas, 2009), in order to convert relational databases (e.g., Access, Oracle, and SQL Server) into the archival SIARD format, edit the SIARD format and reactivate an archived database, restoring from the SIARD Format to a database.

The SIARD format is a nonproprietary and published open standard, based on open standard (e.g., ISO norms Unicode, XML, SQL1999) and the industry standard ZIP. In May 2008, the European PLANETS project accepted SIARD format as the official format for archiving relational databases (Archives, 2008).

The SIARD format is a ZIP64 (PKWARE, 2007) uncompressed package based on an organizational system of folders, storing the metadata in the header folder and table data in the content folder. This organization is shown in Figure 3.

For database's metadata characterization a single XML file is used that contains the entire structure of the database (schemas, tables, attributes, keys, views, functions...) and the corresponding XSD[4] schema for XML validation.

As to the primary data, each schema is stored in different folders and sequentially numbered, as well as the tables of each schema. The data from each table is stored in an XML file with simplified structure (only rows and columns) and its XSD. If there are Large Objects—LOB (BLOB—Binary Large Objects; and CLOB—Character Large Objects), these data are stored in binary files or text, within a folder for each attribute of these types, being referred to its path in the respective XML of the table.

One of the major benefits of this segmented archiving of the primary data is that it will reduce the size of each XML file, because the data will be

Figure 3. Structure of the SIARD archive file

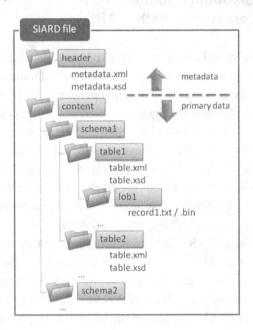

distributed into the corresponding XML table files. This will increase the efficiency of parsing and querying of the XML data and can be extremely useful for parsing and querying of simultaneous XML table files, in order to solve a query involving more than one XML file (table).

Another reason for using the SIARD format is the existence of a tool that already allows us to create these packages from relational databases in Oracle, MSAccess and MSSQLServer.

The SIARD project produced a set of tools— SIARD Suite (Thomas, 2009)—comprised of three components: the *SiardEdit*, a graphical user interface for migration and metadata processing; the *SiardFromDb*, a command line application for extracting and storing a database generating the SIARD file; and the *SiardToDb*, a command line application to reactivate a database from a SIARD file.

Thus, the effort in this work will focus on the description of the dimensional model, complementing the existing one for the relational metadata format. The migration of the primary data into an XML format according to SIARD has also to be ensured.

However, the reuse and expansion of an existing open format like SIARD should not prevent the use of the applications that supports it, the SIARD Suite. Existing applications should be executed as if no changes to the format were made. Thus, using SIARD Suite it must be possible to manage the relational level metadata and the primary data.

DWXML Definition

As XML languages exist for many domains and applications, existing XML representations for data warehouses were considered. There are some works in this area (Jensen, Muller, & Pedersen, 2001; Hummer, Bauer, & Harde, 2003). These works concern a multidimensional schema representation, i.e. data cubes. The XCube (Hummer, Bauer, & Harde, 2003) is a data cube XML representation and it was developed to exchange data warehouse data over networks. The XCube was designed for interoperability purposes in MOLAP systems. The representation of the cube is divided into several XML documents to characterize each entity involved in the multidimensional system. This approach is interesting in the context in which it was developed, as it allows slicing the cube and sending small packets of information over the network, just as requested by the client. Even trying to adapt it for dimensional models, the diversity of documents produced would obscure the representation of the data warehouse. Moreover, it does not have any reference to tables (which store the facts and the dimensions in ROLAP systems), views, and star or snowflake schemas.

To extend the SIARD format for archiving data warehouses in ROLAP systems, providing dimensional metadata to the SIARD format, a new XML file is added for characterizing the data warehouse and providing the concepts associated with the dimensional model, which are not covered by the base SIARD format. The XML schema (XSD) will also be added for validation of the XML file produced. This new XML representation was named Data Warehouse Extensible Markup Language (DWXML).

As a SIARD format extension for archiving data warehouses, the proposed DWXML bridges the gap between the relational model description and the dimensional model description, adding a metadata file (dw.xml) and its schema definition (dw.xsd[5]). Figure 4 shows an excerpt of the extended SIARD format, which includes the description of a data warehouse.

The data warehouse is composed by a set of stars and a set of dimensions, implemented by tables and views organized in schemas. Data marts are also defined as a set of stars. Figure 5 characterizes the DWXML basic structure and the star element.

The *version* attribute represents the version of the DWXML definition. The element *dwBinding* supports the description of the DWXML file, the information related to the owner of the data, the credentials of the connection to the data warehouse and the names and versions of the applications involved in the DWXML creation, including the DBMS where the data warehouse was working and the migration date.

Table 1 describes the elements of the data warehouse metadata. The column *Opt.* indicates whether the identifier is optional. Table 2 describes the elements of the data warehouse binding metadata.

Stars and Facts

A star is composed by a fact table and a set of "rays" which establish relationships to dimensions and, possibly, bridge tables. The *factTable*

Figure 4. DWXML added to the SIARD archive file

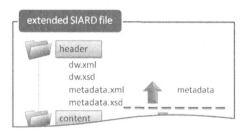

element references the respective table description in the schemas element, indicates the columns responsible for the joins between fact tables and dimensions or bridge tables, and contains information about its granularity and about the facts. Regarding the facts, these elements indicate the table column that represents each of them, as well as their measure type: non-additive, semi-additive or additive. Table 3 describes the elements of the star metadata.

Figure 6 shows the schema of a fact table element, including its facts and possible join column definitions. These are used when a bridge table sits between a fact table and a dimension, with a many-to-many relationship between the fact and the bridge table.

Table 4 describes the elements of the fact table metadata.

Joins with dimensions are dealt by the ray element. The joinColumns element is useful to indicate which column of the fact table is responsible for the relationship with a column of a bridge table. Table 5 describes the elements of the join column metadata. Table 6 describes the elements of the fact metadata.

In a star, each *ray* element represents a relationship between the fact table and a dimension. In special situations, for instance when there is a many to many relationship between the fact table and the dimension, a bridge table may be added. In this case, the ray element is composed by a *bridgeTable* element that references the related table, followed by a reference to the dimension element. Table 7 describes the elements of the ray metadata.

The following example shows a star definition using DWXML. The IPDW_ANSWERS_STAR is composed by the IPDW_ANSWERS fact table, which holds the data of the additive fact ANSWER_F represented on the fact table's column ANSWER, and by two ray elements. One of them establishes a connection to the dimension QUESTION_DIM (see Algorithm 2).

Figure 5. DWXML schema showing the star element

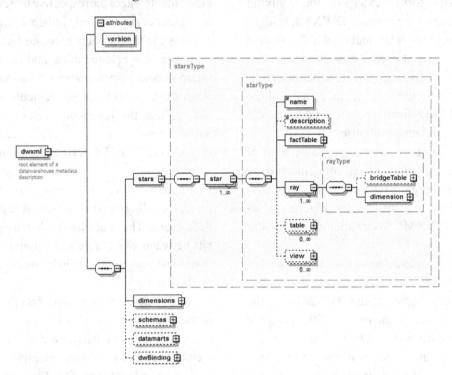

Table 1. Data warehouse metadata description

Identifier	Opt.	Description
version	no	DWXML format version
stars	no	List of stars in the data warehouse
dimensions	no	List of dimensions, dimensional tables and views in the data warehouse
schemas	yes	List of schemas in the data warehouse
datamart	yes	List of datamarts in the data warehouse
dwBinding	yes	Additional metadata for data warehouse connection description and DWXML file generation

Table 2. Data warehouse binding metadata description

Identifier	Opt.	Description
description	yes	Description of the data warehouse's meaning and content
dataOwner	no	The owner of the data, who has the right to grant the access to the data
xmlApplication	yes	Name and version of program that produced the DWXML from the data warehouse
migrationDate	yes	Date when the DWXML was produced from the data warehouse
dwProduct	no	Product name and version of the DBMS containing the data warehouse
dwUser	no	The user of the data warehouse who carried out the XML migration
dwConnection	no	The connection string to the data warehouse that contains the dimensional model

Table 3. Star metadata description

Identifier	Opt.	Description
name	no	Name of the star
description	yes	Description of the star meaning and content
factTable	no	Fact table implementing the star
ray	no	Ray of the star connecting the fact table with a dimension or a bridge table (referenced by schema and name).
table	yes	List of extra tables to accommodate special cases (referenced by schema and table name)
view	yes	List of views which may represent a virtual fact table (referenced by schema and view name)

Figure 6. DWXML schema showing a fact table element

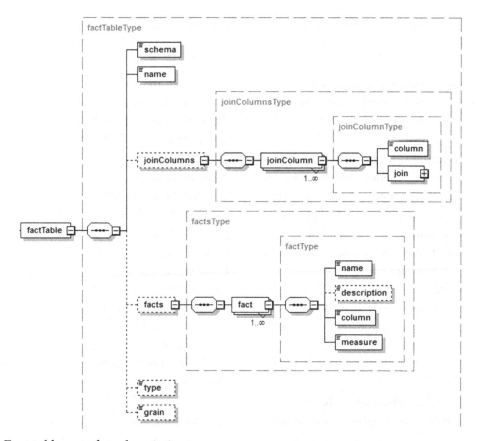

Table 4. Fact table metadata description

Identifier	Opt.	Description
schema	no	Schema of the fact table
name	no	Name of the fact table
joinColumns	yes	List of columns used in the joins between the fact table and possible bridge tables
facts	yes	List of facts represented in the fact table
type	yes	The type of the fact table (TRANSACTIONS, CUMULATIVE, or SNAPSHOT)
grain	yes	The grain of the fact, the meaning and content of a row in the fact table

Table 5. Join column metadata description

Identifier	Opt.	Description
column	no	Fact table column used in the join
join	no	Column of the bridge table involved in the join (schema, table and column)

Table 6. Fact metadata description

Identifier	Opt.	Description
name	no	Name of the fact
description	yes	Fact meaning and content
column	no	Column of the fact table where the fact is stored
measure	no	Measure type (constrained to ADDITIVE, NON- ADDITIVE, or SEMI-ADDITIVE)

As snowflake schemas can be seen as extensions of star schemas, their representation starts as a star schema, but the dimensions of a snowflake schema are implemented by tables (dimension tables) that are partially normalized, resulting in relationships with other tables (sub-dimension). Therefore, inspecting the dimension table's foreign keys, it is possible to differentiate between a snowflake schema and a star schema. If a foreign key of a dimension table refers a sub-dimension, the schema is a snowflake schema.

Datamarts are subsets of data warehouses, i.e. sets of star or snowflake schemas. Table 8 describes the elements of the datamart metadata.

Dimensions

Dimensions may be shared by different stars. Therefore, the metadata related to the dimensions is stored in a list of dimension elements that are referenced by the stars. Dimensions explain the meaning of the measures stored in the fact table and support the data analysis. Figure 7 displays the dimensions element schema. The dimension element has been defined following the syntax of the CREATE DIMENSION Oracle SQL statement (Oracle, 2010).

Each dimension element represents a relevant entity in the problem domain and is characterized by a set of attributes. Attributes may be grouped in levels, which are organized in hierarchies. Dimensions and levels have keys. The tables and views elements contain the references to the tables and views (schema and name) that support the declared dimensions; their structure is described in the schemas element.

Table 9 describes the elements of the dimension metadata.

Figure 8 displays the level element schema in a dimension. Levels have a level key that identifies each level. The level key of the lowest level

Table 7. Ray metadata description

Identifier	Opt.	Description
bridgeTable	yes	Reference to the bridge table (schema and name)
dimension	no	Reference to the dimension (schema and name)

Algorithm 2. Example of a DWXML star definition

```
<?xml version="1.0" encoding="UTF-8"?>
<dwxml version="1.0" xsi:noNamespaceSchemaLocation="dw.xsd"
    xmlns:xsi="http://www.w3.org/2001/XMLSchema-instance">
    <stars>
        <star>
            <name>IPDW_ANSWERS_STAR</name>
            <description>Star related to the answers</description>
            <factTable>
                <schema>CALDEIAS</schema>
                <name>IPDW_ANSWERS</name>
                <facts>
                    <fact>
                        <name>ANSWER_F</name>
                        <column>ANSWER</column>
                        <measure>ADDITIVE</measure>
                    </fact>
                </facts>
            </factTable>
            <ray>
                <dimension>
                    <schema>CALDEIAS</schema>
                    <name>QUESTION_DIM</name>
                </dimension>
            </ray>
            <ray>
                ...
            </ray>
        </star>
    </stars>
    ...
</dwxml>
```

Table 8. Datamart metadata description

Identifier	Opt.	Description
name	no	Name of the datamart
description	yes	Description of the datamart meaning and content
stars	no	List of the names of the stars that defines the datamart

Figure 7. Dimensions element schema

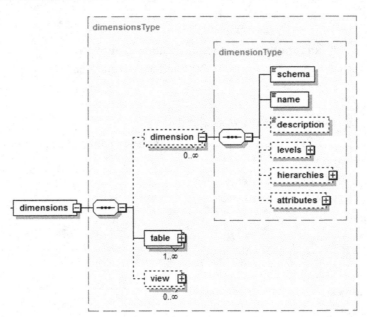

corresponds to the dimension key. This key represents the dimension in the data warehouse.

Table 10 describes the elements of the level metadata.

Figure 9 displays the hierarchy element schema in a dimension.

Table 11 describes the elements of the hierarchy metadata. Table 12 describes the elements of the attribute metadata. Attributes represent the characteristics of a level, which is identified by its level key.

When a dimension is implemented by just one table, each record contains attributes for all the levels. If some levels are detached in a subdimension (snowflake or partially normalized schema) an extra join attribute must be included in the main dimension to reference the subdimension.

Figure 10 displays the attribute element schema in a dimension.

Table 13 describes the identifiers of the level referenced by an attribute.

The next example shows a dimension definition using DWXML. This dimension (CLASS_DIM) is composed by the levels COURSE and CLASS, identified by their level keys COURSE_ID and CLASS_ID, respectively. Both these levels are implemented by the IPDW_CLASS relational table. The dimension has a defined hierarchy of levels named (CLASS_ROLLUP) stating that CLASS level is child of COURSE level, according to the order of appearance (the first is parent of the second and so on). The attribute element states which attributes are defined by each level. Therefore, the attributes COUR_PREVIOUS_COD, COUR_TYPE, COUR_NAME, COUR_ACRONYM belong to the COURSE level and the attributes TYPE, NAME, ACRONYM belong to the CLASS level (see Algorithm 3).

Tables and Views

The schemas, tables, and views follow a simplified representation with respect to the SIARD format and some elements are replicated in this description to make the data warehouse metadata self-contained. However, this DWXML version does not contemplate the representation of the primary

Table 9. Dimension metadata description

Identifier	Opt.	Description
schema	no	Schema of the dimension
name	no	Name of the dimension
description	yes	Description of the dimension meaning and content
levels	yes	List of levels in the dimension
hierarchies	yes	List of hierarchies in the dimension
attributes	yes	List of attributes in the dimension

Figure 8. Level element schema

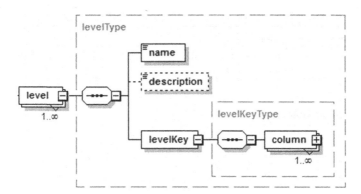

Table 10. Level metadata description

Identifier	Opt.	Description
name	no	Name of the level
description	yes	Description of the level meaning and content
levelKey	no	Key of the level (one or more columns in the dimension table)

Figure 9. Hierarchy element schema

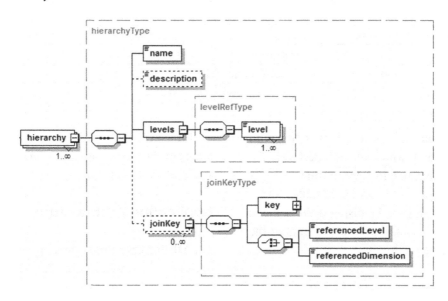

Table 11. Hierarchy metadata description

Identifier	Opt.	Description
name	no	Name of the hierarchy
description	yes	Description of the hierarchy meaning and content
levels	no	List of the levels of the hierarchy, starting with the more general level
joinKey	yes	The key that joins the levels of the hierarchy when they are implemented using different dimension tables.

Table 12. Attribute metadata description

Identifier	Opt.	Description
attributeName	yes	Name of the attribute
evel	no	Identifies the level and the attributes determined by its level key. There must be at least one level element

Figure 10. Attribute element schema

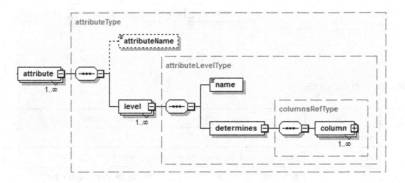

Table 13. Attribute levels metadata description

Identifier	Opt.	Description
name	no	Name of the level
determines	no	Attribute determined by the level

data in XML, since it is used in conjunction with the SIARD format, which already performs the primary data migration to XML format.

A schema contains a group of tables and a group of views. Figure 11 displays the schema element. Table 14 describes the elements of the schema metadata.

Tables 15, 16, 17, 18, and 19 describe the elements of the table, column, primary key, foreign key, and view metadata.

Application Architecture

The DBPreserve Suite, the application that supports the data warehouse migration process to the

Algorithm 3. Example of a DWXML dimension definition

```
<?xml version="1.0" encoding="UTF-8"?>
<dwxml version="1.0" xsi:noNamespaceSchemaLocation="dw.xsd"
 xmlns:xsi="http://www.w3.org/2001/XMLSchema-instance">
 ...
 <dimensions>
  <dimension>
    <schema>CALDEIAS</schema>
   <name>CLASS_DIM</name>
   <levels>
    <level>
      <name>CLASS</name>
      <description />
      <levelKey>
        <column>
            <schema>CALDEIAS</schema>
            <table>IPDW_CLASS</table>
            <column>CLASS_ID</column>
        </column>
      </levelKey>
    </level>
    <level>
    <name>COURSE</name>
    <levelKey>
      <column>
        <schema>CALDEIAS</schema>
        <table>IPDW_CLASS</table>
        <column>COURSE_ID</column>
      </column>
     </levelKey>
    </level>
   </levels>
  <hierarchies>
    <hierarchy>
       <name>CLASS_ROLLUP</name>
       <levels>
         <level>COURSE</level>
         <level>CLASS</level>
       </levels>
    </hierarchy>
   </hierarchies>
   <attributes>
     <attribute>
```

continued on following page

Algorithm 3. Continued

```
            <attributeName>COURSE</attributeName>
            <level>
              <name>COURSE</name>
              <determines>
                  <column>
                      <schema>CALDEIAS</schema>
                      <table>IPDW_CLASS</table>
                      <column>COUR_PREVIOUS_COD</column>
                  </column>
                  <column>
                      <schema>CALDEIAS</schema>
                      <table>IPDW_CLASS</table>
                      <column>COUR_TYPE</column>
                  </column>
              ...
              </determines>
              </level>
          </attribute>
          <attribute>
          ...
          </attribute>
          </attributes>
      </dimension>
      ...
    </dimensions>
    ...
</dwxml>
```

proposed preservation format, had the following general requirements:

- Migrate the data warehouse model implemented using relational database technologies to the SIARD format;
- Acquire the metadata to describe the dimensional model of the data warehouse;
- Help in the process of building a DWXML representation, upon the metadata collected;
- Enable metadata editing supported by graphical interfaces;

- Generate the DWXML from the metadata collected/edited and embed it into the generated SIARD format;
- Enable primary data browsing using the proposed preservation format.

The DBPreserve Suite application is a Windows desktop application that has a modular and extensible architecture, composed by 5 major new modules as shown in the overall architecture of the application in Figure 12.

It has been developed using the NetBeans IDE 7.0 RC1 and Netbeans Platform[6], with support

Figure 11. The schema element

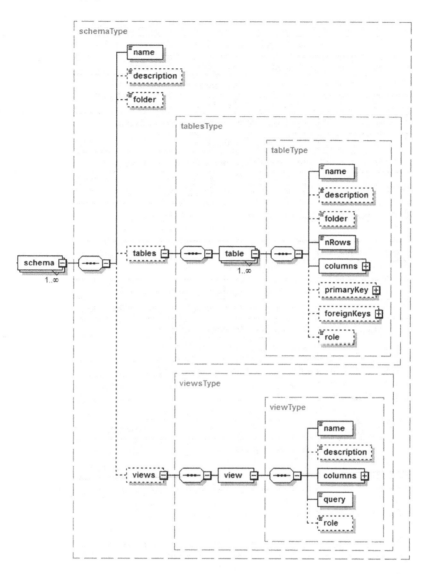

Table 14. Schema metadata description

Identifier	Opt.	Description
name	no	Name of the schema
description	yes	Description of the schema meaning and content
folder	yes	The name of the folder in the SIARD format
tables	yes	List of tables of the schema and their definition
views	yes	List of views of the schema and their definition

Table 15. Table metadata description

Identifier	Opt.	Description
name	no	Name of the table
description	yes	Description of the table meaning and content
folder	yes	The name of the data folder in the SIARD format
nRows	no	Number of rows of the table
columns	no	List of columns of the table and their definition
primaryKey	yes	The primary key of the table
foreignKeys	yes	List of foreign keys of the table and their definition
role	yes	The role of the table in the dimensional model (FACT TABLE, DIMENSION TABLE, BRIDGE TABLE, DEGENERATED DIMENSION TABLE)

Table 16. Column metadata description

Identifier	Opt.	Description
name	no	Name of the column
description	yes	Description of the column meaning and content
folder	yes	The name of the folder in the SIARD format for LOBs storage
type	yes	Data type of the column in the data warehouse
defaultValue	yes	Default value of the column
nullable	no	Indicates if the column value can be null

Table 17. Primary key metadata description

dentifier	Opt.	Description
name	no	Name of the primary key
description	yes	Description of the primary key's meaning and content
column	no	Column that belongs to the primary key. There must be at least one column element

Table 18. Foreign key metadata description

Identifier	Opt.	Description
name	no	Name of the foreign key
description	yes	Description of the foreign key's meaning and content
referencedSchema	no	Name of the schema of the referenced table
referencedTable	no	Name of the referenced table
reference	no	Name of the referencing column and referenced column (must be non-empty)

Table 19. View metadata description

Identifier	Opt.	Description
name	no	Name of the view
description	yes	Description of the view's meaning and content
columns	no	List of the columns of the view (schema, table and column names)
query	no	Query that represent the view
role	no	The role of the view in the dimensional model

for Java 1.7[7], using the JDOM[8] library (Hunter, 2002) for XML processing of metadata. This application integrates a tool from the SIARD Suite that manages the migration of a relational database to the SIARD format, the *SIARDfromDB* application.

The Connection Module enables the abstraction of the data warehouse connection, using Java Database Connectivity (JDBC). The application already supports connections to Oracle database using Oracle JDBC (OJDBC), due to the DBMS used in the proposed case study. However, this module is prepared for an easy extension to connect with other DBMS, adding just a file that rewrites some metadata retrieval methods.

The Metadata Module handles all the metadata imported from the DBMS and the metadata import process itself. The imported metadata is related with schemas, tables, views, columns, primary keys, foreign keys, dimensions, levels, level keys, hierarchies, attributes, table comments, and column comments. Through the analysis of the acquired metadata, this module proposes a possible DWXML that describes the dimensional model.

The SIARD Module allows the integration of the *SIARDfromDB* tool from SIARD Suite (Thomas, 2009) that creates the SIARD format of the relational data in the data warehouse. This format still lacks the dimensional model description. It looks at the data warehouse from a relational model point of view. This module also manages the generated SIARD format, accessing the relational metadata, enabling the primary data browsing and embedding the DWXML with the dimensional model description.

The DWXML Module handles the dimensional metadata, creating the DWXML file to embed it into the SIARD format or reading it from the SIARD format if already recorded.

The Output Module manages all the graphical interfaces, such as connection management, SIARD format generation through *SIARDfromDB*

Figure 12. DBPreserve suite general architecture

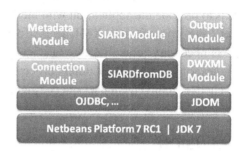

integration, table and view roles visual editing, graphical representation of star or snowflake schemas and dimensions, hierarchical viewing of schemas, star and dimension, editing of the DWXML through several graphical user interfaces, viewing of the DWXML file added to the SIARD format and browsing of the primary data when selecting a star schema or dimension.

This work has been applied to a real world case study from DBPreserve project, to test the migration process, in order to validate all the features implemented in the DBPreserve Suite application.

FUTURE RESEARCH DIRECTIONS

The DBPreserve Suite application can be extended with new features, such as the implementation of the reverse migration process, i.e. starting from the XML preservation format, reactivate the data warehouse through its reconstruction in a DBMS and then loading it with the primary data. Notice that, as DWXML is meant for preservation and not as a backup utility, instrumental database objects useful in a running database like sequences or materialized views have not been included, and so they must be recreated to revive the DW. Another new feature could be the implementation of a module to generate the initial SIARD format, untying the DBPreserve Suite application from the SIARD Suite tool and making it completely autonomous. One of the most important improvements is to provide the application with methods to query the primary data XML files. To this end, it is necessary to analyze the efficiency of techniques for large XML document processing, and to choose a convenient user query language.

CONCLUSION

The proposed format for data warehouse preservation, combining the DWXML (that describes the dimensional model) with the SIARD format (for relational model description and primary data storage), proved to be a useful way to represent a data warehouse in XML-based files. In fact, the DBPreserve Suite application uses this extended SIARD format to represent star and snowflake schemas, as well as dimension structures (hierarchies, levels and attributes), and it enables the browsing of primary data from the dimensional model perspective (through stars and dimensions). Thus, extending the SIARD format with a DWXML dimensional model metadata layer, a long-term preservation format for data warehouses is achieved.

Looking at the major implemented features of DBPreserve Suite application, the integration of the *SIARDfromDB* command line application from the SIARD Suite enables the standard SIARD format generation, migrating all relational metadata and primary data according to that format, with a total control of this process from the developed application. The reuse of this model has allowed us to concentrate on the description of the dimensional model, by importing the metadata from the data dictionary, automating the creation of DWXML after analysis of the imported metadata, providing user interfaces for a friendly DWXML editing, embedding it into the SIARD format and enabling the access to primary data through the dimensional model perspective. All the implemented features were tested and refined using the project case study.

The proposed preservation format is not in itself a guarantee of success regarding long-term digital preservation. As a preservation format for data warehouses implemented with relational databases technologies, it fulfills part of the requirements for an OAIS. The fact that it is platform independent and captures the dimensional model metadata is a contribution to that goal.

REFERENCES

Brandl, S., & Keller-Marxer, P. (2007). Long-term archiving of relational databases with chronos. In *Proceedings of the First International Workshop on Database Preservation – PresDB 2007*. PresDB.

CCSDS. (2002). *Reference model for an open archival information system (OAIS) - Blue book*. Washington, DC: National Aeronautics and Space Administration.

Christophides, V., & Buneman, P. (2007). Report on the first international workshop on database preservation, PresDB 2007. *SIGMOD Record*, *36*(3), 55–58. doi:10.1145/1324185.1324197

Consortium, W. (2008). *Extensible markup language (XML) 1.0 (5th ed.)*. W3C Recommendation. Retrieved from http://www.w3.org

Date, C. J. (2004). *An introduction to database systems* (8th ed.). Reading, MA: Addison Wesley.

Ferreira, M. (2006). *Introdução à preservação digital - Conceitos, estratégias e actuais consensos*. Minho, Portugal: Escola de Engenharia da Universidade do Minho.

Force, A. T. (2002). *Requirements for assessing and maintaining the authenticity of electronic records. Technical Report*. Vancouver, Canada: InterPARES Project.

Hackney, D. (1997). *Understanding and implementing successful data marts*. Boston, MA: Addison-Wesley Longman Publishing Co.

Hedstrom, M., & Lampe, C. (2001). Emulation vs. migration: Do users care?. *RLG DigiNews, 5*(6).

Hoeven, J. (2007). Emulation for digital preservation in practice: The results. *The International Journal of Digital Curation, 2*(2), 123–132.

Hummer, W., Bauer, A., & Harde, G. (2003). XCube: XML for data warehouses. In *Proceedings of the 6th ACM International Workshop on Data Warehousing and OLAP (DOLAP 2003)*, (pp. 33-40). New York, NY: ACM Press.

Hunter, J. (2002, September-October). JDOM in the real world - JDOM makes XML manipulation in java easier than ever. *Oracle Magazine*.

Inmon, W. H. (1992). *Building the data warehouse*. New York, NY: John Wiley & Sons, Inc.

Jensen, M. R., Muller, T. H., & Pedersen, T. B. (2001). Specifying OLAP cubes on XML data. In *Proceedings of the 13th International Conference on Scientific and Statistical Database Management, SSDBM 2001*, (p. 101). Washington, DC: IEEE Computer Society.

Kimball, R., & Ross, M. (2002). *The data warehouse toolkit: The complete guide to dimensional modeling* (2nd ed.). New York, NY: John Wiley & Sons, Inc.

Lagoze, C., Payette, S., Shin, E., & Wilper, C. (2006). Fedora: An architecture for complex objects and their relationships. *International Journal on Digital Libraries, 6*(2), 124–138. doi:10.1007/s00799-005-0130-3

Oracle. (2010). *Oracle database SQL reference 11g release 1 (11.1), part number B28286-06*. Retrieved April 30, 2011, from http://docs.oracle.com/cd/B28359_01/server.111/b28286.pdf

PKWARE. (2007). ZIP file format specification, version: 6.3.2, revised: September 28. *PKWARE Inc*. Retrieved April 30, 2011, from http://www.pkware.com/documents/casestudies/APPNOTE.TXT

PLANETS. (2009). *PLANETS: Tools and services for digital preservation. PLANETS Product Sheet*. New York, NY: PLANETS.

Pokorny, J. (2002). XML data warehouse: Modelling and querying. In *Proceedings of the Baltic Conference, BalticDB&IS 2002*, (Vol. 1, pp. 267-280). BalticDB&IS.

Rahman, A. U., David, G., & Ribeiro, C. (2010). Model migration approach for database preservation. In *Proceedings of the Role of Digital Libraries in a Time of Global Change, 12th International Conference on Asia-Pacific Digital Libraries, ICADL 2010*, (pp. 81-90). Gold Coast, Australia: Springer.

Ramalho, J. C. Ferreira. M., Faria, L., & Castro, R. (2007). Relational database preservation through XML modelling. In *Proceedings of Extreme Markup Languages 2007*. IEEE.

SFA. (2008). *SIARD format description. Technical Report*. Berne, Switzerland: Federal Department of Home Affairs.

Sinclair, P. (2010). *The digital divide: Assessing organizations' preparations for digital preservation*. PLANETS White Paper. New York, NY: PLANETS.

Sperberg-McQueen, C. M., & Burnard, L. (1994). *A gentle introduction to SGML*. Oxford, UK: Thibodeau, K. (2002). Overview of technological approaches to digital preservation and challenges in coming years. In *the State of Digital Preservation: An International Perspective. Documentation Abstracts, Inc*. New York, NY: Institutes for Information Science.

Thomas, H. (2009). *SIARD suite manual*. Berne, Switzerland: Federal Department of Home Affairs.

Zierau, E., & Wijk, C. (2008). *The PLANETS approach to migration tools*. Bern, Switzerland: Society for Imaging Science and Tech.

ADDITIONAL READING

Barbedo, F., Corujo, L., Faria, L., Castro, R., Ferreira, M., & Ramalho, J. C. (2007). *RODA: Repositório de objectos digitais autênticos*. Paper presented at the 9º Congresso Nacional de Bibliotecários, Arquivistas e Documentalistas. Ponta Delgada, Portugal.

Christophides, V., & Buneman, P. (2007). Report on the first international workshop on database preservation, PresDB 2007. *SIGMOD Record, 36*(3), 55–58. doi:10.1145/1324185.1324197

Committee, P. E. (2011). *Data dictionary for preservation metadata: PREMIS version 2.1*. New York, NY: PREMIS Editorial Committee.

Dappert, A., & Farquhar, A. (2009). Implementing metadata that guides digital preservation services. In *Proceedings of iPress 2009*, (pp. 5-6). San Francisco, CA: iPress.

Day, M. (1998). Issues and approaches to preservation metadata. In *Conference Guidelines for Digital Imaging*. Coventry, UK: University of Warwick.

Farquhar, A., & Hockx-Yu, H. (2007). PLANETS: Integrated services for digital preservation. *International Journal of Digital Curation, 2*(2), 88–99.

Freitas, R. A. P., & Ramalho, J. C. (2007). Using ontologies in database preservation. In *Proceedings of XATA 2011 - XML: Aplicações e Tecnologias Associadas*. Vila do Conde, Portugal: XATA.

Freitas, R. A. P., & Ramalho, J. C. (2011). New dimension in relational database preservation: Rising the abstraction level. In *Proceedings of iPRES 2011 - 8th International Conference on Preservation of Digital Objects*. Singapore, Singapore: iPRES.

Garrett, J., & Waters, D. (1996). *Preserving digital information, report of the task force on archiving of digital information. Technical Report*. Washington, DC: The Commission on Preservation and Access and The Research Libraries Group.

Hedstrom, M. (1997). Digital preservation: A time bomb for digital libraries. *Computers and the Humanities, 31*, 189–202. doi:10.1023/A:1000676723815

Lee, K., Slattery, O., Lu, R., Tang, X., & McCrary, V. (2002). The state of the art and practice in digital preservation. *Journal of Research of the National Institute of Standards and Technology, 107*(1), 93–106. doi:10.6028/jres.107.010

Lorie, R. A. (2001). Long-term archiving of digital information. In *Proceedings of the 1st ACM/IEEE-CS Joint Conference on Digital Libraries*. Roanoke, VA: ACM/IEEE Press.

Lorie, R. A., & van Diessen, R. J. (2005). UVC: Long-term preservation of complex processes. In *Proceedings of the IS&T Archiving Conference*, (pp. 26-29). Washington, DC: IS&T.

Mellor, P., Wheatley, P., & Sergeant, D. (2002). Migration on request, a practical technique for preservation. In *Research and Advanced Technology for Digital Libraries* (pp. 516–526). Berlin, Germany: Springer. doi:10.1007/3-540-45747-X_38

Testbed, D. P. (2003). *From digital volatility to digital permanence: Preserving databases. Technical Report*. Amsterdam, The Netherlands: Dutch National Archives and the Dutch Ministry of the Interior and Kingdom Relations.

Verdegem, R. (2003). Databases preservation issues. In *Proceedings of the Erpanet Workshop on Long-Term Preservation of Databases*. Bern, Switzerland: Digital Preservation Testbed.

Waugh, A., Wilkinson, R., Hills, B., & Dell'oro, J. (2000). Preserving digital information forever. In *Proceedings of the International Conference on Digital Libraries Proceedings of the Fifth ACM Conference on Digital Libraries,* (pp. 175–184). ACM Press.

KEY TERMS AND DEFINITIONS

Data Warehouse: Data warehouse s are complex digital objects, based on a dimensional model, where star and snowflake schemas, facts, dimensions with levels and hierarchies, bridges tables and datamarts can be identified. Data warehouses are often implemented on relational databases (ROLAP), keeping the data in tables, views and schemas.

Digital Preservation: Is a process or a set of processes that must follow a concrete plan of activities, with allocation of adequate resources and use of technologies and practices that ensure access to a digital object, in the long-term perspective.

Dimensional Model Metadata: Includes the concepts of the dimensional model, like facts, dimensions, bridges, hierarchies, levels, data marts, star schemas, or snowflake schemas, which are essential for the full description of a data warehouse.

DWXML: Stands for Data Warehouse Extensible Markup Language, and it is an XML format used for characterizing the data warehouse and providing the concepts associated with the dimensional model, which are not covered by the base SIARD format. As a SIARD format extension for archiving data warehouses, the DWXML bridges the gap between the relational model description and the dimensional model description, adding a metadata file related to the dimensional model characterization and its schema definition.

OAIS: An Open Archival Information System is an organization of people and systems that has accepted the responsibility to preserve information and make it available for a designated community. The OAIS reference model introduces the appropriate terminology in the context of long-term preservation, as well as defining the functional components necessary to an archive implementation.

SIARD Format: The SIARD format is a nonproprietary and published open standard, based on other open standards (e.g., ISO standard Unicode, XML, SQL1999), and the industry standard ZIP. It was developed by the Swiss Federal Archives. In May 2008, the European PLANETS project accepted SIARD format as the official format for archiving relational databases.

XML: Stands for Extensible Markup Language and it is an open standard defined by the World Wide Web Consortium (W3C). This standard is a very flexible text format derived from SGML (ISO8879), and it is widely used to structure, exchange and store data.

ENDNOTES

1. Information System of Faculty of Engineering, University of Porto, Portugal.
2. http://www.w3.org/TR/xquery
3. http://www.w3.org/TR/xpath
4. http://www.w3.org/XML/Schema
5. https://www.fe.up.pt/si/wikis_paginas_geral.paginas_view?pct_pagina=43194
6. http://netbeans.org/features/platform/
7. http://download.java.net/jdk7/docs/api/
8. http://www.jdom.org/index.html

Chapter 9
New Dimension in Relational Database Preservation:
Using Ontologies

Ricardo André Pereira Freitas
Lusiada University, Portugal

José Carlos Ramalho
University of Minho, Portugal

ABSTRACT

Due to the expansion and growth of information technologies, much of human knowledge is now recorded on digital media. A new problem in the digital universe has arisen: Digital Preservation. This chapter addresses the problems of Digital Preservation and focuses on the conceptual model within a specific class of digital objects: Relational Databases. Previously, a neutral format was adopted to pursue the goal of platform independence and to achieve a standard format in the digital preservation of relational databases, both data and structure (logical model). The authors address the preservation of relational databases by focusing on the conceptual model of the database, considering the database semantics as an important preservation "property." For the representation of this higher layer of abstraction present in databases, they use an ontology-based approach. At this higher abstraction level exists inherent Knowledge associated to the database semantics that the authors tentatively represent using "Web Ontology Language" (OWL). From the initial prototype, they develop a framework (supported by case studies) and establish a mapping algorithm for the conversion between databases and OWL. The ontology approach is adopted to formalize the knowledge associated to the conceptual model of the database and also a methodology to create an abstract representation of it. The system is based on the functional axes (ingestion, administration, dissemination, and preservation) of the OAIS reference model.

DOI: 10.4018/978-1-4666-2669-0.ch009

INTRODUCTION

In the current paradigm of information society more than one hundred exabytes of data are used to support information systems worldwide (Manson, 2010). The evolution of the hardware and software industry causes that progressively more of the intellectual and business information are stored in computer platforms. The main issue lies exactly within these platforms. If in the past there was no need of mediators to understand the analogical artifacts, today we depend on those mediators (computer platforms) to understand digital objects.

Our work addresses this issue of Digital Preservation and focuses on a specific class of digital objects: Relational Databases (RDBs). These kinds of archives are important to several organizations (they can justify their activities and characterize the organization itself) and are virtually in the base of all dynamic content in the Web.

In previous work (Freitas & Ramalho, 2009) we adopted an approach that combines two strategies and uses a third technique—migration and normalization with refreshment:

- Migration which is carried in order to transform the original database into the new format—Database Markup Language (DBML) (Jacinto, Librelotto, Ramalho, & Henriques, 2002);
- Normalization reduces the preservation spectrum to only one format;
- Refreshment consists on ensuring that the archive is using media appropriate to the hardware in usage throughout preservation (Freitas, 2008).

This previous approach deals with the preservation of the Data and Structure of the database, i.e., the preservation of the database logical model. We developed a prototype that separates the data from its specific database management environment (DBMS). The prototype follows the Open Archival Information System (OAIS) reference model (by the Consultative Committee for Space Data Systems, 2002) and uses DBML neutral format for the representation of both data and structure (schema) of the database.

Conceptual Preservation

In this work, we address the preservation of relational databases by focusing on the conceptual model of the database (the Information System – IS). It is intended to raise the representation level of the database up to the conceptual model and preserve this representation. For the representation of this higher level of abstraction on databases, we use an ontology-based approach. At this level there is an inherent Knowledge associated to the database semantics that we represent using OWL (McGuinness & Harmelen, 2004). We developed a prototype (supported by case study) and established an algorithm that enables the mapping process between the database and OWL.

In the following section we overview the problem of digital preservation, referring to the digital object, preservation strategies and the preservation of relational databases. Section 3 describes our previous work and states the open issue (database semantic representation) the lead us to the current approach. In Section 4, we outline the relation between ontologies and databases establishing the state-of-the-art and referring to related work. The prototype and the mapping process from RDBs to OWL is detailed in section 5. At the end, we draw some conclusions and specify some of the future work.

DIGITAL PRESERVATION

A set of processes or activities that take place in order to preserve a certain object (digital) addressing its relevant properties, is one of the several definitions. Digital objects have several associated aspects (characteristics or properties) that we should consider whether or not to preserve. The designated community plays an important role and helps to define:

The characteristics of digital objects that must be preserved over time in order to ensure the continued accessibility, usability, and meaning of the objects, and their capacity to be accepted as evidence of what they purport to record (Wilson, 2007).

The Digital Object

Some distinction can be established between digital objects that already born in a digital context, and those that appear from the process of digitization: analog to digital. In a comprehensive way and encompassing both cases above, we can consider that a digital object is characterized by being represented by multiple bitstreams, i.e., by sequences of binary digits (zeros and ones).

We can question if the physical structure of the object (original system) is important, and if so, think about possible strategies for preservation at that level, e.g. "technology preservation" (museums of technology) (Ferreira, 2006). Nev-

ertheless, the next layer—the logical structure or logical object—which corresponds to the string of binary digits have different preservation strategies. The bitstream have a certain distribution that will define the format of the object, depending on the software that will interpret it. The interpretation by the software, of the logical object, provides the appearance of the conceptual object, that the human being is able to understand (interpret) and experiment. The strategy of preservation is related to the level of abstraction considered important for the preservation (Thibodeau, 2002). From a human perspective, one can say that what is important to preserve is the conceptual object (the one that the humans are able to interpret). Other strategies defend that what should be preserved is the original bitstream (logical object) or even the original media. Figure 1 shows the relationship between the different levels of abstraction (digital object) and the correspondent preservation formats adopted for RDBs in this research.

Relational Databases Preservation

By focusing on a specific class or family of digital objects (relational databases), questions emerge

Figure 1. Levels of abstraction and preservation policy

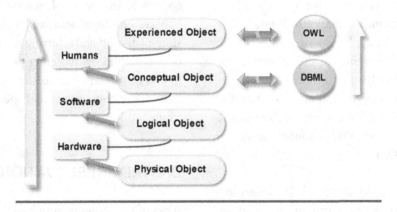

ConceptualObject + Humans = ExperimentedObject <=> Ontology

LogicalObject + Software = ConceptualObject <=> DBML

PhysicalObject + Hardware = LogicalObject

such as: what are the effects of cutting/extracting the object from its original context? Can we do this even when we are referring to objects that are platform (hardware/software) dependent? The interaction between the source of the digital object and the platform results on a conceptual object that can be different if the platform changes (Wilson, 2007); the output can be different (will the object maintain its original behavior?). The important is the preservation of the essential parts that purport what the object where made for. Either the source or the platform can be altered if what is essential is obtained and also maintaining the meaning of the digital object over long periods of time (long-term scope).

Considering the nature of the digital artifacts that we are addressing—relational databases—there is an European strategy encompassed in the Planets Project[1] to enable their long term access. The project adopted the SIARD[2] solution, which is based on the migration of database into a normalized format (XML – eXtensible Markup Language by the World Wide Web Consortium, 1996-2003). The SIARD was initially developed by the Swiss Federal Archives (SFA).

Another approach, also based on XML, relies on the main concept of "extensibility"—XML allows the creation of other languages (Ramalho & Henriques, 2002) (it can be called as a meta language). The DBML (Database Markup Language) was created in order to enable representation of both DATA and STRUCTURE of the database.

Both approaches (SIARD and DBML) adopt the strategy of Migration of the database to XML, why? A neutral format that is hardware and software (platform) independent is the key to achieve a standard format to use in digital preservation of relational databases. This neutral format should meet all the requirements established by the designated community of interest.

PREVIOUS WORK AND CURRENT APPROACH

In previous work, we address the preservation of the RDBs data and structure by developing an archive prototype that uses the DBML format for preservation. Our first approach covers the preservation of the logical model of databases (tables, structure, and data). However, neither this approach nor others (e.g., SIARD) are concerned with the database semantics. The focus of our research then turned into this problem related conceptual model of the database, i.e., the information system on the top of the operational database.

First Approach

The prototype is based on a Web application with multiple interfaces. These interfaces have the mission to take a certain database and ingest it into the archive. The access to the archive in order to do all the necessary interventions on the system is also done through those Web interfaces.

Conceptually, the prototype is based on the OAIS reference model. The OAIS model of reference does not impose rigidity with regard to implementation; rather it defines a series of recommendations. The OAIS model is accepted and referenced for digital preservation purposes since it is concerned about a number of issues related to preservation of digital artifacts: the process of information Ingestion into the system, the information storage as well as its administration and preservation, and finally information access and dissemination (Day, 2006; Lavoie, 2004). Three information packages are the base of the archival process: Submission Information Package (SIP), Archival Information Package (AIP), and Dissemination Information Package (DIP).

Proposed Approach

Based on the first prototype we now intend to include in the information packages (SIP, AIP, and DIP) a higher representation level of the database—the conceptual model of the database. Ontologies are used to address semantics and conceptual model representation.

Our hypothesis concentrates on the potentiality of reaching relevant stages of preservation by using ontologies to preserve of RDBs. This leads us to the preservation of the higher abstraction level present in the digital object, which corresponds to the database conceptual model. At this level, there is an inherent Knowledge associated to the database semantics (Figure 2).

We intend to capture the experienced object (knowledge) through an ontology-based approach. This experienced or knowledge object is the "final abstraction." The ontology approach is adopted to formalize the knowledge present at the

experienced object level and also a methodology to create an abstract representation of it. The system has evolved into an OAIS based architecture that allows the ingestion, preservation, and dissemination of relational databases at two levels of abstraction—logical and conceptual (Figure 2). This approach is also an extension to previous approaches in terms of metadata since the ontology provides information about the data at a conceptual level. Figure 3 also shows a possible preservation "lifecycle" of RBDs.

ONTOLOGIES AND DATABASES

There is a direct relation between ontologies and databases: a database has a defined scope and intends to model reality within that domain for computing (even when it is only virtual or on the Web); ontology in ancient and philosophical

Figure 2. Preservation policy

Digital Object	Preservation Levels	Relational Database
Experimented Object	Ontology	**Conceptual Model**
Conceptual Object	DBML	Logical Model
Logical Object	–	Original Bitstream
Physical Object	–	Physical Media

Figure 3. RDBs preservation framework

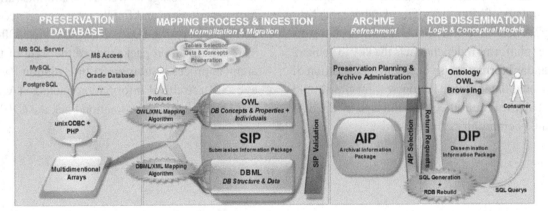

significance means the study of being, of what exists (Berners-Lee, Hendler, & Lassila, 2001).

The (strong) entities present in relational databases have an existence because they were model from the real world: they relate to each other and have associated attributes. In information society and computer science, an ontology establishes concepts, their properties, and the relationships among them within a given domain (Gruber, 2008).

Database Semantics

A database can be defined as a structured set of information. In computing, a database is supported by a particular program or software, usually called the Database Management System (DBMS), which handles the storage and management of the data. In its essence, a database involves the existence of a set of records of data. Normally these records give support to the organization information system; either at an operational (transactions) level or at other levels (decision support—data warehousing systems). In particular, the relational databases model is designed to support an information system at its operational level. Thus, RDBs are complex and their data can be distributed into several entity relations that related to each other through specific attributes (foreign to primary keys) in order to avoid redundancy and maintain consistency (Codd, 1970).

If we intend not only to preserve the data but also the structure of the (organization) information system, we should endorse efforts to characterize (read) the database semantics. It is intended to raise the representation level of the database up to the conceptual model and preserve this representation. In other words, we represent the conceptual model of the database using an ontology for preservation.

Ontologies

The study of ontologies in computer science received new impetus due to the growth of the Web, their associated semantics and the possibility of

extracting knowledge from it. Tim Berners-Lee realized that years ago giving origin to the "Semantic Web" supported by W3C (World Wide Web Consortium) which works on establishing a technology to support the *Web of data* (Semantic Web). Notice that a tremendous part of the Web is based in (relational) databases—especially dynamic information.

Behind the ontology, there is the need of knowledge representation for machine interpretation. Two technologies: a) the RDF (Resource Description Framework) triples give support for the meaning in simple sentences; b) and XML is used for structuring documents (Berners-Lee, Hendler, & Lassila, 2001). The RDF document consist on a set of triples—*object, property, value*—that we can also define as—*subject, predicate, object* (Zarri, 2006).

The notion of ontology then emerges due to the need of expressing concepts in different domains (ontologies as collections of information). An ontology can provide readable information to machines (Santoso, Hawa, & Abdul-Mehdia, 2010) at a conceptual level (higher abstraction level). They also enable the integration and interpretability of data/information between applications and platforms. Ontologies benefit from the fact that they are not platform/system dependent when compared to traditional relational databases.

Related Work

Work related to RBDs and ontologies transformations proliferate and is addressed continuously. Considering the RDF, OWL, ontologies and RDBs, several frameworks, mapping approaches and tools exist: Virtuoso RDF Views (OpenLink Virtuoso Platform); D2RQ (Bizer & Cyganiak, 2007); Triplify (Auer, Dietzold, Lehmann, Hellmann, & Aumueller, 2009); RDBToOnto (Cerbah, 2008); R2O (Barrasa & Gomez-Perez, 2006); Dartagrid Semantic Web toolkit (Chen & Wu, 2005); SBRD Automapper (Fisher & Dean, 2007); XTR-RTO (Xu & Li, 2007); RDB2OWL (Bumans & Cerans,

2011); DB2OWL(Cullot, Ghawi, & Yetongnon, 2007); R2RML(Das, Sundara, & Cyganiak, 2011); OntER (Trinkunas & Vasilecas, 2007); DM2OWL (Albarrak & Sibley, 2009); OWLFromDB (He-Ping, Lu, & Bin, 2008), among others.

Several of these approaches and tools are referenced and analyzed in the W3C Incubator group survey (W3C Incubator Group, 2009) and also in the "Concept hierarchy as background knowledge" proposal from Santoso, Hawa, and Abdul-Mehdia (2010).

The conversion from databases into an ontology could be characterized as a process in the scope of reverse engineering (Trinkunas & Vasilecas, 2007). While some approaches and works try to establish a mapping language or a mapping process (Myroshnichenko & Murphy, 2009), others use different techniques and strategies for the database translation (Albarrak & Sibley, 2009) into an ontology (e.g. OWL).

The R2RML(RDB to RDF Mapping Language [Das, Sundara, & Cyganiak, 2011]) working draft submitted to W3C is designed for mapping the data within the attributes of a table into pairs: property, object. Each record within a table share the same subject in this RDF triple map relation. This approach supports the input of "logical" tables from the source database, which can be an existing table, a view, or a valid SQL query. Also in cases where attributes are foreign keys it is generated a pair (property, object) referencing the correspondent table. The rules for this mapping are then organized in a vocabulary with several classes and subclasses (*TripleMapClass, SubjectMapClass, PredicateMapClass, ObjectMapClass, RefPredicateMapClass, etc.*).

For example, R2O (Barrasa & Gomez-Perez, 2006) approach is based on a mapping document generation (mapping language). Virtuoso RDF Views establishes a set of RDF statements by defining for each table: *primary key* (subject), *attribute* (predicate), *value* (object). In the RDB2OWL (Bumans, & Cerans, 2011) a different strategy is used since it is created a mapping RDB

schema. The "Concept hierarchy as background knowledge" proposal (Santoso, Hawa, & Abdul-Mehdia, 2010) gives special attention to the data preparation before conversion and to the knowledge that resides on the database.

FROM RDB TO OWL

This section presents the work developed to convert databases to ontology, based on a mapping process (mapping algorithm), for preservation. We intend to preserve a snapshot of the database (or a frozen database) by preserving the OWL generated from the database. We start by concentrating our efforts on detailing the mapping process and analyzing the created algorithm. Then, the conducted tests and some of the results are also presented.

Mapping Process of RDBs to OWL: Prototype

Our work implements the conversion from RDBs into OWL through an algorithm that performs the mapping process. The developed prototype enables the connection to a DSN (Data Source Name), extracts the data/information needed, and gives the initial possibility of selecting the tables of interest (for conversion). It is assumed that the source database is normalized (3NF). We start by enumerating the properties of RDBs that are addressed and incorporated in the ontology (OWL):

- Tables names;
- Attributes names and data types;
- Keys primary keys, foreign keys (relationships between tables);
- Tuples data;

These elements are extracted from the database into multidimensional arrays. Figure 4 shows the arrays structure.

For each table on the database we define a class on the ontology with the exception of those

Figure 4. Multidimensional array structure

```
tables = Array{ [1] => t1, ... , [n]=> tn }

columns = Array{
              [t1] => Array{
                      [a1] => Array{ [Name] => 'a1_name', [Type] => 'a1_type' },
                      [an] => Array{ ... }},
              [tn] => Array{...}}

p_keys = Array{
              [t1] => Array{ [a1] => 'pk_t1', ..., [an] => 'pk_t1' },
              [tn] => Array{...}}

f_key = Array{
              [t1] => Array{
                      [a1] => Array{ [pk_table] => 'tref', [pk_column] => 'tref.aref'},
                      [an] => Array{...}},
              [tn] => Array{...}}

tables_data= Array{
              [t1] => Array{
                      [1] => Array{ [a1]=> 'a1_data', ..., [an] => 'an_data'},
                      [m] => Array{...}},
              [tn] => Array{...}}
```

tables where all attributes constitute a composed primary key (combination of foreign keys). These link tables used in the relational model to dismount a many-to-many relationship, are not mapped to OWL classes, instead they give origin to object properties in the ontology. These object properties have on their domain and range the correspondent classes (database tables) involved in the relationship (Figure 5).

The foreign keys of the tables mapped directly to OWL classes also give origin to object properties of the correspondent OWL classes (tables). The attributes of the several tables are mapped to data properties within the analogous OWL classes with the exception of the attributes that are foreign keys (Figure 6).

The algorithm generates inverse object properties for all relationships among the classes. If

Figure 5. Algorithm: classes and non-classes

```
//   Classes (tables) & ObjectProperties (link tables - non_classes)
FOREACH [ table ]
        IF [ ( |columns[table]| = |p_keys[table]| ) AND ( |p_keys[table]| = |f_keys[table])| ) ] THEN
                non_class[] = table
                FOREACH [ columns[table] - 1 ]

                NEW 'ObjectProperty'
                        Property_Description = 'is_' + f_keys[table][columns[table]][pk_table] + '_of'
                        Domain = f_keys[table][columns[table]][pk_table]
                        Range = f_keys[table][next(columns[table])][pk_table]

                NEW 'ObjectProperty'
                        Property_Description = 'has_' + f_keys[table][columns[table]][pk_table]
                        Domain = f_keys[table][next(columns[table])][pk_table]
                        Range = f_keys[table][columns[table]][pk_table]

                NEW 'InverseObjectProperties'
                        Property_Description = 'is_' + f_keys[table][columns[table]][pk_table] + '_of'
                        Property_Description = 'has_' + f_keys[table][columns[table]][pk_table]

                END FOR
        ELSE
        class[] = table
        END IF
END FOR
```

Figure 6. Algorithm: structure generation

```
//   Sub Classes of Thing & Disjoint all & Object and Data Properties
class_disjoint[] = class
FOREACH [ class ]
        NEW class 'SubClassof' owl:Thing
        FOREACH [ class_disjoint ]
                IF [ class IN class_disjoint ] THEN
                        NEW 'DisjointClasses'
                                Class_Description = class
                                Class_Description = class_disjoint
                END IF
        END FOR
        pop(class_disjoint)

        FOREACH [ f_keys[table] as fk ]
                NEW 'ObjectProperty'
                        Property_Description = 'is_' + fk['pk_table'] + '_of'
                        Domain = fk['pk_table']
                        Range = class
                NEW 'ObjectProperty'
                        Property_Description = 'has_' + fk['pk_table']
                        Domain = class
                        Range = fk['pk_table']
                NEW 'InverseObjectProperties'
                        Property_Description = 'is_' + fk['pk_table'] + '_of'
                        Property_Description = 'has_' + fk['pk_table']
                NEW 'FunctionalObjectProperty'
                        Property_Description = 'is_' + fk['pk_table'] + '_of'
        END FOR

        FOREACH [ columns[table] as table_data ]
                IF [ f_keys[$table][table_data['Name']]['pk_column'] != table_data['Name'] ] THEN
                        NEW 'DataProperty'
                                Property_Description = 'has_' + table_data['Name']
                                Domain = class
                                Range = data_type
                END if
        END FOR
END FOR
```

Figure 7. Algorithm: individuals

```
//   tuples -> Individuals    //
FOREACH [ class ]
        FOREACH [ tables_data[table] as tuple ]
                primary_key = class
                FOREACH [ p_keys[table] as pk)
                        primary_key = primary_key + pk
                END FOR

                NEW 'ClassAssertion'
                        Class_Description = class
                        NamedIndividual = primary_key
                FOREACH [ tuple as kt=>t ]
                        IF [ NOT [ kt IN array_keys(f_keys[table]) ] ]
                                NEW 'DataPropertyAssertion'
                                        DataProperty = class + '_has_' + kt
                                        NamedIndividual = primary_key
                                        Literal = t
                        ELSE
                                NEW 'ObjectPropertyAssertion'
                                        ObjectProperty = f_keys[table][kt]['pk_table']
                                        NamedIndividual = primary_key
                                        NamedIndividual = f_keys[table][kt]['pk_table'] + '_' + t
                        END IF
                END FOR
        END FOR
END FOR
//   tuples -> ObjectProperties (link tables)    //
FOREACH [ non_class ]
        FOREACH [ columns[table] - 1 ]
                FOREACH [ tables_data[table] as tuple ]
                        NEW 'ObjectPropertyAssertion'
                                ObjectProperty = f_keys[table][columns[table]]['pk_table']
                                NamedIndividual = f_keys[table][next(columns[table])]['pk_table'] +
                                        '_' + tuple[f_keys[table][next(columns[table])]['pk_column']]
                                NamedIndividual = f_keys[table][columns[table]]['pk_table'] +
                                        '_' + tuple[f_keys[table][columns[table]]['pk_column']]
                END FOR
        END FOR
END FOR
```

the object properties are generated directly from a 1-to-many relationship (which is the last case), it is possible to define one of the object properties as functional (in one direction).

The tuples of the different tables are mapped to individuals in the ontology and are identified by the associated primary key in the database. A tuple in a database table is mapped to an individual of a class (Figure 7).

The object properties that relate individuals in different classes are only defined in one direction. If in the inverse pair of object properties exists one property that is functional, is that one that it is defined; if not, the generated object property assertion is irrelevant.

In the next table (Figure 8), we summarize the mapping process. From the conceptual mapping approach and some DBMS heuristics, we start to manually convert a relational database (case study database) into OWL using Protégé (http://protege.stanford.edu/). The algorithm was then designed based on the defined mapping and from the code analysis (Protégé – OWL/XML format).

Prototype: Tests and Results

The algorithm was then tested with the case study database. Figure 9 presents the database logical model and the ontology conceptual approach. It was necessary to do some adjustments in order to achieve a consistent ontology.

Then we successfully use the HermiT 1.3.3 reasoner to classify the ontology. The inverse "object properties assertions" that the algorithm do not generates for the individuals were inferred. Some equivalent (and inverse functionality) object properties were also inferred.

In Figure 10, we present an example of the generated ontology. This example focus on the relationship that exists between the two tables ("Authors" and "Bibliography") where the link table "AuthorsBibliography" is mapped into an object property (and inverse object property) relating the correspondent mapped classes. It is also shown a portion of the generated OWL document where we demonstrate the results of mapping a table attribute into a data property of a class.

The next step consisted on testing the algorithm with other databases. We use one MySQL database and two MSSQL Server databases (the maximum tables size were about tens of thousands records). All databases used in this research are from the University Lusíada information system.

The results were very satisfactory because the algorithm achieve similar results of the ones obtained with the case study database only with

Figure 8. Mapping process summarized

RDB	OWL
Tables	Classes
If (#attributes = #primary keys = #foreign keys) → Object Property	
Foreign Keys	Object Properties
Primary Keys	Individuals Identification
Other Attributes	Data Properties
Tuples	Individuals
	• Inverse Object Properties Generation • Functional Object Properties Definition • Disjoin All Classes

Figure 9. RDB logical model vs. ontology overview

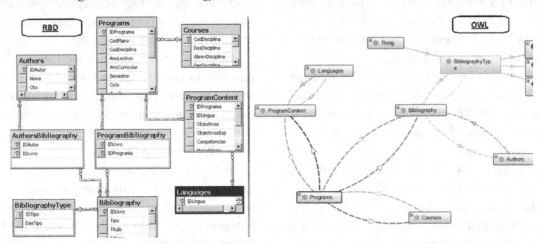

Figure 10. Results portion: tables "authors" and "bibliography" relationship and "authors" attribute mapping

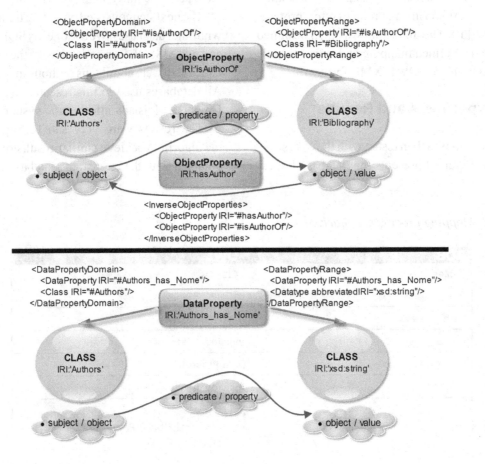

minor inconsistencies related with naming and encoding problems. The processing time is an issue directly related to the dimension of the database (it is necessary to test the algorithm with huge databases [millions of records] in machines with powerful processing capability).

CONCLUSION AND FUTURE WORK

Ontologies and databases are related to each other because of their characteristics. Using ontologies in database preservation is an approach to capture the "knowledge" associated to the conceptual model of the database.

In previous work, we preserve the database data and structure (logical model) by ingesting the database in a XML based format (DBML introduce by Jacinto, Librelotto, Ramalho, & Henriques, 2002) into an OAIS based archive.

Here, we present the work developed in order to convert databases to ontology, based on a mapping process (mapping algorithm), for preservation. In order to preserve a snapshot of the database (or a frozen database) we preserve the ontology (OWL, also a XML based format) obtained from the application of developed algorithm to the source database. We tested the algorithm with few databases and the results were acceptable in terms of consistency of the generated ontology (and comparing to the results obtained with the case study database).

This generated ontologies will induce the development of a new database browser/navigation tool. Ontologies also have other potentialities such as the asset of providing answers to questions that other standards are limited. For example, in terms of metadata, one issue that we intend to also address in future work.

We also anticipate the possibility of integration between Web Ontology Language (OWL) and Semantic Web Rule Language (SWRL – Horrocks, Patel-Schneider, Boley, Tabet, Grosof, & Dean, 2004) to consolidate the asserted and inferred knowledge about the database and its information system.

REFERENCES

W3C Incubator Group. (2009). *A survey of current approaches for mapping of relational databases to RDF*. Retrieved from http://www.w3.org

W3C International Community. (2011). *Website*. Retrieved from http://www.w3.org/

Albarrak, K. M., & Sibley, E. H. (2009). Translating relational & object-relational database models into OWL models. In *Proceedings of the 10th IEEE International Conference on Information Reuse & Integration*. Las Vegas, NV: IEEE Press.

Auer, S., Dietzold, S., Lehmann, J., Hellmann, S., & Aumueller, D. (2009). Triplify – Light-weight linked data publication from relational databases. In *Proceedings of WWW 2009*. Madrid, Spain: IEEE.

Barrasa, J., & Gomez-Perez, A. (2006). Upgrading relational legacy data to the semantic web. In *Proceedings of the 15th International Conference on World Wide Web Conference (WWW 2006)*. Edinburgh, UK: IEEE.

Berners-Lee, T., Hendler, J., & Lassila, O. (2001). The semantic web. *Scientific American*. doi:10.1038/scientificamerican0501-34

Bizer, C., & Cyganiak, R. (2007). D2RQ–*Lessons learned*. Paper presented for the W3C Workshop on RDF Access to Relational Databases. Cambridge, MA.

Bumans, G., & Cerans, K. (2011). RDB2OWL: A practical approach for transforming RDB data into RDF/OWL. In *Proceedings of the 6th International Conference on Semantic Systems ISEMANTICS*. Retrieved 2011, from http://portal. acm.org/citation.cfm?id=1839739

Cerbah, F. (2008). Learning highly structured semantic repositories from relational databases: The RDBToOnto tool. In *Proceedings of the 5th European Semantic Web Conference*. IEEE.

Chen, H., & Wu, Z. (2005). DartGrid III: A semantic grid toolkit for data integration. In *Proceedings of the First International Conference on Semantics, Knowledge, and Grid*. Beijing, China: IEEE.

Codd, E. (1970). A relational model of data for large shared data banks. *Communications of the ACM, 13*(6), 377–387. doi:10.1145/362384.362685

Consultative Committee for Space Data Systems. (2002). *Reference model for an open archival information system (OAIS) – Blue book*. Washington, DC: National Aeronautics and Space Administration.

Cullot, N., Ghawi, R., & Yetongnon, K. (2007). DB2OWL: A tool for automatic database-to-ontology mapping. In *Proceedings of 15th Italian Symposium on Advanced Database Systems (SEBD 2007)*, (pp. 491-494). Torre Canne, Italy: SEBD.

Das, S., Sundara, S., & Cyganiak, R. (2011). *R2RML: RDB to RDF mapping language*. W3C Working Draft. Retrieved from http://www.w3.org

Day, M. (2006). *The OAIS reference model*. Bath, UK: University of Bath.

Ferreira, M. (2006). *Introdução à preservacao digital – Conceitos, estratratégias e actuais consensos*. Guimarães, Portugal: Escola de Engenharia da Universidade do Minho.

Fisher, M., & Dean, M. (2007). Automapper: Relational database semantic translation using OWL and SWRL. In *Proceedings of the IASK International Conference E-Activity and Leading Technologies*. Porto, Portugal: IASK.

Freitas, R. A. P. (2008). *Preservação digital de bases de dados relacionais*. (MSc Dissertation). Universidade do Minho. Minho, Portugal.

Freitas, R. A. P., & Ramalho, J. C. (2009). *Relational databases digital preservation*. Paper presented at the Inforum: Simpósio de Informática. Lisboa, Portugal.

Gruber, T. (2008). Ontology. In Liu, L., & Ozsu, M. (Eds.), *Encyclopedia of Database Systems*. Berlin, Germany: Springer-Verlag.

He-Ping, C., Lu, H., & Bin, C. (2008). Research and implementation of ontology automatic construction based on relational database. In *Proceedings of the International Conference on Computer Science and Software Engineering*. IEEE Computer Society.

Hermit Reasoner. (2011). *Information systems group, department of computer science, University of Oxford*. Retrieved from http://hermit-reasoner. com/

Horrocks, I., Patel-Schneider, P. F., Boley, H., Tabet, S., Grosof, B., & Dean, M. (2004). *SWRL: A semantic web rule language combining OWL and RuleML*. W3C Member Submission. Retrieved 2011, from http://www.w3.org/Submission/SWRL/

Jacinto, M., Librelotto, G., Ramalho, J. C., & Henriques, P. (2002). *Bidirectional conversion between documents and relational data bases.* Paper presented at the 7th International Conference on CSCW in Design. Rio de Janeiro, Brasil.

Lavoie, B. F. (2004). The open archival information system reference model: Introductory guide. *Technology Watch Report Watch Series Report.* 04-01.

Manson, P. (2010). *Digital preservation research: An evolving landscape.* Geneva, Switzerland: European Research Consortium for Informatics and Mathematics.

McGuinness, D. L., & Harmelen, F. (2004). *OWL – Web ontology language: Overview.* Retrieved from http://www.w3.org/TR/owl-features/

Myroshnichenko, I., & Murphy, M. C. (2009). Mapping ER schemas to OWL ontologies. In *Proceedings of the 2009 IEEE International Conference on Semantic Computing,* (pp. 324-329). IEEE Press.

OpenLink Virtuoso Platform. (2010). *Automated generation of RDF views over relational data sources.* Retrieved from http://docs.openlinksw.com/virtuoso/rdfrdfviewgnr.html

Ramalho, J., & Henriques, P. (2002). *XML and XSL - Da teoria à prática.* Lisbon, Portugal: FCA Editora Informática.

Resource Description Framework. (2010). *Website.* Retrieved 2011, from http://www.w3.org/RDF/

Santoso, H., Hawa, S., & Abdul-Mehdia, Z. (2010). *Ontology extraction from relational database: Concept hierarchy as background knowledge.* London, UK: Elsevier. doi:10.1016/j.knosys.2010.11.003

Semantic Web. (2010). *Website.* Retrieved 2011, from http://www.w3.org/standards/semanticweb/

Stanford Center for Biomedical Informatics Research. (2011). *Website.* Retrieved from http://protege.stanford.edu/

Thibodeau, K. (2002). *Overview of technological approaches to digital preservation and challenges in coming years.* Paper presented at the State of Digital Preservation: An International Perspective. Washington, DC.

Trinkunas, J., & Vasilecas, O. (2007). Building ontologies from relational databases using reverse engineering methods. In *Proceedings of the International Conference on Computer Systems and Technologies – CompSysTech 2007.* ACM Press.

Wilson, A. (2007). *Significant properties report.* InSPECT Work Package 2.2, Draft/Version 2.

World Wide Web Consortium. (2003). *XML: Extensible markup language.* Retrieved from http://www.w3.org/XML/

Xu, J., & Li, W. (2007). Using relational database to build OWL ontology from XML data sources. In *Proceedings of the International Conference on Computational Intelligence and Security Workshops.* Washington, DC: IEEE Computer Society.

Zarri, G. P. (2006). RDF and OWL. In *Encyclopedia of Knowledge Management.* Academic Press. doi:10.4018/978-1-59140-573-3.ch101

ENDNOTES

[1]   PLANETS – Preservation and Long-Term Access through NETworked Services [Online]. Available: http://www.planets-project.eu/

[2]   SIARD – Format Description, Swiss Federal Archives – SFA.

173

Chapter 10
Managing Research Data at the University of Porto:
Requirements, Technologies, and Services

João Rocha da Silva
University of Porto, Portugal

Cristina Ribeiro
University of Porto, Portugal

João Correia Lopes
University of Porto, Portugal

ABSTRACT

This chapter consists of a solution for the management of research data at a higher education and research institution. The chapter is based on a small-scale data audit study, which included contacts with researchers and yielded some preliminary requirements and use cases. These requirements led to the design of a data curation workflow involving the researcher, the curator, and a data repository. The authors describe the features of the data repository prototype, which is an extension to the widely used DSpace repository platform and introduced a set of features mentioned by the majority of the interviewed researchers as relevant for a data repository. The data repository platform contributes to the curation workflow at the university, with XML technology at its core—data is stored using XML documents, which can be systematically processed and queried unlike its original-format counterpart. This system is capable of indexing, querying, and retrieving, in whole or in part, datasets represented in tabular form. There is also the possibility of using elements from domain-specific XML schemas for the cataloguing process, improving the interoperability and quality of the deposited data.

DOI: 10.4018/978-1-4666-2669-0.ch010

INTRODUCTION

It is currently recognized in most research areas that data is not only an essential component of the scientific process but that research is more and more driven by the data itself. The so-called "data deluge" (Hey & Trefethen 2003) has prompted research institutions, funding agencies, data specialists, editors and researchers in many areas to find solutions for managing research data and to comply with the requirements of their research processes.

Current technologies and devices generate an immense flow of data, most of it even prior to the application of any scientific process; but even data that are not created in the scope of research can become the subject of research if it is recorded, making it available and interpretable. This "data deluge" is raising concerns about the possibilities that may be missed if all this data cannot be stored, explored, and made available.

This increasingly widespread use of powerful computing infrastructures has led to the coining of the term "e-Science." E-Science is a general term used to designate research activities that are supported by large quantities of data and substantial computational resources. The growth in computational capability in the recent decades has led to the emergence of the so-called "Fourth Paradigm" of research, through which scientific research is built on massive quantities of data captured by instruments or generated by simulations. These data assets are leveraged using federated resources designed to support researchers in their collaborative efforts, aiding them in the analysis, visualization and dissemination of their results (Hey, et al., 2009).

The publication of research, which relies on extensive exploration of data, tends to be limited without the publication of the data itself and major publishers have made very concrete proposals in this direction. Nature, for instance, provides for the availability of "supporting online material" on the published papers, and even considers software in this category (Hanson, et al., 2011).

Another line of inquiry related to the wider availability of data is data sharing and reuse. The Open Data movement advocates free access to data as the path to improving research, policy making and transparency in many domains (Foundation, 2011). The concern with data reuse and the possibilities of promoting new "digital data products" has also been raised (Faniel & Zimmerman, 2011).

A recent overview (Borgman, 2011) has shown that preserving research data is relevant for many reasons—but there are four main drivers for the implementation of these practices. These are ensuring the reproducibility and verifiability of the research findings, making the results of publicly funded research available to the public, enabling others to ask new questions based on existing data, and finally, advancing the state of research and innovation.

Research data is especially hard to preserve because of its complex underlying semantics and its heterogeneity. Researchers use many file formats, often relying on proprietary software or even software that they wrote themselves. Datasets can also vary greatly in volume depending on the domain and on the type of data that is to be stored. However, it is important to point out that big data storage issues are not within the scope of this work—we are instead tackling the issue of how to provide better ways for researchers to retrieve the preserved data.

The underlying semantics of research datasets must be captured in a set of relevant metadata that can help researchers who wish to reuse those datasets ("re-users") to understand their original context of production. If a dataset is not sufficiently well annotated, it may be difficult for the potential re-user to evaluate that data in terms of its relevance to their work or verify its authenticity and correctness—which would most certainly mean that such data would not be reused at all.

Managing research data at a research institution requires knowledge on many different research fields, from ethics to low-level data representation formats. In this chapter, we will start with an overview of the requirements that have been identified in a small-scale data audit performed at U.Porto. We will also try to clarify the scope of the work and decompose the problem into several smaller issues. In the case of this experiment, we decided to focus on the role of the researchers because U.Porto is at an early stage of development in the field of data preservation. Thus, we believed that the best way to start this work was to understand the perspective of the "end-user" of the prototype repository platform that we implemented. This software solution will also be presented in detail, including both a description of its architecture and of its usage throughout the whole deposit, curation, and data retrieval workflow.

RELATED WORK

To establish the context of the developed work and provide a general overview of the subject, we will analyze several projects related to research data management in this section. Data management is a research subject that spans across several domains, so we decided to split these projects into several categories, according to their application domains, technical and expertise sectors and also according to the stakeholders that drive them. All these projects show the increasing interest in research data management and institution-level projects have served as an important source of inspiration for this work.

DATA PRESERVATION PROJECTS

Some specific domains have already implemented successful strategies and platforms for the preservation of their data. Biology (genetics research), chemistry (crystallography in particular), and social sciences are some examples of data intensive research in which there are already highly sophisticated tools for data. A brief description of some of these platforms follows.

Research in the domain of biology, particularly genetics, has benefitted greatly from the recent growth in computation capabilities. As a consequence of these improvements, researchers required the creation of a highly sophisticated platform that not only is capable of preserving molecular biology data but also of performing heavy computing operations over the deposited data–all in a collaborative environment. These are some of the objectives of the NCBI (Information, 2011), a full-fledged e-Science platform that indexes several genome databases, data curation services, and offers a platform for running specific algorithms over the stored datasets using domain specific programs such as BLAST (Information, 2011).

The Interuniversity Consortium for Political and Social Research (ICPSR) is a public data repository for the deposit and retrieval of datasets from the social sciences. According to its website (Michigan, 2011), it "offers more than 500,000 digital files containing social science research data. Disciplines represented include political science, sociology, demography, economics, history, (…) mental health, and more." This particular repository service uses detailed descriptions of all the variables represented in the data tables stored in the repository to help researchers understand the meaning of the datasets and also offers an online data analysis and visualization tool that can represent the stored datasets in the form of charts.

CERN (The European Organization for Nuclear Research) has performed studies to gather feedback on the opinion of researchers about data preservation. A recent survey (Holzner, 2009) was performed to study its perceived importance and urgency. As a side-note, CERN also promotes an Open Access policy on all its research results (CERN, 2011).

Several other projects are not focused in finding a solution for managing the data produced in a specific research domain but instead on improving data management practices at the institution level.

The DISC-UK is a forum for data professionals working in UK higher education who support their institutions' staff and students in managing their data (DISC-UK, 2010). DISC-UK fosters the implementation of data management policies across research institutions in the UK, performing workshops, guides for policy making and promoting large projects such as the Data Asset Framework.

The Data Asset Framework or DAF (Glasgow & Centre, 2011), previously named Data Audit Framework, was a project led by the HATII[1] at the University of Glasgow, in conjunction with the DCC[2]. The project was funded by the JISC[3] and tested by four prominent academic institutions in the UK: the Imperial College London, the University College London, King's College London and the University of Edinburgh. The DAF yielded, among other results, several reports and also a methodology (Jones, et al., 2009) to help institutions implement their own data management plans.

The Edinburgh DataShare (Edimburgh, 2011), is a digital repository of multi-disciplinary datasets produced at the University of Edinburgh. It provides, among other capabilities, a data self-deposit mechanism to the university researchers while offering persistent identifier and citation services for these datasets. This platform also encourages researchers to contact the university's Collection Administrators to help them throughout the dataset deposit process.

The demand for data preservation is increasing as funding agencies require data management plans to be added to every grant proposal (Borgman, 2011; Foundation, 2011) and prominent research publishers demand the annexing of the original data to each of their published articles.

Looking at this issue at the highest levels of policy-making, it is encouraging to see the degree of commitment that some countries are showing towards research data preservation.

Australia has invested greatly in e-Research since 2004 through funding programs such as the NCRI (Australia, 2008), and projects such as the ANDS (Services, 2011). The country expressed its commitment to this policy by investing heavily in eResearch projects like the *Building eResearch Support Capabilities and Capacity* project (Jennifer, 2011).

The United Kingdom has also funded large projects—like the DAF—through its Joint Information Systems Committee, or JISC. The JISC funds various kinds of infrastructure, services, and research projects at UK's Higher Education and Further Education institutions. As of present time, it is funding more than 170 ongoing projects spread across 29 programs and supports two of the most renowned services of data preservation and curation: The Digital Curation Centre (DCC) in Edinburgh, and the United Kingdom Office for Library and Information Networking (UKOLN) at the University of Bath (England, 2011).

In the United States, we underline the work of the National Institutes of Health (NIH), which offers a series of policies for data sharing. These data sharing guidelines are associated to grant applications at the NIH, which has required, since 1996, the sharing of specific research materials produced by projects funded by its grants. Examples of such materials are DNA sequences, mapping information and crystallographic coordinates (Services, 2004).

Finally, the National Science Foundation (or NSF)—a major research grant provider in the US—has spurred the data management efforts at research institutions by requiring the annexing of a Data Management Plan to all research grant applications, starting in January 18, 2011 (Foundation, 2011).

Data Curation Services

Some institutions have begun to offer data curation as a service. As we will show, professional data curation is essential to ensure the proper conversion of file formats between the original sources that may depend on their creation software into more "preservation-friendly" formats. Another vital role for professional data curators is to ensure the consistency, validity, and thorough annotation of these datasets so that they can be reused.

The UK Data Archive is responsible for curating the UK's largest collection of digital social and economic research data. Its curation service follows a high standard, comprehensive data curation process that is divided in 9 steps that go from the initial contact with the researcher, ensuring the proper transmission of the data, to the delivery and publishing of curated data. This is a very mature process that has been built on years of practice (Essex, 2011).

The need for data sharing has long been a concern in the research community (Norman, 1985; Glass, 1986). Proper research data management is, however, a premise for the implementation of any data sharing policy and also a domain where there is much room for improvement from a technical standpoint—namely in building appropriate software tools to support data management tasks.

It becomes apparent that researchers have to be committed to become a part of the curation workflow. However, many are unsure of their role, but most of them agree that research data should be preserved so that it can retain its value for secondary use. Others also make clear that the preservation effort involved is too great—in human and material resources—especially when the data has such a short lifecycle that there is no point in preserving it. Others are afraid to become a part of the research data management because of complicated legal constraints. These can be a consequence of the nature of the data itself but also of the tools that were used to produce it—proprietary software being a clear example. Simple practices such as systematic data backup procedures and essential cataloguing are gradually becoming part of researchers' workflow but there are relevant opportunities for improvement.

LESSONS LEARNED FROM SIMILAR DATA AUDITS

Since there are many ongoing research and development efforts in the field of scientific data management, we decided to analyze their reports to avoid some common pitfalls and learn from their experiences. One of such projects, the DAF, involved four of UK's large education institutions. Each of these institutions developed a pilot project to test the developed platform and implement the DAF guidelines, which divide the audit process into four stages: Planning the Audit, Identifying and Classifying Assets, Assessing Management of Data Assets and Reporting and Recommendation. We followed a similar sequence of this audit, which had as its primary objective the determination of the user requirements of the repository platform. The reports summarizing the conclusions of these projects also provided valuable insight for the writing of the interview guides used throughout the requirements elicitation phase. In this part of the experiment, we studied the most relevant data management needs of some U.Porto researchers who kindly responded to our challenge to take part in the this experiment.

The timing of the data gathering is another relevant issue when implementing data management practices in a research institution. An interesting conclusion came from project SPECTRA (Tonge & Morgan, 2007) when they determined that there is a "golden moment" for researchers to become actively involved in the curation process. This is the point at which the researcher best understands the process, possesses a comprehensive package of information to describe it, and is motivated to take part in the curation process (Initiative, 2011), something that we confirmed during the conducted interviews.

Experienced active researchers and students in the final years of their PhD or Master's Degree were prime sources of real-world experience when handling data in research contexts, since they are at a moment when they have already gone through the process of having to search for baseline data for result comparison or as a guide to help them bootstrap their research process. In addition, they are still actively involved in the research effort, so their knowledge of the data is excellent. It is a time when many of them have already published the conclusions of their work, so a data curation intervention is more likely to successfully retrieve publicly shareable datasets.

Evaluating the Maturity of a Data Management Process

When proposing any improvements to a current system it is important to provide a scale that can be used do evaluate the situation at the start of the improvement process and also at the end, so that the improvement can be measurable. For this purpose, we have selected the DISC-UK's Data Sharing Continuum (Rice, 2007) concept.

Building on previous experience, we have looked to the Edinburgh DataShare project, which introduced the notion of "Data Sharing Continuum," which is a scale for measuring the maturity of a curation process. Figure 1 shows the different maturity levels for the classification of a data curation context and the requirements for attaining those levels. We will use these criteria to evaluate the improvements provided by our solution.

THE DATA AUDIT AT U.PORTO

The data management initiative at U.Porto has the goal of providing a data curation service for the researchers who need assistance in managing their data assets. Designing and installing a prototype data repository has been established as the first main goal. To achieve it, the first step has been to lead a data audit following the recommendations issued by similar initiatives, namely the methodology proposed in the Data Asset Framework (University of Glasgow, DCC, 2009).

The DAF framework prescribes an identification of the data assets created in the institution followed by an analysis concerning storage, management, sharing, and reuse. It also recommends an identification of the risks faced by research data and gathering the views of researchers on the data creation and sharing processes. This knowledge is then to be used to inform initiatives towards the improvement of data management policies.

The interviews with the researchers have confirmed our initial assumption that the design of a solution for a data repository should be determined by the needs of the researchers, rather than by any abstract data management convenience (Borgman, 2011). The interviews also showed more concern with functionalities such as data browsing and querying than with strict data preservation or management.

Dataset Gathering and Cataloguing

Taking into account the fact that no data curation policies exist at the university level, it was decided to conduct the data audit giving preference to the diversity of domains. After selecting a set of researchers that were motivated to take part in this experience, we have interviewed them following a script that allowed for many open questions. In some cases, the researchers agreed to provide sample datasets, and follow-up interviews were scheduled for discussing data formats, the meaning of the data and also their terms of use.

Table 1 lists the nature of the collected datasets and the access conditions established by the researchers. Interviews have been a rich source of information on their needs, where we can highlight data preservation and data exchange with research partners, either within the research groups or externally in international projects or other partnerships.

Figure 1. The data sharing continuum, based on the original image by Robin Rice (Rice, 2007)

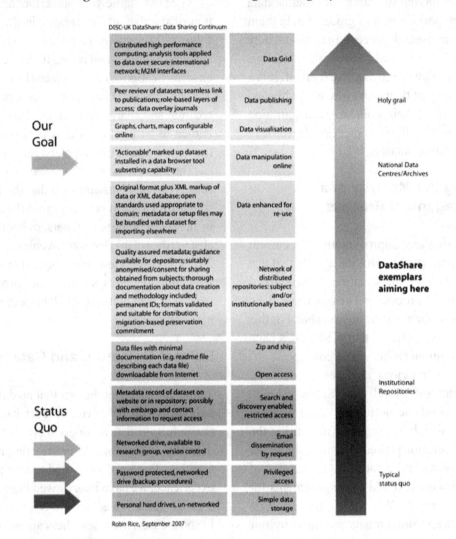

Designing a Curation Workflow

After the dataset gathering phase, we were able to determine the most valued features of a research data repository in the researchers' point of view. Most researchers pointed out that useful repository tools should focus on four main aspects:

1. Allowing for easy sharing of datasets, reducing the need for individual follow-up contacts with researchers interested in the data—this means enriching the annotations to effectively capture the datasets' meaning and production context;

2. Making it easy to find datasets by their dimensions, regardless of their production domain. Such dimensions are measurable quantities or characteristics such as age, length, substance names, latitude or height;

3. Exploring and querying deposited datasets using domain dimensions;

4. Retrieving and downloading results of queries on the deposited data, which requires the existence of support for partial retrieval of datasets.

Table 1. Domains and access conditions for the gathered datasets

Domain	Dataset	Access
Astronomy	Gravimetry	Free
Chemical Engineering	Pollutant analysis	Contract pending
Mechanical Engineering	Material fracture	Embargoed
Civil Engineering	High-speed railways	Embargoed
Educational Science	Interviews	Embargoed
Psychology	Interaction records	Embargoed
Economy	Population	Embargoed
Ecology	Plant distribution	Embargoed

The data representation formats used by researchers are, in most cases, not suitable for direct data retrieval and querying. As a consequence, traditional approaches such as saving whole files and associated metadata are ill-suited for this purpose. Finding a way to reduce the granularity of data beyond the file level is a pre-requisite for building automated data manipulation capabilities.

Development of the Prototype Repository Platform

The user stories that we gathered during the interviews conducted in the first phase of the project were prioritized according to their complexity in terms of implementation effort involved and perceived usefulness, in order to select those that offered the most beneficial compromise between the two factors. We took care to select the most relevant features that were pointed out by the majority of the researchers so as to not skew the proposed solution in favour of the specific needs of any specific research groups.

We gathered datasets from various kinds during our interviews—from audio archives to text processing documents and even entire relational databases. There were also some cases where the files delivered as part of the dataset could only be read using programs written by the researchers themselves. There was, however, a kind of data that was common to all datasets—tabular data. Usually

tabular data is associated with spreadsheet editing programs such as Excel, but broadly speaking, what we are interested in are conceptual tables, regardless of the file format they are stored in. One of the examples was a geo-referencing dataset used by Ecology researchers, which was edited using a specific program. However, we noticed that in many occasions such as this, the programs used in specific domains could export data in a tabular format such as Excel or Comma-Separated Values. Since there were currently no repositories specifically designed for the cataloguing of data at U.Porto, we decided to start by building a Web-based tool capable of better managing this type of data.

There are several open-source repository platforms currently available, such as Fedora, e-Prints or DSpace. They are primarily designed as publication repositories, but include many generic modules (such as workflow engines for document deposit) that can be reused in a data management repository.

The DSpace platform was selected to be the basis for this experiment because U.Porto already has two operational public repositories built using this solution—the Open Repository and the Thematic Repository (Porto, 2011). Contributing to DSpace can also help raise awareness on the topic of research data management since the platform already has a large user base, with more than 1000 running instances (Duraspace, 2011) mainly at educational institutions. It is also open-source software, meaning that contributions can be submitted to the developer community and be integrated in future releases.

The Data Explorer extension was designed around the workflow presented in Figure 2. The data is deposited as part of a dataset using the built-in deposit capabilities of DSpace. This deposited package will, at the end of the deposit workflow, be a DSpace Item. Items are the smallest-granularity element to which metadata can be added, in a standard DSpace installation.

After the new Item is deposited in the system and associated to a specific Collection, the Bit-streams that it contains ("files" in DSpace terms) can be curated using one of the tools in the developed extension. Each collection has its own group of administrators, which are e-Persons (DSpace registered "users") in charge of approving Item submissions to their collections. The curation feature is available to the administrators of the Collection that contains that Item.

Platform Installation and User Feedback Gathering

We have successfully completed the process of installed and setting up the finished repository tool on a test server[4]. Another step was the writing of support materials such as the user's manual and other relevant technical manuals, as well as the production of several demonstration videos, available at the project wiki[5]. There is still an ongoing process of evaluating the results of the experiment, which means gathering feedback from the interviewed researchers on the implemented repository features.

Figure 2. The data curation workflow using the DSpace data explorer extension

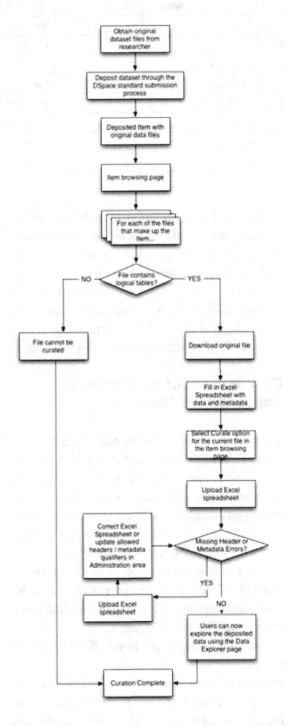

THE PROTOTYPE REPOSITORY: DSPACE DATA EXPLORER

As part of this experiment, we have designed and implemented an extension for the DSpace repository software which aims to provide users with the most requested data preservation features—easy data sharing, better searching, sub-dataset querying, and partial download of datasets.

After analyzing the datasets gathered during the course of the experiment, we have concluded that researchers use many different formats for storing their data, which makes it difficult to develop tools to automate its processing. We have also determined that the main cause of data loss is the common lack of annotation and the use of proprietary file formats. The analyzed data has, generally speaking, quite simple models and multidimensional or hierarchical data are not very common. Most scientific data can therefore be organized into tables because the most prevalent types of files are spreadsheets, text files or other formats, which can be converted into spreadsheets by the original programs used to create the data.

For these reasons, creating a better way to manage tables in a repository platform was considered, in our case, a good starting point towards better preservation of research data.

To make it possible for the repository to extract the relevant information from a dataset, we are designing a system that ingests specially formatted Excel spreadsheets to facilitate the interaction between the repository and the end users (either data curators or researchers). We decided to adopt this format because Excel is a common format among researchers in many areas and also because the creation of a dedicated Web-based deposit interface would mean heavier implementation efforts while being somewhat superfluous, since any spreadsheet program is an excellent tool for manipulating this kind of data. A sample layout for a data deposit spreadsheet is shown in Figure 3.

Following this format, first we have a metadata section with a series of [metadata element]—[value] pairs. These metadata elements can be taken from established metadata schemas from each research domain and reused here to take advantage of domain-specific terminology in the

Figure 3. Excel spreadsheet layout for curating one file

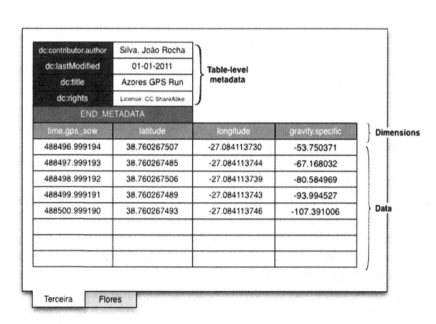

classification of the data. After this metadata section, there is a separator tag—a single line separating the metadata section of the table from the data itself. The data section of the table is composed of a header line with metadata qualifiers (which can also be taken from existing schemas) and a series of rows containing the data itself.

This particular example (which will be used throughout this section) shows a series of records from a gravimetry run (gravimetry is the study of the gravity acceleration in different parts of the globe). We can see in the first column the time instant (in GPS Seconds of Week, a specific unit of this domain); the next two columns are georeferencing values to know the point over the Earth's surface was the record taken. Lastly, we have the value of the specific gravity in that location in a differential scale (another domain specific measurement).

The spreadsheet is to be filled in manually by the repository curators, starting from the data, which must be previously self-deposited by the original creator in its original format and layout. Since the data annotation process requires specific domain knowledge, it must be conducted in strict cooperation with the data creator. If an original data file contains several conceptual tables, each must be placed in a separate sheet of the Excel document—in this example, they are labeled "Terceira" and "Flores."

Depositing Data in the Platform

Different data formats and domain diversity mean that researchers have to collaborate with the repository services if the data is to be correctly indexed and annotated for later searching. After the dataset is deposited using the DSpace standard workflow engine, there must be a meeting between the researcher who created the data and a data curator. During this meeting, the researcher would help the curator with the task of describing the data before a curated version of the original dataset can be added to the repository.

By the end of this meeting (there can be more than one, depending on the number of files to be curated), the curator would have produced a series of Excel spreadsheets for depositing in the DSpace Data Explorer. The curation procedure is the following:

1. Parameterize header and table-level metadata in the dedicated administration panel as required
2. Access the DSpace visualization page for the item that contains the dataset to be curated
3. Select the file (or *Bitstream)* that contains the data and download it
4. Fill in the Excel spreadsheet with the data extracted from the original file, as well as the any relevant metadata—this is to be done during a meeting with the researcher that created the original data
5. Select the curation option for the data file that contains the data
6. Upload the Excel spreadsheet containing the dataset
7. The data becomes available through the data-exploring interface and is now retrievable through the dataset querying option in the repository's homepage.

As can be seen in Figure 3, the Excel format for data deposit includes data and table-level metadata for each of the logical tables contained in the dataset file to be curated. For each of the sheets/tables, the curator must then specify its related metadata, which includes the table's creator, original creation date, etc. This is because a data file can contain several series of data, each produced in its own context.

As an example, let us analyze the case of a certain file that contains chemical experiment data spread across several logical tables. A table can be related to an experiment where a specific substance was analyzed and another table may also contain results of another experiment on a different substance. The correct way to curate such a dataset would be to specify a table metadata element meaning "substance name" or "substance chemical formula" such as the "cml:moleculeid" element from the CML metadata schema, including it in two separate sheets inside the workbook and fill in the corresponding values.

After the spreadsheet is submitted, the system will validate the headers and table metadata elements to ensure that they match the elements parameterized in the system, and will signal an error otherwise. The deposited data may be numeric or textual, but to ensure the matching between headers/metadata elements and XML schemas, the former must adhere to the "<schema short id>.<element name>[.<qualifier>]?" format. This is to encourage a more uniform format for headers and the reuse of metadata elements from existing XML Schemas from the datasets' own domains. An example Excel spreadsheet after the initial curation process is shown in Figure 4.

Platform Administration and Parametrization

The Data Explorer extension offers two configuration panels for the parameterization of the metadata that can be used to catalogue scientific datasets. During the curation process, the system validates the submitted Excel spreadsheets according to the parameters set in these two panels.

The Data Explorer Table Metadata administration panel allows DSpace Administrators to specify the relevant metadata for the logical tables contained in a specific file. These are the tables that are inserted into the system during the submission process via an Excel spreadsheet containing all logical tables of a given Bitstream or "file."

Figure 5 shows the link to the table metadata panel, available in the DSpace administration area; it is very similar in appearance to the DSpace Metadata Registry included in the standard DSpace

Figure 4. Example of a finished Excel spreadsheet

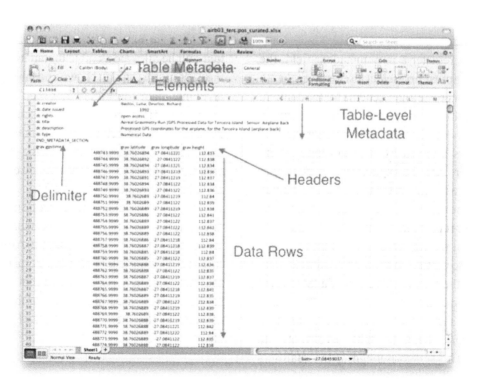

Figure 5. Table metadata management tool in the DSpace administration tools

platform. To register a new metadata field, the administrator must first select an existing schema from the list or create a new schema for the domain. By selecting the option just below the one shown in Figure 5, administrators can parameterize the table headers allowed by the curation system. Table headers are the metadata qualifiers that can be used as headers for the tables contained in each of the sheets of a curation Excel workbook and are represented in Figure 3 by the cells highlighted in green and labeled as "Dimensions." The parameterization of an allowed table header is similar to the parameterization of a table-level metadata element.

Figure 6 shows the process of registering a new metadata schema for table-level metadata annotation. This schema will group the qualifiers that will be allowed as table metadata—these are the cells highlighted in brown and labeled "Table-level metadata" on Figure 3.

Adding fields to a metadata schema can be performed by selecting the schema to which a new field will belong and entering the element name, for example "creator" in "dc.creator" and a qualifier, if required (Figure 7).

The user must also enter a "scope note," which is a brief description of the metadata element within the schema's scope domain. After submitting the new metadata element parametrization, the data curation page will accept new Excel spreadsheets containing values for that metadata element in the metadata section of each table/sheet.

Figure 6. Adding a new metadata schema for table-level metadata

Figure 7. Adding a new metadata field

Data Retrieval and Subsetting

The interface that users will have to use to access and retrieve data from the repository was called the "Data Explorer." The Data Explorer view is available for all Bitstreams ("files") in an Item, provided they have gone through the curation process. It allows users to view the data contained in a file without having to download the entire data and explore it locally on their computer's filesystem, thus requiring the potential re-used to have access to the software that was originally used to produce that data.

To access the Data Explorer view and explore a file's data, the user must access the page of its parent Item. The system will show an "Explore Data" option next to all files which have been curated (See Figure 8).

The user may select the "Explore Data" option to access the curated data. The system will then show a grid and a series of tabs, one for each logical table contained in the file. The user may select a tab and the system will show only that table. When the user selects one of these options, he/she gains access to the Data Explorer view for that specific file.

An example of the data explorer interface is shown in Figure 9.

Atop of the visualization area, there is a toolbar with 3 buttons:

- Download Current Data
  - This option allows the user to download the data currently displayed in the selected tab to the local file system. This is useful for retrieving rel-

Figure 8. Data exploring functionality is available for the files in this item

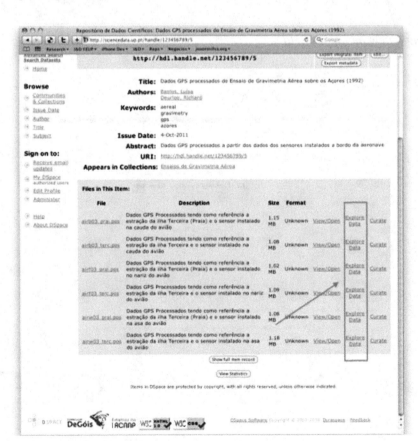

Figure 9. Data retrieval options toolbar

evant parts of data tables that correspond to the results of the application of filters that can be specified by the user.

- Download Current Sheet
  - This option allows the user to download the table containing the data that corresponds to the table currently selected (disregarding any filters that may have been applied).
- Download Workbook
  - Retrieve the whole workbook containing all the data (with one sheet per tab shown in the data explorer page and disregarding any filters).
  - All downloaded files will contain the relevant table metadata for each table

they include the headers and data rows. The download format is Office 97 Excel Spreadsheet (XLS extension) for increased compatibility.

The data explorer view also allows user to see the relevant metadata for the table that is being viewed. The user accesses this metadata by selecting the corresponding option (see Figure 10).

The Data Explorer view also allows users to filter the data that they want to view. To do this, users may specify filters to apply to the data by combining sets of restrictions on data columns (see Figure 11). The numbers shown in the figure show the normal flow of interaction with the system. The text box on the right of the two combo boxes in the "Search…" area is where the

Figure 10. Showing table metadata

Figure 11. Options for adding and combining data filters

user will input the value parameter for the filter. Button 3 allows users to add as many restrictions as they wish, while button 4 allows them to apply the combination of all of them to the data in the table.

Retrieving Datasets using Domain-Specific Restrictions

Metadata exists in DSpace at the Item level, but we decided to add table-level metadata because this allows users to retrieve individual data tables contained in a single Bitstream. This also allows for easier cross-referencing of scientific domains. For example, finding all tables that contain 'latitude' and 'longitude' columns allows a researcher to cross-reference data from different domains but which are georeferenced. Still in the context of this example, after retrieving the relevant data tables, users can use the filtering capabilities described in the previous section to retrieve all records, which occurred in a specific geographical area, which can help them build an overlay of georeferenced occurrences of certain phenomena. The restrictions available do not offer the detail level of a full-fledged GIS[6], but can serve as an illustrative scenario.

The Data Explorer extension for DSpace includes a dataset-searching page that can be used to retrieve data tables which contain specific columns or which include certain metadata characteristics. This page can be accessed through the left-side tool bar in the DSpace Main Page (see Figure 12).

To look for tables that contain specific columns, users may add them to the restriction by specifying their metadata name. The system will assist the user in filling in the correct metadata parameter (see Figure 13).

Users can combine the header-based restrictions with table metadata-level restrictions (See Figure 14). The metadata field also provides the same automatic completion capabilities present for table headers.

Figure 12. Dataset search option in the DSpace data explorer

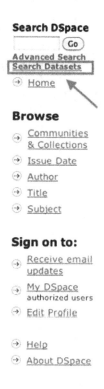

After submitting the search request, the results are shown in a list, which includes, for each matching table, its owning item and the link to the original file which contains that logical table (see Figure 15).

If the user selects an item in the "Table" column, the system will display the corresponding table in the Data Explorer view already described in the "Data retrieval and subsetting" section. By selecting an item in the "Owning Item" column, the DSpace page for the item that contains the table will be shown. Lastly, the user can have direct access to the original file that contains the table (as the researcher first deposited it) by selecting the corresponding item in the "Original File" column.

Figure 13. Dataset search automatic completion feature

Figure 14. Combining header and data table-level restrictions

Figure 15. Dataset search results

Figure 16. DSpace data explorer extension high-level architecture

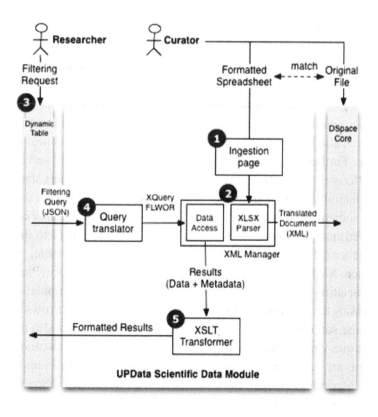

System Architecture

The system makes extensive use of XML technologies since the structure of the tables is not known beforehand; it had to be possible to query the deposited data through a dynamic user interface that did not depend on the names of the columns in the dataset's tables or on the types of data that they hold (string, numeric, float, etc.). XML is also a very "preservation-friendly" format—much more so than a series of conventional relational database tables, which would be obvious alternative solution for storing the data. XML is platform-agnostic, excellent for data exchange because there are countless open-source solutions for parsing XML documents in almost every programming language. In addition, since it is represented in plain text, the technologies in which it relies are reduced to a bare minimum—just the encoding formats of the documents, such as UTF-8 or ANSI.

The deposit and indexing of datasets pose several challenges to the DSpace platform. Since dataset tables can have many different structures depending on their domain subject, a conventional relational model for such a heterogeneous reality might probably resemble the Associative Model of Data (Williams, 2000) with clear performance issues. XML Documents, on the other hand, have the required flexibility to represent all these different table formats and can also be queried through the XQuery language. Furthermore, one of the main goals of this platform is to offer better ways to access stored data—simply storing and retrieving whole data files is something DSpace already supports, so we believed that reducing this granularity is a pre-requisite for offering better access methods. In this solution, XML markup language is at the core of such capability, since XML documents can be queried using the XQuery language. It a weak-typed language, something that makes it easier to build generic querying interfaces where the querying statements are generated on the fly. Using a strong-typed language such as SQL would mean that we would have to restrict the operators that are to be applied to certain columns of a data table, depending on the column's datatype. With XQuery and XML documents, the user is freed from this kind of low-level technical details of the data access.

The high-level architecture of the DSpace extension is depicted in Figure 16 and is made up of the following modules:

1. The ingestion page can be accessed through the item-viewing page in DSpace. Collection curators can upload a single formatted spreadsheet representing the data content of each of the files that make up the deposited item.

2. The XML Manager module takes care of all the operations on the XML-represented data. These include the translation of specially formatted spreadsheets—using the Apache POI library (Foundation, 2011)—and running XQuery FLWOR[7] statements over deposited data to select parts of the dataset.

3. When the user interacts with the dynamic table, a filtering statement (in the form of a JSON[8] request) is sent to the server. These filtering statements contain the column to filter by, the operator to be applied and the argument value, and can be combined using OR/AND operators to build more complex queries. The server must then implement the required business logic to filter the data. In this case, the server side querying logic generates XQuery statements to be executed over the XML data stored in the repository.

4. The Dynamic Table component presents an XML document to the user in the form of an interactive table, which is generated by the jqGrid library (Plugin, 2011). It supports basic data manipulation functionality, such as ordering data rows by specific columns in the dataset and also more complex column filtering features (numeric and string-based operators). An example table generated by the developed DSpace extension using this library is shown in Figure 5.

5. The XSLT Transformer module was created to provide flexible means for presenting the data stored in the repository and the results of data selection. It is used to transform the preserved data (which is stored in a rich format, complete with the relevant metadata) into a generic XML format that the jqGrid Javascript library can understand, so that it can create the dynamic tables shown to the repository users. XSL stylesheets are adequate for this sort of export operations because the engine can be easily modified to export just the metadata for all tables or transform the original XML-formatted data into other file formats or make it easier to turn the DSpace repository into a data source for other applications. At the same time, XSLT technology allows us to offload the server by performing the transformations on the original data on the client using Javascript—something that is relevant since the analyzed datasets may be small to medium-sized (the gravimetry example included tables with 10000 rows, for example).

CONCLUSION AND FUTURE TRENDS

Starting from the experiences of several data preservation projects, we outlined a plan for an experiment with the goal of identifying possible improvements to the data management practices at U.Porto, using open-source tools to support these changes when needed.

Data sharing and Open Access policies are undoubtedly connected issues but are also outside the scope of this experiment. This work is primarily a technical approach to data preservation aiming to build tools to support a preservation workflow. We believe that the decision to encourage or even enforce these policies rests in the hands of certain stakeholders such as funding agencies and scientific publications—currently, we are focusing on ensuring that stakeholders have better tools to support these practices, should they become a reality.

This experiment has provided an insight on the data management requirements of several U.Porto research groups. This analysis was conducted through several interviews with researchers, during which sample datasets were collected. From the opinions gathered in the interview phase, we elicited several use cases that would, if implemented, benefit the majority of the interviewed researchers.

The documented use cases were implemented in a DSpace repository, through extensive use of XML technologies and the development of a data explorer extension. This extension includes features for depositing datasets through Excel spreadsheets, and the possibility of adding metadata at the table level as well as at the item, or dataset, level. Another interesting feature is the ability to retrieve individual data tables based on their dimensions.

As a first approach to improve the semantic richness and exchangeability of the deposited data, the prototype repository allows curators to reuse metadata elements from existing domain-specific XML schemas as table-level metadata elements and table headers. This was a first approach at minimizing the issues that arise from the existence of several different metadata "standards" for research data annotation. We believe that this is an area where there is potential for improvements in the future.

If we look at the proposed data repository in the light of the DataShare Data Curation Continuum scale, there is a considerable improvement of the maturity of the curation process, moving up from a "Simple Data Storage" level of unpreserved data stored on personal hard drives or sometimes networked data to a "Data Manipulation Online" level where there is assistance in the data deposit, XML representations for the deposited data and also a browser-based tool for exploring datasets, querying the data and performing data subsetting, which allows the user to download just the data he/she needs.

The next step in the evaluation and further development of the prototype requires its use by the researchers with their own data, and this will provide the opportunity to test the curation workflow. We are convinced that the contact of the researchers with this prototype will have two major outcomes. The first is to highlight the strengths and weaknesses of the tool and contribute to define more challenging requirements. The second is to provide a concrete evaluation of the effort required for setting up a data curation service at the university level, as well as defining the professional profiles required for the curation personnel.

REFERENCES

Australia. (2008). *National collaborative research infrastructure strategy*. Retrieved from http://ncris.innovation.gov.au/Pages/default.aspx

Borgman, C. L. (2011). *The conundrum of sharing research data*. Retrieved from http://papers.ssrn.com/sol3/papers.cfm?abstract_id=1869155

CERN. S. I. S. (2011). *Supporting open access publishing*. Retrieved from http://library.web.cern.ch/library/OpenAccess/OpenAccessPolicy.html

DISC-UK. (2010). *DISC-UK home*. Retrieved from http://www.disc-uk.org/

Duraspace. (2011). *About DSpace*. Retrieved from http://www.dspace.org/about

Edimburgh. (2011). *What is Edinburgh datashare?* Retrieved from http://datashare.is.ed.ac.uk/

England. (2011). *JISC - Services*. Retrieved from http://www.jisc.ac.uk/whatwedo/services.aspx

Essex. (2011). *How we curate data - The process*. Retrieved December, 2011, from http://www.data-archive.ac.uk/curate/process

Faniel, I. M., & Zimmerman, A. (2011). Beyond the data deluge: A research agenda for large-scale data sharing and reuse. *International Journal of Digital Curation, 6*(1), 1297–1298. doi:10.2218/ijdc.v6i1.172

Foundation. (2011a). *Grants: Gov application guide*. Retrieved from http://www.nsf.gov

Foundation. (2011a). *The open data foundation*. Retrieved from http://www.opendatafoundation.org/

Foundation. (2011b). *Apache POI - The Java API for microsoft documents*. Retrieved from http://poi.apache.org/

Foundation. (2011b). *NSF data management plan requirements*. Retrieved from http://www.nsf.gov/eng/general/dmp.jsp

Glasgow, & Centre. (2011). *Data asset framework - Implementation guide JISC*. Glasgow, UK: Academic Press.

Glass, G. V. (1986). Sharing research data. *Contemporary Psychology, 31*(10), 774–775.

Hanson, B. (2011). Making data maximally available. *Science, 331*(6018), 649. doi:10.1126/science.1203354

Hey, A. (2009). *The fourth paradigm: Data-intensive scientific discovery*. New York, NY: Microsoft Research.

Hey, A. J. G., & Trefethen, A. E. (2003). *The data deluge: An e-science perspective*. New York, NY: Wiley and Sons.

Holzner, A., & Mele, S. (2009). *Data preservation, re-use and (open) access: A case study in high-energy physics*. Retrieved from http://www.parse-insight.eu/downloads/PARSEInsight_event200909_casestudy_HEP.pdf

Information. (2011a). *About NCBI*. Retrieved December 2011, from http://www.ncbi.nlm.nih.gov/About/index.html

Information. (2011b). *Basic local alignment search tool*. Retrieved December 2011, from http://blast.ncbi.nlm.nih.gov/Blast.cgi

Initiative. (2011). *Open archives initiative - Frequently asked questions (FAQ)*. Retrieved from http://www.openarchives.org/documents/FAQ.html

Jennifer, T. (2011). Future-proofing: The academic library's role in e-research support. *Library Management, 32*(1/2), 37–47. doi:10.1108/01435121111102566

Jones, S. (2009). *Data audit framework methodology*. Glasgow, UK: University of Glasgow.

Michigan. (2011). *Inter-university consortium for political and social research*. Retrieved December 2011, from http://www.icpsr.umich.edu/icpsrweb/ICPSR/access/index.jsp

Norman, C. (1985). Sharing research data urged. *Science, 229*(4714), 632. doi:10.1126/science.229.4714.632

Plugin, J. G. (2011). *jQuery grid plugin - Grid plugin*. Retrieved from http://www.trirand.com/blog/

Porto, U. (2011). *Open repository and thematic repository - Repositorio.up.pt*. Retrieved from http://repositorio.up.pt/repos.html

Rice, R. (2007). *DISC-UK DataShare: Data sharing continuum*. Retrieved November, 2011, from http://www.disc-uk.org/docs/data_sharing_continuum.pdf

Services. (2004). *Data sharing - Frequently asked questions*. Retrieved December, 2011, from http://grants.nih.gov/grants/policy/data_sharing/data_sharing_faqs.htm - 898

Services. (2011). *Australian national data service website*. Retrieved November 20, 2011, from http://ands.org.au

Tonge, A., & Morgan, P. (2007). *SPECTRa - Submission, preservation and exposure of chemistry teaching and research data*. Cambridge, UK: Cambridge University.

Williams, S. (2000). *The associative model of data*. New York, NY: Lazy Software.

ENDNOTES

1. Humanities Advanced Technology and Information Institute.
2. Digital Curation Centre (http://www.dcc.ac.uk/).
3. Joint Information Systems Committee.
4. http://sciencedata.up.pt/dspace
5. http://sciencedata.up.pt/doc
6. Geographical Information System.
7. For, Let, Where, Order By, Return.
8. JavaScript Object Notation.

Chapter 11
Using Semantics in XML Information Access:
Application to the Portuguese Emigration Museum

Flavio Xavier Ferreira
University of Minho, Portugal

Pedro Rangel Henriques
University of Minho, Portugal

Alda Lopes Gancarski
Institut Telecom, France

ABSTRACT

This chapter presents an ongoing work in the context of the Portuguese Emigration Museum about information access in XML collections associated with semantic information. The museum asset is made up of documents of more than 8 kinds, ranging from passport records to photos/cards and building-drawings. In this chapter, the authors discuss the approach used to create the exhibition rooms of the virtual Web-based museum. Each room consists of the information contained in those single or interrelated resources. The information exhibited in each room is described by an ontology, written in OWL. The authors also discuss the approach used to take advantage of a combination of structural and semantic information to efficiently retrieve documents from the MEC collection. Both approaches can be automatised to allow a very systematic way to deal with the huge and rich museum assets.

INTRODUCTION

This chapter introduces a system that addresses the task of accessing information contained in XML documents of the Portuguese Emigration Museum ("Museu da Emigração e das Comunidades," MEC, in www.museu-emigrantes.org).

This system has two approaches. One approach uses ontologies to specify different views over the information, and then offer navigation functionalities to explore them, using context sensitive behaviour. The second approach uses a query system that takes advantage of a combination of structural and semantic information contained in the museum archive.

DOI: 10.4018/978-1-4666-2669-0.ch011

Fafe, as many other Portuguese towns and villages, mainly at the north, has a huge cultural heritage characterising the social phenomena of emigration (especially to Brazil) along the nineteenth and first half of twentieth centuries.

In this context, Miguel Monteiro, supported by the staff of Fafe's Town Hall (via Cultural Department), started some years ago collecting information from passport governmental records into a database and soon aroused the idea to gather all sorts of documentation into a repository and create a Web-based virtual museum that makes easily accessible this rich cultural heritage. This kind of museum is important and interesting for Emigrants and their descendants as well as for Historian researching in that area, and of course for the general public. The Museum was born in 2001; its material was inherited mainly from official documents or personal writings reporting on the departure, travel, and stay abroad, but there are also a large number of assets bearing witness to the less usual phenomena of emigrants' *return*. Besides the documents, a large set of buildings (private or public, professional or philanthropic, and other non-physical evidences) left by the emigrants around the country can be also considered assets.

At the moment MEC virtual rooms are handmade, making them difficult to maintain and to add new information, and most important, lacking a systematic way for information acquisition, treatment and exhibition. In addition, some inconsistencies are evident from room to room but even inside the same room.

This fact gave the motivation for the project here reported, that aims to build a systematic approach for the acquisition, archiving, treatment, and exploration of the Museum's documental resources. In our perspective, each room is seen just as a specific view over a common information repository. The repository should be a digital archive (in database format or as a collection of XML files) of all the information resources referred above as museum's assets. Each view (the

knowledge enclosed in the respective room) can be specified by an ontology, as traditionally done by philosophers to organise the discourse over a certain closed-world. The extraction process can be automatised adopting a standard notation for the ontology description; moreover, the Web page that implements the user-interface in each room can also be automatically built.

Along the chapter, we will describe the research work exploring RDF/OWL to define the semantics associated to the XML information of the MEC. The W3C proposal for semantic descriptions is the Resource Description Framework (RDF) (Manola & Miller, 2004). RDF Schema (RDFS) (Brickley & Guha, 2004) is an extension to RDF that contains the basic builders for the description of ontologies. RDFS has some limitations as a standalone ontology language (does not allow for example the equivalence between two objects or two classes). To overcome these deficiencies, the W3C defined the Web Ontology Language (OWL), which is now the standard for ontologies definition.

Structured query languages are currently being used to retrieve information from both XML documents and semantic descriptions. To query XML documents, XPath (Berglund, et al., 2007) and XQuery (Boag, et al., 2007) were proposed by the W3C. In XQuery, the user can base his query not only on the textual contents of documents, but also from their structure. The result of a query is the set of structural elements that satisfy all the restrictions of the query.

To access semantic information three methods can be used: a simple expression in natural language (Finin, et al., 2005); through a navigation structure (Fluit, et al., 2005), or using a dedicated query language like SPARQL (Corby, et al., 2004). The SPARQL query language was defined by the W3C to find information in RDF descriptions (Prud'hommeaux & Seaborn, 2007).

Accessing information over resources is generally made directly on the documents or indirectly on semantic descriptions to find the associated resources, thus not mixing the resources and their semantics during research. Gançarski et al. (2008) suggest the use, not only of XML documents, but also their semantic descriptions to search for information, supposing that both can be interesting to the user, helping him to find the desired information. In this chapter, we want to explore the access to XML information by taking into account documents and their associated semantics.

This chapter is organised as follows. We start by introducing the Portuguese Emigration Museum, the ontology concept and the most used standards for ontology description. Then we present the ontology describing the MEC information resources (the Museum's assets) that are the basis for all the exhibition rooms and give the motivation to our work and proposal. Afterwards we describe MusVis, the extraction and navigation component of our system; its architecture is defined and technical implementation details are provided. We then explore the approach to document retrieval combining XQuery with SPARQL in an interactive environment. The chapter ends with the traditional remarks and future work.

THE INFORMATION SYSTEM OF THE PORTUGUESE EMIGRATION MUSEUM

The MEC is a Web-museum (although it also has physical headquarters and some exhibitions), that gathers knowledge, and resources about the Portuguese emigration.

The MEC wants to discover and show the effects of mixing people and cultures, in the social, cultural and economical history of Portugal. It focus, mainly on the past Portuguese migration to Africa and the more recent emigration to Brazil (19th and 1st half of 20th century) and to Europe (2nd half of the 20th century), but it is by no means restricted to them[1].

The MEC assets are vast and multifaceted due the fact that emigration documents and objects come from the most diversified sources, ranging from official government records to old newspapers and photo albums. The document types are themselves heterogeneous (from official travel reports to local stories). Some documents were converted to an electronic format (plain ASCII text, Ms-Word, Ms-Excel, Ms-Access, HTML, etc.), but many others are still in paper format stored in Archives and Libraries.

This tremendous amount of resources and their variety gives the MEC an enormous potentiality as a museum, but at the same time, it is very difficult to organise and display all this information in a straightforward way. In order to overcome this problem the sources of information (the so-called museum's assets) were catalogued. The conceptual map (a graph of concepts) in Figure 1 shows the organisation of the sources and the types of the documents (ellipses denote document types). Based on that classification, we have defined (using XSD) an XML format to enable the encoding of those documents to a structured (annotated) digital format, adequate for archiving and subsequent processing. We are also developing an editor to assist the acquisition phase and the creation of the XML files.

ONTOLOGIES AND THEIR NOTATION

An ontology is originally a philosophic concept concerned with the study of being or existence and forms the basic subject matter of metaphysics. In computer science, an ontology represents a set of concepts and their relations in a given domain; it can also be used to infer knowledge and information about the domain's objects (Gruber, 1993).

Technically speaking, an ontology is defined by a set of classes, individuals, attributes, and relations. Classes or concepts are abstract sets of objects, which can contain other individuals and other classes (subclasses). Individuals or instances are the actual objects we want to represent (e.g.

Figure 1. MEC ontology

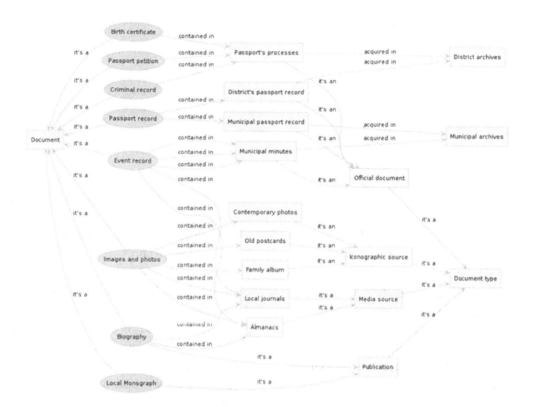

people, animals, numbers, Web pages, etc.). The ontology objects can be described using attributes where each attribute is a name/value pair. Relations are connections between the ontology objects and allow the representation of concepts and the creation of associations within the ontology objects. In the example shown in Figure 2, we can identify the classes Vehicle, Car, Truck and Place; and the individuals China and Opel Corsa; the licence plate 12-31-AA can be seen as an attribute; and there are also the relations built-in, subclass-of and instance-of.

To use ontologies in the MEC we still need a specific notation to write them. There are several ontology description languages available (Corcho & Gomez-Perez, 2000), but our attention (in the next subsections) goes to: World WideWeb Consortium (W3C) standards Resource Description

Framework (RDF), RDF Schema (RDFS), and Web Ontology Language (OWL). All three are part of the W3C semantic Web effort[2].

OWL was chosen to represent the ontologies for the MEC, but OWL is not a standalone technology, it beneffts and uses many RDF and RDFS constructs, and is considered an extension of these languages. As such, we will take a deeper look into those three W3C recommendations.

RDF and RDFS

RDF language was design as metadata model, but is largely used as a general method for modeling information. RDF metadata model is based upon the idea of making statements about resources in the form of subject-predicate-object expressions, called triples in the RDF terminology.

Figure 2. An ontology example

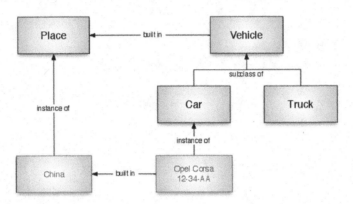

A RDF resource is any data or information source we want to describe. It can be anything from physical objects to Web resources (e.g. a city, a database, a Web page, etc.). A resource is always represented using a Universal Resource Identifier (URI). The URI does not need to be on a Web accessible path, nor has any normalisation rules; it will just suffice that its meaning is known by the reading application.

The subject is the resource we are describing. The predicate or property denotes a characteristic and expresses a relation between the subject and the object; it is represented by a RDF resource. The value or object is represented either by a literal string or a resource (Librelotto, 2007). As an example, the sentence "Ana lives in Portugal" in RDF, is the triple "Ana" (subject), "lives in"

(predicate) and "Portugal" (object). This example is defined using RDF/XML[3] (shown in Algorithm 1).

RDFS is a RDF extension, which allows the definition of classes of resources, restrictions, and properties over RDF, in a way that establishes the application vocabulary. Figure 3 illustrates this new abstraction layer over RDF.

RDFS adds some constructs to the RDF language like, rdfs:Class, rdfs:subClassOf, rdf:Property, they allow the creation of a class hierarchy. The RDFS description for the sample sentence used above ("Ana lives in Portugal") is written in Algorithm 2.

RDFS has some limitations as a standalone ontology language because: there is no distinction between the language constructs and the ontol-

Algorithm 1. Example

```
1 <rdf:RDF
2 xmlns:rdf="http://www.w3.org/1999/02/22/rdf-syntax-ns#"
3 xmlns:pro="http://people.org/predicates#">
4
5 <rdf:Description rdf:about="http://people.org/Ana">
6 <pro:livesin>
7 <rdf:Description rdf:about="http://countries.org/Portugal"/>
8 </pro:livesin>
9 </rdf:Description>
10 </rdf:RDF>
```

Figure 3. A RDF statement and its corresponding RDF schema

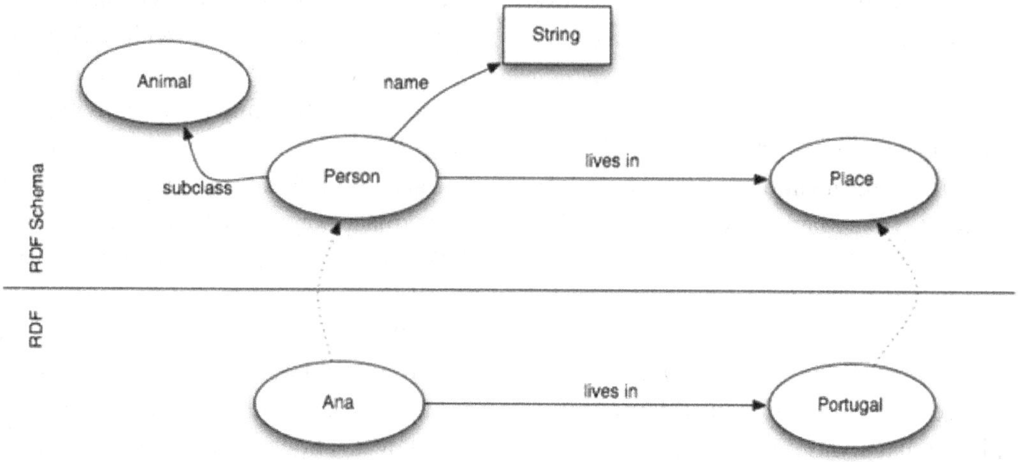

Algorithm 2. "Ana lives in Portugal"

```
1  <rdf:RDF
2  xmlns:rdf-"http://www.w3.org/1999/02/22/rdf-syntax-ns#"
3  xmlns:rdfs="http://www.w3.org/2000/01/rdf-schema#"
4  xml:base="http://people.org/rdf#">
5
6  <rdfs:Classrdf:ID="Animal" />
7  <rdfs:Classrdf:ID="Person">
8  <rdfs:subClassOfrdf:resource="#Animal"/>
9  </rdfs:Class>
10 <rdfs:Classrdf:ID="Place"/>
11
12 <rdf:Propertyrdf:ID="livesin">
13 <rdfs:rangerdf:resource="#Place"/>
14 <rdfs:domainrdf:resource="#Person"/>
15 </rdf:Property>
16 <rdf:PropertyID="name">
17 <rdfs:rangerdf:resource="rdfs:Literal"/>
18 <rdfs:domainrdf:resource="#Person"/>
19 </rdf:Property>
20
21 <Personrdf:ID="Ana">
22 <name>Ana</name>
23 <livesin>
24 <Placerdf:ID="Portugal"/>
25 </livesin>
26 </Person>
27 </rdf:RDF>
```

ogy vocabulary; it does not allow the definition of class and property restrictions; thus, it is too weak to describe resources in detail[4] (Librelotto, 2007).

The example listed above is written in the RDFS abbreviated format; the extended format is much similar to the notation of RDF. However, both formats have the same meaning.

OWL

The OWL was created on the top of RDF and RDFS as a language for the represention of Web ontologies. This language was designed to be used by applications that process the information content instead of just presenting it to humans (Horrocks & Patel-Schneider, 2003; Librelotto, 2007).

An OWL ontology includes class descriptions, along with their associated properties and instances, as well as related restrictions. Algorithm 3 is an example of an OWL description written according to RDF/XML syntax.

As can be seen in the listing above, an OWL file starts with *namespace* declarations, followed by the owl:Ontology element; this element contains the ontology URI (line 10), generic informations about the ontology (rdfs:comment – line 11), version control (owl:priorVersion) and imported ontologies (owl:imports – line 12).

OWL uses the constructs owl:Class (lines 15 and 16) and rdfs:subClassOf (line 17) to represent classes and subclasses. Ontology relations are defined in OWL by the owl:ObjectProperty element (lines 20 and 23). Ontology attributes are defined by owl:DatatypeProperty (line 28). This element relates a OWL class to an XML Schema (XSD) datatype. In OWL, the individuals are created using the class identifiers (lines 35 and 37).

The code presented above is a straitforward example, but there are some things to consider: the usage of the elements rdfs:domain (lines 22 and 30) and rdfs:range (lines 21 and 29) within owl:ObjectProperty to define the domain and range of a property; the element owl:inverseOf (line

25) allows the definition of inverse properties; the declaration of the individual Portugal (line 37) is inside another individual Ana (line 35), which is completely valid and serves to show the OWL syntax flexibility; the individual Portugal (line 37) does not belong to a local class (Place), in fact this individual belongs to the ontology http://places.org/places, this happens because in OWL it is possible to extend existing ontologies in other files.

OWL also offers various other elements such as owl:Restriction, owl:cardinality, owl:intersectionOf and owl:disjointWith, they allow restrictions, cardinality, class intersection and disjoint classes respectively. They, along with other elements such as owl:TransitiveProperty, owl:SymmetricProperty, owl: FunctionalProperty, and owl:FunctionalInverseProperty are specialised types of owl:ObjectProperty.

In the same listing, it can also be noticed that the addressof property is not present in the individual Portugal, but it could be inferred from its inverse (the livesin property) by using an OWL reasoner. A reasoner is a tool that produces valid logical conclusions about an ontology.

OWL has three sub-languages, OWL Lite, OWL DL, OWL Full. OWL lite is the most simple as it uses only a subset of OWL constructs, therefore is very simple to implement. OWL Full is the full language without any semantic restrictions, it is very close to RDFS. We used OWL DL because it is an intermediate solution, which is very expressive, but also maintains a computable completeness and decidability (Horrocks & Patel-Schneider, 2003).

USING ONTOLOGIES TO CREATE MUSEUM ROOMS

The MEC needs a simple and organised way to show its assets to the public. For that purpose, we created theme oriented museum exhibitionrooms, or as we call them, views. Those views are

Algorithm 3. OWL description

```
1 <rdf:RDF
2 xmlns:="http://people.org/owl#"
3 xmlns:per="http://people.org/owl#"
4 xmlns:pla="http://places.org/places#"
5 xmlns:rdf="http://www.w3.org/1999/02/22-rdf-syntax-ns#"
6 xmlns:owl="http://www.w3.org/2002/07/owl#"
7 xmlns:xsd="http://www.w3.org/2001/XMLSchema#"
8 xmlns:rdfs="http://www.w3.org/2000/01/rdf-schema#">
9
10 <owl:Ontologyrdf:about="http://people.org/owl">
11 <rdfs:comment>This document contains the class definition of people and
animals, the reproperties and some instances.</rdfs:comment>
12 <owl:importsrdf:resource="http://places.org/places"/>
13 </owl:Ontology>
14
15 <owl:Classrdf:ID="Animal"/>
16 <owl:Classrdf:ID="Person">
17 <owl:subClassOfrdf:resource="#Animal"/>
18 </owl:Class>
19
20 <owl:ObjectPropertyrdf:ID="livesin">
21 <rdfs:rangerdf:resource=pla:#Place"/>
22 <rdfs:doainrdf:resource="#Person"/>
23 </owl:ObjectProperty>
24 <owl:ObjectPropertyrdf:ID="addressof">
25 <owl:inverseOfrdf:resource="#livesin"/>
26 </owl:Ob jectProperty>
27
28 <owl:DatatypePropertyrdf:ID="name">
29 <rdfs:rangerdf:resource="xsd:#string"/>
30 <rdfs:domain>
31 <owl:Classrdf:about="#Person"/>
32 </rdfs:domain>
33 </owl:DatatypeProperty>
34
35 <Personrdf:ID="Ana">
36 <livesin>
37 <pla:Placerdf:ID="Portugal"/>
38 </livesin>
39 <name>Ana</name>
40 </Person>
41 </rdf:RDF>
```

described in a rigorous way by means of semantic networks, this is, concept maps. This is a new approach, that uses related information gathered from the various information sources rather than just showing each one of them (Figure 4). This approach allows the user to browse in an interactive and differentiated way through the information, and also allows the user to create more than one perspective over the same information. Views are represented by ontologies. Therefore, an OWL ontology is defined for each created view. For each view there is only one ontology, however many OWL files per view can exist (the definition file, and many files with individuals).

Each view is intended to focus in a particular aspect or theme, for instance:

- **Emigrants by Date:** View that shows, for a given time interval, all the known emigrants and associated data.
- **Event Surroundings:** Taking as input an event in the life of a given emigrant (ex. departure), this view will show information about the physical and social surrounding environment at the epoch and place where the event occurred.
- **Emigrant's Places (V1):** View that reports on the different places of emigration cycle (birth, departure, arrival, etc.).

We now take a closer look at this last view and its specification. V1 shows the main events of the emigrant's life and their location, along with images of the events and places. That information is retrieved from passport petitions, passport records, birth certificates, criminal records, events records, and images, postal cards and photos, as can be seen in Figure 5.

Figure 5 shows the ontology specification, i. e. classes, their properties and attributes. Analysing this ontology, it is clear that the Emigrant class is the centrepiece, followed by the Event, Place and Image classes. These four classes represent the main idea of V1: *the emigrant, the events occurring during his life, the places where those events happened, and the emigrant, events, and places images.*

MusVis: AN ONTOLOGY NAVIGATION SYSTEM FOR THE

Museum Visitors

In this section, our ontology navigation system (MusVis) is presented.

MusVis is more than a browser, it is a modular software system that allows the automatic construction of the museum exhibition rooms, based on the following principal: having gathered all the MEC basic information (provided by the various

Figure 4. The ontology and resources planes interaction

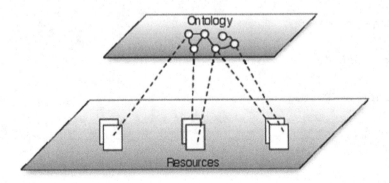

Figure 5. V1 ontology (inverse properties are not represented in the image)

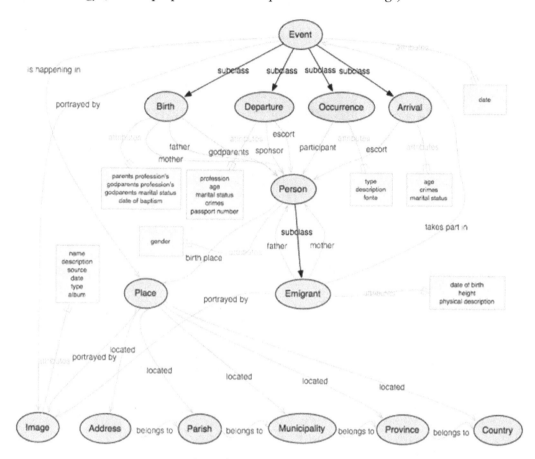

sources) into one single repository, and using an ontology to describe the knowledge that should be exposed in each room, extract from the repository the concrete data to instantiate the abstract ontology and create a Web-based navigator over that data guided by the ontology relations.

The MusVis architecture is presented in Figure 6; the core is made up of four main modules, each with a specific data transformation task, as will be described in detail below. Some extra modules were added to improve the Users' Interaction: a Context Adaptor, in the museum front-end side, to make the visits to the exhibition rooms easier; and two Query Processors, in the back-end side, to facilitate the searches over the museum repository making the document retrieval more powerful.

The MEC assets are multifaceted, so a common digital file format for the various documents presented in Figure 1 was needed: XML markup language was elected. An XML-Schema was defined for each type of document, setting up the XML tags that can be used each time a new document has to be added to the Museum's digital repository.

The Data Acquisition module assists in this task; it is similar to a graphical text editor and allows an historian to translate and markup documents. The markup is done by means of colours and symbols, always hiding the XML backend from the historian. This module is based upon previous work developed inside our research group (Rafael Félix, 2002; Flavio Ferreira, et al., 2007).

Figure 6. The MusVis architecture

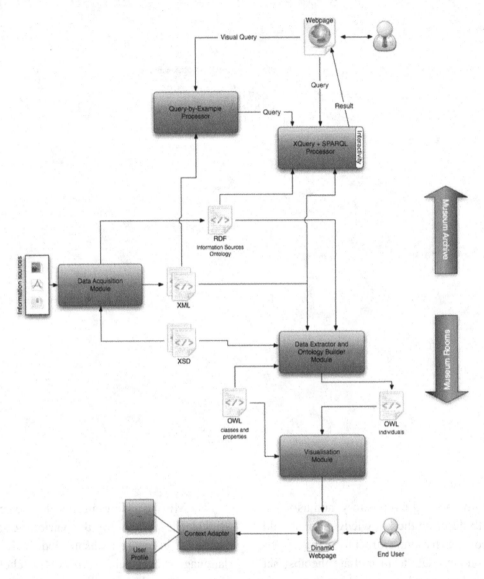

The Extractor module is responsible for indexing and organising in a common repository all the information obtained from the XML files created in the previous module.

The data model chosen for the information repository allows a straightforward implementation of the next module, the Ontology Builder as an information retrieval system.

The Ontology Builder module is responsible, as said above, for the creation of MEC ontologies

that support each museum's room. This module is view specific which means that needs a different instantiation (although with a similar behaviour) for each view. Taking into account the ontology definition (classes, properties, etc.) and the view specific input, it extracts all the information relevant to set up that view, and creates the ontology individuals with the information repository data.

Finally, the Visualisation module traverses the semantic network (corresponding to the ontology that describes the exhibition rooms), and outputs or displays the ontology content (actually, the information intended to be exhibited in that room).

The Visualisation module accomplishes this by using the ontology data and a set of standard presentation rules to generate a set of dynamic Web pages (JSP); the rules are also customizable. Those pages are entity-oriented, and centred on the attributes and connections of each individual.

Figure 7, a screenshot of V1, illustrates such a Webpage; it is precisely the Webpage generated by MusVis from the V1 ontology presented in Figure 5.

The first three modules update the ontologies with new instances, or concept occurrences, every time a XML file is added to the repository; the new data, integrated automatically, will also be visualised immediately because the last module, responsible for generating the pages, retrieves the information from the ontologies dynamically, without any previous configuration.

All the modules of MusVis are implemented in Java. JAXP (Java API for XML Processing) framework is used to parse (with Saxon) and process XML (using XPath). Jena OWL framework with Pellet as a reasoner, for RDF/OWL processing. Sqlite is used for the database.

Working environments are: Protege for OWL editing; XMLSpy to create XSD and XML documents; and Eclipse for Java programming.

MEC ARCHIVE COMPONENT

The museum archive component (above referred to as the museum back-end or back-office), allows the exploration of the information resources using diverse and complex queries. This kind of functionalities is useful for researchers, and is not meaningful for common visitors. The information access that we propose to apply in the MEC back-office is based in the iterative and semantic approach proposed in (Gancarski, et al., 2008) This approach combines XQuery and SPARQL query languages in a more expressive one.

In the following, we introduce XQuery and SPARQL languages. Then, we explain the semantic search using both query languages and its

Figure 7. A MusVis screenshot

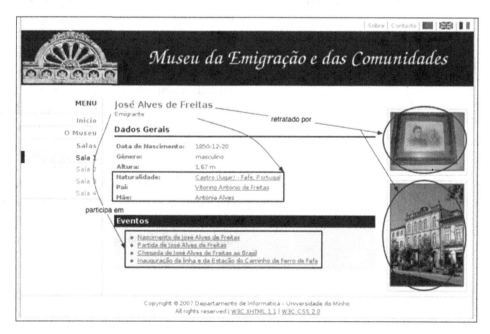

application to MEC. Finally, the iterative feature of the retrieval system is presented, together with the query specification interface.

XQuery is formed by expressions of several kinds, including XPath location paths and *for.. let..where..order by..return* (FLWOR) expressions based on typical database query languages, such as SQL. To pass information from one operator to another, variables are used. As an example, assume a document that stores information about articles, including title, author, and publisher. Algorithm 4 returns articles of author Kevin ordered by the respective title.

XQuery operates in the abstract, logical structure of an XML document, rather than in its surface syntax. The corresponding data model represents documents as trees where nodes correspond to a document, an element, an attribute, a textual block, a namespace, a processing instruction, or a comment. Each node has a unique identity.

Similar to XQuery, SPARQL query language allows the search for information inside RDF descriptions. To illustrate a SPARQL query, consider Algorithm 5.

To get products with a price greater than 100, the SPARQL query is shown in Algorithm 6.

Algorithm 4. Kevin ordered by title

```
for $a in /articles/article
where $a/author = "Kevin"
order by $a/title
return $a
```

Algorithm 5. SPARQL query

```
Product1.xml   price      10.
Product2.xml   price     290.
Product3.xml   price     300.
```

Algorithm 6. SPARQL query with price greater than 100

```
SELECT     ?p
WHERE (?p price ?u)   AND ?u > 100
```

In this query, variable *?p* stores products which price is given by variable *?u*. The restriction over variable *?u* filters products with an adequate price.

Information Access using Semantics

When an XML document is associated to semantic descriptions in RDF format, Gançarski and Henriques (2007) suggest the use of SPARQL queries inside XQuery, yielding the language they call XQuery+SPARQL.

To show an example, let us consider a visitor wishing to explore MEC's resources. Suppose he is interested in searching for travelling details registered in Fafe related to the emigrant *Antonio Serra*; the details considered below are the date of departure and the destination (target country). Travelling information is obtained accessing passport records (remember MEC ontology in Figure 1); an excerpt of a simplified record of this kind is shown in Algorithm 7.

The XQuery+SPARQL query that yields to the desired information is shown in Algorithm 8.

In this query, variable $d stores the passport records elements of the document (line 1) of "Antonio Serra" (line 2). In the metadata clause of this query, the SPARQL query (lines 4 to 10) searches for documents contained in municipal passport records (stored in variable ?p) that were acquired in Fafe. The content of variable $d in the external XQuery statement is intersected with the content of the ?d variable in internal SPARQL query, yielding the set of desired answer.

Algorithm 7. Simplified record

```
<passportRecord  ...> ...
    <name>Antonio Serra</name> ...
    <place of="destination">Brasil</place>
    <place of="source">Portugal</place>...
    <date normDate="1866-11-13">...</date>
</passportRecord>
```

Algorithm 8. XQuery+SPARQL query

```
1   for $d in doc("passportRecords.xml")//passportRecord
2   where $d/name = "Antonio Serra"
3   metadata $d in
4     select ?d
5     where {
6         ?d   rdf:type   Passport_Record   .
7         ?d   contained_in   ?p .
8         ?p   rdf:type   Municipal_passport_record .
9         ?p   acquired_in Fafe .
10    }
11  return $d(place | date/@normDate)
```

Iterative Information Access

Suppose, now, the visitor is interested in searching for images and photos related to some family he knows. Let us assume a user from the city of *Braga*.

Family photos can be found in the respective family album. Identifiers such as "Freitas_Fam_Album" for the "Freitas" family represent instances of family albums.

Image and photo documents have a structure/content similar to Algorithm 9.

In the metadata clause, the list of identifiers of the family albums found is displayed, as the answer computed in the third triple pattern of the SPARQL query (stored in *variable ?f*). The visitor may, then, immediately identify those belonging to families he knows. He can, then, select those albums using the *msf:select* function associated to the FILTER clause. In this query, the user selected albums from *"Freitas"* and *"Silva"* families.

The iterative XQuery+SPARQL information search engine should be completed with an user-friendly interface to help users specify their needs. To accomplish that idea, the interface under development provides capabilities to:

- Specify an XQuery query using a query-by-example mechanism. Looking at a sample document, chosen from the collection, the user may select the interesting elements and make filters over them.
- Specify a *metadata* clause in the XQuery statement to insert a SPARQL query. The results of this query are intersected with the one in the XQuery external query.
- Specify a SPARQL query navigating on the ontology shown in Figure 1. While writing the SPARQL triples, nodes in the ontology may be selected with a simple click on the ontology graphical representation.

Algorithm 9. Image and photo document structure

```
<image>
    <name>Family address of José Freitas</name>...
    <city>Braga</city>
    <date normDate="1885-01-01">…</date>
    <img>http://.../jose_freitas.jpg</img>   ...
</image>
```

Then, the query satisfying the current example is shown in Algorithm 10.

Algorithm 10. Query satisfying example

```
for $i in doc("image1.xml")/image
where $i/city ="Braga"
metadata $i in
select ?i
where {
    ?i rdf:type Images_and_photos  .
    ?i contained_in ?f .
    ?f rdf:type Family_album .
    FILTER msf:select(?f, (Freitas_Fam_Album, Silva_Fam_Album))
    }
return $i/img
```

CONCLUSION

After many years of cooperation with the MEC and many fruitful discussions, after many theoretical studies and different technological trials, and after various prototypes, we came up with an ontology-based approach to manage the assets of MEC and to automatize the construction of the rooms of a virtual museum.

In that context, in this chapter, we have defended the idea that the virtual exhibition rooms are no more than structured views over the documents of the Emigration Museum digital archive (its assets). Although it was assumed along the chapter that the repository is made up from XML documents, if a subset of them is supported in databases, or whatever digital format, the approach can be the same. In addition, ontologies assumed to be described by OWL documents, can be represented in their XML standard notation or using a traditional database.

Future work goes in two directions. On one hand, more implementation work should be done to finish the first and last modules, the Data Acquisition and the Visualiser. Additionally, some extra analysis must be made to improve the automatisation process. After that, MusVis can be deployed and real tests carried on to measure its performance, effective impact and usability. On the other hand, other views (than V1 that was used in our prototype and described in the chapter) should be specified, in order to build the ontologies and generate the respective rooms. It is a crucial step for corroborating the proposed approach.

The museum archive component, included in the architecture proposed, opens the possibility for a sophisticated information search engine. This search is specified in a new query language, a combination of XQuery and SPARQL that we are developing. Due to the complexity of query formulation, an ergonomic, user-friendly, and simple to use interface is being studied. It includes mechanisms such as query-by-example and graphical ontology navigation.

REFERENCES

Berglund, A., Boag, S., Chamberlin, D., Fernandez, M., Kay, M., Robie, J., & Siméon, J. (2007). *XML path language (XPath) 2.0*. Retrieved from http://www.w3.org/TR/xpath20/

Boag, S., Chamberlin, D., Fernandez, M., Florescu, D., Robie, J., & Siméon, J. (2007). *XQuery 1.0: An XML query language*. Retrieved from http://www.w3.org/TR/xquery/

Bouzeghoub, A., Do, K. N., & Lecocq, C. (2007). Contextual adaptation of learning resources. In *Proceedings of IADIS International Conference Mobile Learning*. IADIS.

Bray, T., Paoli, J., Sperberg-McQueen, C., Maler, E., & Yergeau, F. (2006). *Extensible markup language (XML) 1.0* (4th ed). Retrieved from http://www.w3.org/TR/2006/REC-xml-20060816/

Brikley, D., & Guha, R. (2004). *RDF vocabulary description language 1.0: RDF schema*. Retrieved from http://www.w3.org/TR/rdf-schema/

Burrell, J., & Gay, G. K. (2002). E-graffiti: Evaluating real-world use of a context-aware system. *Interacting with Computers*, *14*(4), 301–312. doi:10.1016/S0953-5438(02)00010-3

Chabeb, Y. (2002). *Introduction aux systèmes sensibles au contexte pour la découverte de services*. Paper presented at Dans les Journées Recherche du Département Informatique, Telecom et Management Sud. Paris, France.

Corby, O., Dieng-Kuntz, R., & Faron-Zucker, C. (2004). *Querying the semantic web with corese search engine*. Paper presented at 3rd Prestigious Applications Intelligent Systems Conference (PAIS). Valencia, Spain.

Corcho, O., & Gomez-Perez, A. (2000). A roadmap to ontology specification languages. In *Proceedings of the 12th International Conference Knowledge Engineering and Knowledge Management: Methods, Models, and Tools*. IEEE.

Fallside, D., & Walmsley, P. (2004). *XML schema part 0: Primer second edition*. Retrieved from http://www.w3.org/TR/xmlschema-0/

Félix, R. (2002). *Sistemas de digitalização e anotação de documentos. Technical Report*. Minho, Portugal: Universidade do Minho.

Ferreira, F. X., & Henriques, P. R. (2008). *Using OWL to specify and build different views over the emigration museum resources*. Paper presented at the National Conference XML Aplicações e Tecnologias Associadas 2008 (XATA 2008). Évora, Portugal.

Ferreira, F. X., Pacheco, H., & Vilas-Boas, J. (2007). *PDA's no levantamento de informação em arquivos históricos. Technical Report*. Minho, Portugal: Universidade do Minho.

Finin, T., Ding, L., Pan, R., Joshi, A., Kolari, P., Java, A., & Peng, Y. (2005). *Swoogle: Searching for knowledge on the semantic web*. Paper presented at the National Conference on Artificial Intelligence (AAAI) 2005, Intelligent Systems demo. Pittsburgh, PA.

Fluit, C., Sabou, M., & Harmelen, F. (2005). Ontology-based information visualization: Towards semantic web applications. In Geroimenks, V. (Ed.), *Visualising the Semantic Web* (2nd ed.). Berlin, Germany: Springer Verlag. doi:10.1007/1-84628-290-X_3

Gançarski, A. L., Ferreira, F. X., & Henriques, P. R. (2008). Iterative XML search based on data and associated semantics. In *Proceedings of International Conference on Web Information Systems (ICEIS)*. ICEIS.

Gruber, T. R. (2003). A translation approach to portable ontology specifications. *Knowledge Acquisition, 5*(2), 199–220. doi:10.1006/knac.1993.1008

Horrocks, I., & Patel-Schneider, P. F. (2003). Reducing OWL entailment to description logic satisfiability. In *Proceedings of the International Semantic Web Conference (ISWC)*, (pp. 17-29). ISWC.

Librelotto, G. R. (2007). *Topic maps: Da sintaxe à semântica*. (PhD Thesis). University of Minho. Minho, Portugal.

Librelotto, G. R., Ramalho, J. C., & Henriques, P. R. (2006). *Topic maps aplicados ao sistema de informação do Museu da Emigração*. Paper presented at XML: Aplicações e Tecnologias Associadas: Actas da 4.ª Conferência Nacional. Portalegre, Portugal.

Manola, F., & Miller, E. (2004). *RDF primer*. Retrieved from http://www.w3.org/TR/rdf-primer/

Prud'hommeaux, E., & Seaborn, A. (2008). *SPARQL query language for RDF*. Retrieved from http://www.w3.org/TR/rdfsparqlquery/

KEY TERMS AND DEFINITIONS

Ontology: An ontology formally represents knowledge as a set of concepts within a domain, and the relationships between those concepts. It can be used to reason about the entities within that domain and may be used to describe the domain. An ontology renders shared vocabulary and taxonomy which models a domain with the definition of objects and/or concepts and their properties and relations.

OWL: The Web Ontology Language (OWL) is a family of knowledge representation languages for authoring ontologies. The languages are characterised by formal semantics and RDF/XML-based serializations for the Semantic Web. OWL is endorsed by the W3C and has attracted academic, medical, and commercial interest.

RDF: The Resource Description Framework (RDF) is a family of W3C specifications originally designed as a metadata data model. It has come to be used as a general method for conceptual description or modeling of information that is implemented in Web resources, using a variety of syntax formats.

SPARQL: SPARQL is an RDF query language, that is, a query language for databases, able to retrieve and manipulate data stored in Resource Description Framework format. It was made a standard by the RDF Data Access Working Group (DAWG) of the W3C, and considered as one of the key technologies of semantic Web. On 15 January 2008, SPARQL 1.0 became an official W3C Recommendation.

XML: Extensible Markup Language (XML) is a markup language that defines a set of rules for encoding documents in a format that is both human-readable and machine-readable. It is defined in the XML 1.0 Specification produced by the W3C, and several other related specifications, all gratis open standards.

XML Schema Definition: The XML Schema Definition (XSD) is one of several XML schema languages and it was published as a W3C recommendation in May 2001. Like all XML schema languages, XSD can be used to express a set of rules to which an XML document must conform in order to be considered 'valid' according to that schema.

XQuery: XQuery, an XML Query Language, is a query and functional programming language that is designed to query collections of XML data. XQuery 1.0 was developed by the XML Query working group of the W3C.

ENDNOTES

1   http://www.museu-emigrantes.org/ficha_
     tecnica.htm

2   http://www.w3.org/2001/sw/.

3   http://www.w3.org/TR/rdf-concepts/

4   OWL Web Ontology Language Guide. http://
     www.w3.org/TR/owl-guide/

216

Compilation of References

Albarrak, K. M., & Sibley, E. H. (2009). Translating relational & object-relational database models into OWL models. In *Proceedings of the 10th IEEE International Conference on Information Reuse & Integration*. Las Vegas, NV: IEEE Press.

Anderson, R. (2011). *Can we fix security economics of federated authentication?* Cambridge, UK: University of Cambridge. doi:10.1007/978-3-642-25867-1_4

Antucheviciene, J., Turskis, Z., & Zavadskas, E. K. (2006). Modelling renewal of construction objects applying methods of the game theory. *Technological and Economic Development of Economy, 12*(4), 263–268.

Ardito, C., Costabile, M. F., De Marsico, M., Lanzilotti, R., Levialdi, S., Roselli, T., & Rossano, V. (2006). An approach to usability evaluation of e-learning applications. *Universal Access in the Information Society, 4*, 270–283. doi:10.1007/s10209-005-0008-6

ASPECT. (2011). *EU eContentplus programme's ASPECT (adopting standards and specifications for educational content) best practice network (2008–2011) web site*. Retrieved from http://aspect-project.org/

Auer, S., Dietzold, S., Lehmann, J., Hellmann, S., & Aumueller, D. (2009). Triplify – Light-weight linked data publication from relational databases. In *Proceedings of WWW 2009*. Madrid, Spain: IEEE.

Australia. (2008). *National collaborative research infrastructure strategy*. Retrieved from http://ncris.innovation.gov.au/Pages/default.aspx

Barrasa, J., & Gomez-Perez, A. (2006). Upgrading relational legacy data to the semantic web. In *Proceedings of the 15th International Conference on World Wide Web Conference (WWW 2006)*. Edinburgh, UK: IEEE.

Bartholomaei, M. (2005). *To know is to be: three perspectives on the codification of knowledge*. Sussex, UK: University of Sussex.

Belton, V., & Stewart, T. J. (2002). *Multiple criteria decision analysis: An integrated approach*. Dordrecht, The Netherlands: Kluwer Academic Publishers.

Berglund, A., Boag, S., Chamberlin, D., Fernandez, M., Kay, M., Robie, J., & Siméon, J. (2007). *XML path language (XPath) 2.0*. Retrieved from http://www.w3.org/TR/xpath20/

Berners-Lee, T., Hendler, J., & Lassila, O. (2001). The semantic web. *Scientific American*. doi:10.1038/scientificamerican0501-34

Biron, P. V., & Malhotra, A. (2004). *XML schema part 2: Datatypes* (2nd ed). Retrieved from http://www.w3.org

Bizer, C., & Cyganiak, R. (2007). D2RQ – *Lessons learned*. Paper presented for the W3C Workshop on RDF Access to Relational Databases. Cambridge, MA.

Boag, S., Chamberlin, D., Fernández, M., & Florescu, D. Robie, & Siméon, J. (2010). *XQuery 1.0: An XML query language (second edition)*. W3C Working Draft. Retrieved February 22, 2012, from http://www.w3c.org/TR/xquery

Boekhorst, A., Koers, D., & Kwast, I. (2000). *Informatievaardigheden*. Utrecht, The Netherlands: Uitgeverij Lemma.

Bohere, K., Liu, X., McLaughlin, S., Schonberg, E., & Singh, M. (2003). Object oriented XML query by example. *Lecture Notes in Computer Science, 2814*, 323–329. doi:10.1007/978-3-540-39597-3_32

Böhme, T., & Rahm, E. (2002). XMach-1: A benchmark for XML data management. In *Database Systems in Office, Engineering and Science* (pp. 264–273). Berlin, Germany: Springer-Verlag. doi:10.1007/978-3-642-56687-5_20

Borgman, C. L. (2011). *The conundrum of sharing research data*. Retrieved from http://papers.ssrn.com/sol3/papers.cfm?abstract_id=1869155

Bourret, R. (2005). *XML and databases*. Retrieved from http://www.rpbourret.com/xml/XMLAndDatabases.htm#isxmladatabase

Bouysou, D. (1990). Building criteria: A perquisite for MCDA. In C. A. Bana a Costa (Ed.), *Readings in Multiple Criteria Decision Aid,* (pp. 319-334). Berlin, Germany: Springer-Verlag.

Bouzeghoub, A., Do, K. N., & Lecocq, C. (2007). Contextual adaptation of learning resources. In *Proceedings of IADIS International Conference Mobile Learning*. IADIS.

Braga, D., & Campi, A. (2005). XQBE: A graphical environment to query XML data. *World Wide Web (Bussum)*, *8*(3), 287–316. doi:10.1007/s11280-005-0646-x

Brandl, S., & Keller-Marxer, P. (2007). Long-term archiving of relational databases with chronos. In *Proceedings of the First International Workshop on Database Preservation – PresDB 2007*. PresDB.

Brauers, W. K., & Zavadskas, E. K. (2006). The MOORA method and its application to privatization in a transition economy. *Control and Cybernetics*, *35*(2), 443–468.

Brauers, W. K., Zavadskas, E. K., Peldschus, F., & Turskis, Z. (2008). Multi-objective decision-making for road design. *Transport*, *23*(3), 183–193. doi:10.3846/1648-4142.2008.23.183-193

Bray, T., Paoli, J., Sperberg-McQueen, C., Maler, E., & Yergeau, F. (2006). *Extensible markup language (XML) 1.0* (4th ed). Retrieved from http://www.w3.org/TR/2006/REC-xml-20060816/

Brikley, D., & Guha, R. (2004). *RDF vocabulary description language 1.0: RDF schema*. Retieved from http://www.w3.org/TR/rdf-schema/

Bumans, G., & Cerans, K. (2011). RDB2OWL: A practical approach for transforming RDB data into RDF/OWL. In *Proceedings of the 6th International Conference on Semantic Systems ISEMANTICS*. Retrieved 2011, from http://portal.acm.org/citation.cfm?id=1839739

Burrell, J., & Gay, G. K. (2002). E-graffiti: Evaluating real-world use of a context-aware system. *Interacting with Computers*, *14*(4), 301–312. doi:10.1016/S0953-5438(02)00010-3

Calibrate. (2011). *EU FP6 IST calibrate (calibrating elearning in schools) project (2005 – 2008) web site*. Retrieved from http://calibrate.eun.org

Caudit, E. JISC, & Surf. (2010). *The future of higher education: Beyond the campus*. Retrieved 03-04-2010, from http://net.educause.edu/ir/library/pdf/PUB9008.pdf

CCSDS. (2002). *Reference model for an open archival information system (OAIS) - Blue book*. Washington, DC: National Aeronautics and Space Administration.

Cerbah, F. (2008). Learning highly structured semantic repositories from relational databases: The RDBToOnto tool. In *Proceedings of the 5th European Semantic Web Conference*. IEEE.

CERN. S. I. S. (2011). *Supporting open access publishing*. Retrieved from http://library.web.cern.ch/library/OpenAccess/OpenAccessPolicy.html

Chabeb, Y. (2002). *Introduction aux systèmes sensibles au contexte pour la découverte de services*. Paper presented at Dans les Journées Recherche du Département Informatique, Telecom et Management Sud. Paris, France.

Chang, C., & Sheu, J. (2004). Design and implementation of ad hoc classroom and eschoolbag systems for ubiquitous learning. In *Proceedings of the IEEE International Workshop Wireless and Mobile Technologies in Education*. IEEE Press.

Chen, H., & Wu, Z. (2005). DartGrid III: A semantic grid toolkit for data integration. In *Proceedings of the First International Conference on Semantics, Knowledge, and Grid*. Beijing, China: IEEE.

Chen, Y., et al. (2002). A mobile scaffolding-aid-based bird-watching learning systems. In *Proceedings of the IEEE International Workshop Wireless and Mobile Technologies in Education*. IEEE Press.

Chen, S. Y., Fan, J.-P., & Macredie, R. D. (2006). Navigation in hypermedia learning systems: Experts vs. novices. *Computers in Human Behavior*, *22*, 251–266. doi:10.1016/j.chb.2004.06.004

Christophides, V., & Buneman, P. (2007). Report on the first international workshop on database preservation, PresDB 2007. *SIGMOD Record, 36*(3), 55–58. doi:10.1145/1324185.1324197

Chua, B. B., & Dyson, L. E. (2004). Applying the ISO9126 model to the evaluation of an elearning system. In R. Atkinson, C. McBeath, D. Jonas-Dwyer, & R. Phillips (Eds.), *Beyond the Comfort Zone: Proceedings of the 21st ASCILITE Conference*, (pp. 184-190). Perth, Australia: ASCILITE.

Codd, E. (1970). A relational model of data for large shared data banks. *Communications of the ACM, 13*(6), 377–387. doi:10.1145/362384.362685

Colardyn, D. (2002). From formal education and training to lifelong learning. In Colardyn, D. (Ed.), *Lifelong Learning: Which Ways Forward?* (pp. 17–28). Utrecht, The Netherlands: Lemma.

Cole, J., & Foster, H. (2007). *Using Moodle - Teaching with the popular open source cours management system.* New York, NY: O'Reilly.

Collection, S. W. I. T. C. H. (2008). *The national learning object repository project website.* Retrieved from http://www.switch.ch/it/els/collection/evaluation.html

Consortium, W. (2008). *Extensible markup language (XML) 1.0 (5th ed).* W3C Recommendation. Retrieved from http://www.w3.org

Consultative Committee for Space Data Systems. (2002). *Reference model for an open archival information system (OAIS) – Blue book.* Washington, DC: National Aeronautics and Space Administration.

Corby, O., Dieng-Kuntz, R., & Faron-Zucker, C. (2004). *Querying the semantic web with corese search engine.* Paper presented at 3rd Prestigious Applications Intelligent Systems Conference (PAIS). Valencia, Spain.

Corcho, O., & Gomez-Perez, A. (2000). A roadmap to ontology specification languages. In *Proceedings of the 12th International Conference Knowledge Engineering and Knowledge Management: Methods, Models, and Tools.* IEEE.

Côté, M.-A., Suryn, W., & Georgiadou, E. (2007). In search for a widely applicable and accepted software quality model for software quality engineering. *Software Quality Journal, 15*, 401–416. doi:10.1007/s11219-007-9029-0

Cruz, D., Ferreira, F. X., Henriques, P. R., Gançarski, A. L., & Defude, B. (2009). GuessXQ: An inference web-engine for querying XML documents. In *Proceedings of INForum 2009 - Simpósio de Informática*, (pp. 322-325). Lisboa, Portugal: Faculdade de Ciências da Universidade de Lisboa.

Cullot, N., Ghawi, R., & Yetongnon, K. (2007). DB2OWL: A tool for automatic database-to-ontology mapping. In *Proceedings of 15th Italian Symposium on Advanced Database Systems (SEBD 2007)*, (pp. 491-494). Torre Canne, Italy: SEBD.

Dallas, L. (2008). *XML repositories – If you can't beat 'em – Open source 'em.* Retrieved from http://bigmenoncontent.com/2008/03/26/xml-repositories-if-you-cant-beat-em-open-source-em/

Das, S., Sundara, S., & Cyganiak, R. (2011). *R2RML: RDB to RDF mapping language.* W3C Working Draft. Retrieved from http://www.w3.org

Date, C. J. (2004). *An introduction to database systems* (8th ed.). Reading, MA: Addison Wesley.

Davis, B., Carmean, C., & Wagner, E. D. (2009). *The evolution of the LMS: From management to learning - Deep analysis of trends shaping the future of elearning.* Thousand Oaks, CA: Sage Road Solutions, LLC.

Day, M. (2006). *The OAIS reference model.* Bath, UK: University of Bath.

der Kinderen, G. (2011). *Openfire XMPP server.* Retrieved April 14, 2011, from http://bit.ly/openfireServer

DISC-UK. (2010). *DISC-UK home.* Retrieved from http://www.disc-uk.org/

Drachsler, H. (2009). *Navigation support for learners in informal learning networks.* (Doctoral Thesis). Open Universiteit. Heerlen, The Netherlands. Retrieved from http://dspace.ou.nl/handle/1820/2098

DSpace. (2009). *DSpace repository software website.* Retrieved from http://www.dspace.org/

Dublin Core Metadata Initiative. (2006). *Dublin core metadata initiative: Education application profile*. Retrieved from http://dublincore.org/educationwiki/DC_2 dEducation_20Application_20Profile

Duraspace. (2011). *About DSpace*. Retrieved from http://www.dspace.org/about

Duval, E. (2004). Learning technology standardization: Making sense of it all. *Computer Science and Information Systems, 1*(1), 33–43. doi:10.2298/CSIS0401033D

Dzemyda, G., & Saltenis, V. (1994). Multiple criteria decision support system: Methods, user's interface and applications. *Informatica, 5*(1-2), 31–42.

Edimburgh. (2011). *What is Edinburgh datashare?* Retrieved from http://datashare.is.ed.ac.uk/

EdReNe. (2011). *EU eContentplus programme's educational repositories network project web site*. Retrieved from http://edrene.org/

Ehlers, U., & Pawlowski, J. M. (2006). Quality in European e-learning: An introduction. In Ehlers, U., & Pawlowski, J. M. (Eds.), *Handbook on Quality and Standardisation in E-Learning* (pp. 1–13). Berlin, Germany: Springer. doi:10.1007/3-540-32788-6_1

England. (2011). *JISC - Services*. Retrieved from http://www.jisc.ac.uk/whatwedo/services.aspx

EPrints. (2009). *EPrints repository website*. Retrieved from http://www.eprints.org/

Essex. (2011). *How we curate data - The process*. Retrieved December, 2011, from http://www.data-archive.ac.uk/curate/process

European Credit Transfer System. (2009). *ECTS users' guide*. Brussels, Belgium: Directorate General for Education and Culture.

Falaki, H., Mahajan, R., & Kandula, S. (2010). Diversity in smartphone usage. In *Proceedings of the 8th International Conference on Mobile Systems, Applications, and Services*. New York, NY: ACM Press.

Fallside, D. C. (2004). *XML schema part 0: Primer* (2nd ed). Retrieved from http://www.w3.org

Fallside, D., & Walmsley, P. (2004). *XML schema part 0: Primer second edition*. Retrieved from http://www.w3.org/TR/xmlschema-0/

Faniel, I. M., & Zimmerman, A. (2011). Beyond the data deluge: A research agenda for large-scale data sharing and reuse. *International Journal of Digital Curation, 6*(1), 1297–1298. doi:10.2218/ijdc.v6i1.172

Fedora. (2009). *Fedora repository website*. Retrieved from http://fedoraproject.org/

Félix, R. (2002). *Sistemas de digitalização e anotação de documentos. Technical Report*. Minho, Portugal: Universidade do Minho.

Ferreira, F. X., & Henriques, P. R. (2008). *Using OWL to specify and build different views over the emigration museum resources*. Paper presented at the National Conference XML Aplicações e Tecnologias Associadas 2008 (XATA 2008). Évora, Portugal.

Ferreira, F. X., Cruz, D., Henriques, P. R., Gançarski, A. L., & Defude, B. (2009). *A query by example approach for XML querying*. Paper presented at WISA - Workshop on Intelligent Systems and Applications, Iberic Conference on Information Systems and Technologies. Povoa de Varzim, Portugal.

Ferreira, F. X., Pacheco, H., & Vilas-Boas, J. (2007). *PDA's no levantamento de informação em arquivos históricos. Technical Report*. Minho, Portugal: Universidade do Minho.

Ferreira, M. (2006). *Introdução à preservação digital - Conceitos, estratégias e actuais consensos*. Minho, Portugal: Escola de Engenharia da Universidade do Minho.

Finin, T., Ding, L., Pan, R., Joshi, A., Kolari, P., Java, A., & Peng, Y. (2005). *Swoogle: Searching for knowledge on the semantic web*. Paper presented at the National Conference on Artificial Intelligence (AAAI) 2005, Intelligent Systems demo. Pittsburgh, PA.

Fisher, M., & Dean, M. (2007). Automapper: Relational database semantic translation using OWL and SWRL. In *Proceedings of the IASK International Conference E-Activity and Leading Technologies*. Porto, Portugal: IASK.

Fluit, C., Sabou, M., & Harmelen, F. (2005). Ontology-based information visualization: Towards semantic web applications. In Geroimenks, V. (Ed.), *Visualising the Semantic Web* (2nd ed.). Berlin, Germany: Springer Verlag. doi:10.1007/1-84628-290-X_3

Fonte, D., Carvalho, P., Cruz, D., Gançarski, A. L., & Henriques, P. R. (2010). XML archive for testing: A benchmark for GuessXQ. In *Proceedings of XATA 2010 - XML, Associated Technologies and Applications*, (pp. 127-138). Vila do Conde, Portugal: XATA.

Fonte, D. (2010). *GuessXQ: A query-by-example approach for XML querying. Technical report*. Braga, Portugal: Universidade do Minho.

Fonte, D., Cruz, D., Henriques, P. R., & Gançarski, A. L. (2010). GUI for XML documents access using query-by-example paradigm. In *Proceedings of Interacção 2010: Interacção Humano-Computador* (pp. 89–93). Aveiro, Portugal: Universidade de Aveiro.

Foray, D., & Lundvall, B.-Å. (1998). The knowledge-based economy: From the economics of knowledge to the learning economy. In Neef, D., Siesfeld, G. A., & Cefola, J. (Eds.), *The Economic Impact of Knowledge* (pp. 115–121). London, UK: Butterworth-Heinemann. doi:10.1016/B978-0-7506-7009-8.50011-2

Force, A. T. (2002). *Requirements for assessing and maintaining the authenticity of electronic records. Technical Report*. Vancouver, Canada: InterPARES Project.

Foundation. (2011). *Grants: Gov application guide*. Retrieved from http://www.nsf.gov

Foundation. (2011). *The open data foundation*. Retrieved from http://www.opendatafoundation.org/

Foundation. (2011). *Apache POI - The Java API for microsoft documents*. Retrieved from http://poi.apache.org/

Foundation. (2011). *NSF data management plan requirements*. Retrieved from http://www.nsf.gov/eng/general/dmp.jsp

Freitas, R. A. P. (2008). *Preservação digital de bases de dados relacionais*. (MSc Dissertation). Universidade do Minho. Minho, Portugal.

Freitas, R. A. P., & Ramalho, J. C. (2009). *Relational databases digital preservation*. Paper presented at the Inforum: Simpósio de Informática. Lisboa, Portugal.

Friesen, N. (2005). Interoperability & learning objects: Overview of elearning standardization. *Interdisciplinary Journal of Knowledge and Learning Objects*. Retrieved from http://www.ijello.org/Volume1/v1p023-031Friesen.pdf

Friesen, N. (2004). Semantic and syntactic interoperability for learning object metadata. In Hillman, D. (Ed.), *Metadata in Practice*. Chicago, IL: ALA Editions.

Fuller, A., & Unwin, L. (2003). Learning as apprentices in the contemporary UK workplace: Creating and managing expansive and restrictive participation. *Journal of Education and Work, 16*(4). doi:10.1080/1363908032000093012

Gançarski, A. L., Ferreira, F. X., & Henriques, P. R. (2008). Iterative XML search based on data and associated semantics. In *Proceedings of International Conference on Web Information Systems (ICEIS)*. ICEIS.

Gasperovic, J., & Caplinskas, A. (2006). Methodology to evaluate the functionality of specification languages. *Informatica, 17*(3), 325–346.

Gimson, R., Lewis, R., & Sathish, S. (2006). *Delivery context overview for device independence - W3C working group note*. Retrieved from http://www.w3.org/TR/di-dco

Ginevicius, R., Podvezko, V., & Bruzge, S. (2008). Evaluating the effect of state aid to business by multicriteria methods. *Journal of Business Economics and Management, 9*(3), 167–180. doi:10.3846/1611-1699.2008.9.167-180

Glasgow, & Centre. (2011). *Data asset framework - Implementation guide JISC*. Glasgow, UK: Academic Press.

Glass, G. V. (1986). Sharing research data. *Contemporary Psychology, 31*(10), 774–775.

Global, I. M. S. (2010). *IMS basic learning tools interoperability specification – v.1.0 final specification*. Retrieved from http://www.imsglobal.org/lti/blti/bltiv1p0/ltiBLTIimgv1p0.html

Global, I. M. S. (2012). *IMS-QTI - IMS question and test interoperability: Information model, version 1.2.1 final specification*. Retrieved from http://www.imsglobal.org/question/index.html

Global, I. M. S. (2012). *IMS-CP – IMS content packaging, information model, best practice and implementation guide, version 1.1.3 final specification*. Retrieved from http://www.imsglobal.org/content/packaging

Global, I. M. S. (2012). *IMS application profile guidelines overview, part 1 – Management overview, version 1.0*. Retrieved from http://www.imsglobal.org/ap/apv1p0/imsap_oviewv1p0.html

Global, I. M. S. (2012). *IMS common cartridge profile, version 1.1 final specification*. Retrieved from http://www.imsglobal.org/cc/index.html

Gollmann, D. (2010). *Computer security*. New York, NY: John Wiley & Sons, Inc.

Graf, S., & List, B. (2005). An evaluation of open source e-learning platforms stressing adaptation issues. In *Proceedings of ICALT 2005*. ICALT.

Gruber, T. (2008). Ontology. In Liu, L., & Ozsu, M. (Eds.), *Encyclopedia of Database Systems*. Berlin, Germany: Springer-Verlag.

Gruber, T. R. (2003). A translation approach to portable ontology specifications. *Knowledge Acquisition, 5*(2), 199–220. doi:10.1006/knac.1993.1008

Hackney, D. (1997). *Understanding and implementing successful data marts*. Boston, MA: Addison-Wesley Longman Publishing Co.

Hammer-Lahav, E. (2008). *Security architecture*. Retrieved April 14, 2011, from http://bit.ly/OAuthToken

Hammer-Lahav, E. (2010). *The OAuth 1.0 protocol (RFC5849)*. Retrieved April 14, 2011, from http://tools.ietf.org/html/rfc5849

Hanson, B. (2011). Making data maximally available. *Science, 331*(6018), 649. doi:10.1126/science.1203354

Harold, E. R. (2204). *The XML bible* (3rd ed). New York, NY: Hungry Minds.

Harold, E. R., & Means, W. S. (2002). *XML in a nutshell*. Sebastopol, CA: O'Reilly & Associates, Inc.

Heddergott, K. (2006). The standards jungle: Which standard for which purpose? In Ehlers, U.-D., & Pawlowski, J. M. (Eds.), *Handbook on Quality and Standardisation in E-Learning* (pp. 185–191). Berlin, Germany: Springer. doi:10.1007/3-540-32788-6_13

Hedstrom, M., & Lampe, C. (2001). Emulation vs. migration: Do users care?. *RLG DigiNews, 5*(6).

He-Ping, C., Lu, H., & Bin, C. (2008). Research and implementation of ontology automatic construction based on relational database. In *Proceedings of the International Conference on Computer Science and Software Engineering*. IEEE Computer Society.

Hermit Reasoner. (2011). *Information systems group, department of computer science, University of Oxford*. Retrieved from http://hermit-reasoner.com/

Hey, A. (2009). *The fourth paradigm: Data-intensive scientific discovery*. New York, NY: Microsoft Research.

Hey, A. J. G., & Trefethen, A. E. (2003). *The data deluge: An e-science perspective*. New York, NY: Wiley and Sons.

Hodgins, W. (2006). Out of the past and into the future: Standards for technology enhanced learning. In Ehlers, U.-D., & Pawlowski, J. M. (Eds.), *Handbook on Quality and Standardisation in E-Learning* (pp. 309–327). Berlin, Germany: Springer. doi:10.1007/3-540-32788-6_21

Hoeven, J. (2007). Emulation for digital preservation in practice: The results. *The International Journal of Digital Curation, 2*(2), 123–132.

Holzner, A., & Mele, S. (2009). *Data preservation, re-use and (open) access: A case study in high-energy physics*. Retrieved from http://www.parse-insight.eu/downloads/PARSEInsight_event200909_casestudy_HEP.pdf

Hori, M., Ono, K., Abe, M., & Koyanagi, T. (2004). Generating transformational annotation for web document adaptation: Tool support and empirical evaluation. *Journal of Web Semantics, 2*(1), 1–18. doi:10.1016/j.websem.2004.08.001

Horrocks, I., & Patel-Schneider, P. F. (2003). Reducing OWL entailment to description logic satisfiability. In *Proceedings of the International Semantic Web Conference (ISWC)*, (pp. 17-29). ISWC.

Horrocks, I., Patel-Schneider, P. F., Boley, H., Tabet, S., Grosof, B., & Dean, M. (2004). *SWRL: A semantic web rule language combining OWL and RuleML*. W3C Member Submission. Retrieved 2011, from http://www.w3.org/Submission/SWRL/

Hummer, W., Bauer, A., & Harde, G. (2003). XCube: XML for data warehouses. In *Proceedings of the 6th ACM International Workshop on Data Warehousing and OLAP (DOLAP 2003)*, (pp. 33-40). New York, NY: ACM Press.

Hunter, J. (2002, September-October). JDOM in the real world - JDOM makes XML manipulation in java easier than ever. *Oracle Magazine*.

Hwang, C. L., & Yoon, K. S. (1981). *Multiple attribute decision-making / methods and applications*. Berlin, Germany: Springer-Verlag. doi:10.1007/978-3-642-48318-9

IEEE. (2002). *IEEE LTSC lom learning technology standards committee: Draft standards for learning object metadata, 2002: Final 1484.12.1 LOM draft standard document*. Retrieved from http://ltsc.ieee.org/wg12/files/LOM_1484_12_1_v1_Final_Draft.pdf

Igniterealtime.org. (2011). *Smack API*. Retrieved April 14, 2011, from http://www.igniterealtime.org/projects/smack/

I-Jetty Community. (2011). *I-jetty: Webserver for the android mobile platform*. Retrieved April 14, 2011, from https://code.google.com/p/i-jetty

Information. (2011). *About NCBI*. Retrieved December 2011, from http://www.ncbi.nlm.nih.gov/About/index.html

Information. (2011). *Basic local alignment search tool*. Retrieved December 2011, from http://blast.ncbi.nlm.nih.gov/Blast.cgi

Initiative. (2011). *Open archives initiative - Frequently asked questions (FAQ)*. Retrieved from http://www.openarchives.org/documents/FAQ.html

Inmon, W. H. (1992). *Building the data warehouse*. New York, NY: John Wiley & Sons, Inc.

International Standard ISO. IEC 14598-1:1999. (1999). *Information technology – Software product evaluation – Part 1: General overview*. Retrieved from http://www.itu.int

International Standard ISO. IEC 9126-1:2001(). (2001). *Software engineering – Product quality – Part 1: Quality model. 2001*. Retrieved from http://www.itu.int

Jacinto, M., Librelotto, G., Ramalho, J. C., & Henriques, P. (2002). *Bidirectional conversion between documents and relational data bases*. Paper presented at the 7th International Conference on CSCW in Design. Rio de Janeiro, Brasil.

Jamieson, S. (2004). *Likert scales, how to (ab)use them*. Oxford, UK: Blackwell Publishing. doi:10.1111/j.1365-2929.2004.02012.x

Janssen, J., Hermans, H., Berlanga, A. J., & Koper, R. (2008). *Learning path information model*. Retrieved from http://hdl.handle.net/1820/1620

Janssen, J., Berlanga, A. J., Heyenrath, S., Martens, H., Vogten, H., & Finders, A. (2010). Assessing the learning path specification: A pragmatic quality approach. *Journal of Universal Computer Science, 16*(21), 3191–3209.

Janssen, J., Berlanga, A. J., & Koper, R. (2011). Evaluation of the learning path specification. *Journal of Educational Technology & Society, 14*(3), 218–230.

Janssen, J., Berlanga, A. J., Vogten, H., & Koper, R. (2008). Towards a learning path specification. *International Journal of Continuing Engineering Education and Lifelong Learning, 18*(1), 77–97. doi:10.1504/IJCEELL.2008.016077

Janssen, J., Berlanga, J., & Koper, R. (2009). How to find and follow suitable learning paths. In Koper, R. (Ed.), *Learning Network Services for Professional Development* (pp. 151–166). Berlin, Germany: Springer. doi:10.1007/978-3-642-00978-5_9

Janssen, J., Tattersall, C., Waterink, W., Van den Berg, B., Van Es, R., & Bolman, C. (2007). Self-organising navigational support in lifelong learning: How predecessors can lead the way. *Computers & Education, 49*(3), 781–793. doi:10.1016/j.compedu.2005.11.022

Java OAuth Library. (2011). *OAuth API needz authorized?* Retrieved April 14, 2011, from http://bit.ly/OAuthLib

Jennifer, T. (2011). Future-proofing: The academic library's role in e-research support. *Library Management, 32*(1/2), 37–47. doi:10.1108/01435121111102566

Jensen, M. R., Muller, T. H., & Pedersen, T. B. (2001). Specifying OLAP cubes on XML data. In *Proceedings of the 13th International Conference on Scientific and Statistical Database Management, SSDBM 2001*, (p. 101). Washington, DC: IEEE Computer Society.

Jensen, M., Schwenk, J., Gruschka, N., & Iacono, L. (2009). On technical security issues in cloud computing. In *Proceedings of the IEEE International Conference on Cloud Computing*, (pp. 109-116). IEEE Press.

Johnson, S. (1999). Query-by-example (QB). In Ramakrishnan, R., & Gehrke, J. (Eds.), *Database Management Systems*. New York, NY: McGraw-Hill Publisher.

Jones, S. (2009). *Data audit framework methodology*. Glasgow, UK: University of Glasgow.

Kalibatas, D., & Turskis, Z. (2008). Multicriteria evaluation of inner climate by using MOORA method. *Information Technology and Control*, *37*(1), 79–83.

Kellokoski, K. (1999). *XML repositories*. Retrieved from http://www.tml.tkk.fi/Opinnot/Tik-111.590/2000/Papers/XML_Repositories.pdf

Kendall, M. (1979). *Rank correlation methods*. London, UK: Griffin and Co.

Kessels, J. (1999). Het verwerven van competenties: Kennis als bekwaamheid. *Opleiding & Ontwikkeling*, *12*(1-2), 7–11.

Kessels, J., & Plomp, T. (1999). A systemic and relational approach to obtaining curriculum consistency in corporate education. *Journal of Curriculum Studies*, *31*(6), 679–709. doi:10.1080/002202799182945

Kickmeier-Rust, M. D., Albert, D., & Steiner, C. (2006). *Lifelong competence development: On the advantages of formal competence-performance modeling*. Paper presented at the International Workshop in Learning Networks for Lifelong Competence Development, TENCompetence Conference. Sofia, Bulgaria.

Kimball, R., & Ross, M. (2002). *The data warehouse toolkit: The complete guide to dimensional modeling* (2nd ed.). New York, NY: John Wiley & Sons, Inc.

Kim, L. (2002). *The XMLSPY handbook*. New York, NY: John Wiley & Sons, Inc.

Kiss, C. (2010). *Composite capability/preference profiles (CC/PP): Structure and vocabularies 2.0 - W3C working group note*. Retrieved from http://www.w3.org/TR/CCPP-struct-vocab2/

Klein, M., Fensel, D., Harmelen, F. V., & Horrocks, I. (2000). The relation between ontologies and schemalanguages: Translating OIL-specifications to XMLschema. In *Proceedings of the Workshop on Application of Ontologies and Problem-Solving Methods*. Berlin, Germany: ECAI.

Krogstie, J. (1998). Integrating the understanding of quality in requirements specification and conceptual modeling. *ACM SIGSOFT Software Engineering Notes*, *23*(1), 86–91. doi:10.1145/272263.272285

Kurilovas, E. (2009). Learning content repositories and learning management systems based on customization and metadata. In *Proceedings of the 1st International Conference on Creative Content Technologies (CONTENT 2009)*, (pp. 632-637). Athens, Greece: CONTENT.

Kurilovas, E. (2009). Evaluation and optimisation of elearning software packages: Learning object repositories. In *Proceedings of the 4th International Conference on Software Engineering Advances (ICSEA 2009)*. Porto, Portugal: ICSEA.

Kurilovas, E. (2009). Learning objects reusability and their adaptation for blended learning. In *Proceedings of the 5th International Conference on Networking and Services (ICNS 2009)*, (pp. 542-547). Valencia, Spain: ICNS.

Kurilovas, E., & Dagiene, V. (2009). Learning objects and virtual learning environments technical evaluation criteria. *Electronic Journal of e-Learning*, *7*(2), 127–136.

Kurilovas, E., & Dagiene, V. (2010). Multiple criteria evaluation of quality and optimisation of e-learning system components. *Electronic Journal of e-Learning*, *8*(2), 141–150.

Kurilovas, E., Bireniene, V., & Serikoviene, S. (2011). Methodology for evaluating quality and reusability of learning objects. *Electronic Journal of e-Learning*, *9*(1), 39–51.

Kurilovas, E. (2009). Interoperability, standards and metadata for e-learning. In Papadopoulos, G. A., & Badica, C. (Eds.), *Intelligent Distributed Computing III: Studies in Computational Intelligence* (pp. 121–130). Berlin, Germany: Springer-Verlag. doi:10.1007/978-3-642-03214-1_12

Kurilovas, E. (2012). European learning resource exchange – A platform for collaboration of researchers, policy makers, practitioners, and publishers to share digital learning resources and new e-learning practices. In Cakir, A., & Ordóñez de Pablos, P. (Eds.), *Social Development and High Technology Industries: Strategies and Applications* (pp. 200–243). Hershey, PA: IGI Global.

Kurilovas, E., & Dagienė, V. (2009). Multiple criteria comparative evaluation of e-learning systems and components. *Informatica, 20*(4), 499–518.

Kurilovas, E., & Dagiene, V. (2010). *Evaluation of quality of the learning software: Basics, concepts, methods. monograph*. Saarbrücken, Germany: LAP LAMBERT Academic Publishing.

Kurilovas, E., & Dagiene, V. (2011). Technological evaluation and optimisation of e-learning systems components. In Magoulas, G. D. (Ed.), *E-Infrastructures and Technologies for Lifelong Learning: Next Generation Environments* (pp. 150–173). Hershey, PA: IGI Global.

Kurilovas, E., & Serikoviene, S. (2010). Learning content and software evaluation and personalisation problems. *Informatics in Education, 9*(1), 91–114.

Kurilovas, E., Vinogradova, I., & Serikoviene, S. (2011). Application of multiple criteria decision analysis and optimisation methods in evaluation of quality of learning objects. *International Journal of Online Pedagogy and Course Design, 1*(4), 62–76. doi:10.4018/ijopcd.2011100105

Lagoze, C., Payette, S., Shin, E., & Wilper, C. (2006). Fedora: An architecture for complex objects and their relationships. *International Journal on Digital Libraries, 6*(2), 124–138. doi:10.1007/s00799-005-0130-3

Lahlou, S. (2008). Identity, social status, privacy and face-keeping in digital society. *Social Science Information*. Retrieved from http://ssi.sagepub.com/content/47/3/299.abstract

Lavoie, B. F. (2004). The open archival information system reference model: Introductory guide. *Technology Watch Report Watch Series Report*. 04-01.

Leal, J. P., & Queirós, R. (2009). CrimsonHex: A service oriented repository of specialised learning objects. In *Proceedings of ICEIS 2009: 11th International Conference on Enterprise Information Systems*. Milan, Italy: ICEIS.

Leal, J. P., & Queirós, R. (2010). *Visual programming of XSLT from examples*. Paper presented at 8ª Conferência - XML: Aplicações e Tecnologias Associadas. Vila do Conde, Portugal.

Learning Object Metadata. (2002). *Learning technologies standards committee of the IEEE 148.41.21*. Retrieved from http://ltsc.ieee.org/wg12/files/LOM_1484_12_1_v1_Final_Draft.pdf

Leung, F., & Bolloju, N. (2005). *Analyzing the quality of domain models developed by novice systems analysts*. Paper presented at the 38th Annual Hawaii International Conference on System Sciences. Hawaii, HI.

Lewis, R. (2003). *Authoring challenges for device independence*. Retrieved from http://www.w3.org/TR/acdi/

Li, X., Gennari, J. H., & Brinkley, J. F. (2007). XGI: A graphical interface for XQuery creation. In *Proceedings of the American Medical Informatics Association Annual Symposium*, (pp. 453-457). American Medical Informatics Association.

Librelotto, G. R. (2007). *Topic maps: Da sintaxe à semântica*. (PhD Thesis). University of Minho. Minho, Portugal.

Librelotto, G. R., Ramalho, J. C., & Henriques, P. R. (2006). *Topic maps aplicados ao sistema de informação do Museu da Emigração*. Paper presented at XML: Aplicações e Tecnologias Associadas: Actas da 4.ª Conferência Nacional. Portalegre, Portugal.

Liferay. (2000). *Liferay open source enterprise portal*. Retrieved from http://www.liferay.com

Lin, H.-F. (2010). An application of fuzzy AHP for evaluating course website quality. *Computers & Education, 54*, 877–888. doi:10.1016/j.compedu.2009.09.017

Liu, T., et al. (2002). Applying wireless technologies to build a highly interactive learning environment. In *Proceedings of the IEEE International Workshop Wireless and Mobile Technologies in Education*. IEEE Press.

LRE. (2011). *European learning resource exchange service for schools web site*. Retrieved from http://lre-forschools.eun.org/

Lu, X. (1990). Document retrieval: A structural approach. *Information Processing & Management, 26*(2), 209–218. doi:10.1016/0306-4573(90)90026-X

Manola, F., & Miller, E. (2004). *RDF primer*. Retrieved from http://www.w3.org/TR/rdf-primer/

Manouselis, N., & Vuorikari, R. (2009). *What if annotations were reusable: A preliminary discussion*. Paper presented at the 8th International Conference Advances in Web Based Learning - ICWL 2009. Aachen, Germany.

Manson, P. (2010). *Digital preservation research: An evolving landscape*. Geneva, Switzerland: European Research Consortium for Informatics and Mathematics.

Ma, Q., & Tanaka, K. (2004). Topic-structure based complementary information retrieval for information augmentation. In Yu, J. X., Lin, X., Lu, H., & Zhang, Y. (Eds.), *Advanced Web Technologies and Applications* (pp. 608–619). Berlin, Germany: Springer. doi:10.1007/978-3-540-24655-8_66

Marchibroda, J. M. (2007). Health information exchange policy and evaluation. *Journal of Biomedical Informatics, 40*(6), S11–S16. doi:10.1016/j.jbi.2007.08.008

McClelland, M. (2003). Metadata standards for educational resources. *Computer, 36*, 107–109. doi:10.1109/MC.2003.1244540

MCDM. (2011). *International society on multiple criteria decision making web site*. Retrieved from http://www.mcdmsociety.org/

McGuinness, D. L., & Harmelen, F. (2004). *OWL – Web ontology language: Overview*. Retrieved from http://www.w3.org/TR/owl-features/

McLaughlin, B., & Edelson, J. (2006). *Java and XML*. New York, NY: O'Reilly.

Merriam, S. B., & Caffarella, R. S. (1991). *Learning in adulthood: A comprehensive guide*. San Francisco, CA: Jossey-Bass.

Metadata for Learning Opportunities Advertising. (2008). *Website*. Retrieved from ftp://ftp.cenorm.be/PUBLIC/CWAs/e-Europe/WS-LT/CWA15903-00-2008-Dec.pdf

Michigan. (2011). *Inter-university consortium for political and social research*. Retrieved December 2011, from http://www.icpsr.umich.edu/icpsrweb/ICPSR/access/index.jsp

Mlýnková, I., Thoman, K., & Pokorny, J. (2006). Statistical analysis of real XML data collections. In *Proceedings of the 13th International Conference on Management of Data*. COMAD.

Mlýnková, I. (2009). *XML benchmarking - The state of the art and possible enhancements*. Hershey, PA: IGI Global.

Moody, D. L., Sindre, G., Brasethvik, T., & Sølvberg, A. (2002). *Evaluating the quality of process models: Empirical analysis of a quality framework*. Paper presented at the 21st International Conference on Conceptual Modeling – ER 2002. Tampere, Finland.

Moody, D. L. (2005). Theoretical and practical issues in evaluating the quality of conceptual models: Current state and future directions. *Data & Knowledge Engineering, 55*, 243–276. doi:10.1016/j.datak.2004.12.005

Myers, A., Nichols, J., & Miller, R. (2004). Taking handheld devices to the next level. *IEEE Computer Society*. Retrieved from http://www.cs.cmu.edu/~pebbles/papers/pebblesControlIEEE.pdf

Myroshnichenko, I., & Murphy, M. C. (2009). Mapping ER schemas to OWL ontologies. In *Proceedings of the 2009 IEEE International Conference on Semantic Computing*, (pp. 324-329). IEEE Press.

Nelson, H. J., Poels, G., Genero, M., & Piattini, M. (2005). Quality in conceptual modeling: Five examples of the state of the art. *Data & Knowledge Engineering, 55*, 237–242. doi:10.1016/j.datak.2004.12.004

Net, A. D. L. (2012). *ADL SCORM overview*. Retrieved from http://www.adlnet.gov/Technologies/scorm

Newhouse, S. (2005). *Software repository – Evaluation criteria and dissemination.* Retrieved from http://www.omii.ac.uk/dissemination/EvaluationCriteria.pdf

Newman, S., & Ozsoyoglu, Z. M. (2004). A tree-structured query interface for querying semi-structured data. In *Proceedings of the International Conference on Scientific and Statistical Database Management.* IEEE.

Norman, C. (1985). Sharing research data urged. *Science, 229*(4714), 632. doi:10.1126/science.229.4714.632

Oliver, M. (2000). An introduction to the evaluation of learning technology. *Journal of Educational Technology & Society, 3*(4), 20–30.

Ono, K., et al. (2002). XSLT stylesheet generation by example with WYSIWYG editing. In *Proceedings of the Symposium on Applications on the Internet (SAINT 2002)*, (pp. 150-159). SAINT.

OpenLink Virtuoso Platform. (2010). *Automated generation of RDF views over relational data sources.* Retrieved from http://docs.openlinksw.com/virtuoso/rdfrdfviewgnr.html

Oracle. (2010). *Oracle database SQL reference 11g release 1 (11.1), part number B28286-06.* Retrieved April 30, 2011, from http://docs.oracle.com/cd/B28359_01/server.111/b28286.pdf

Ortega, M., Pérez, M., & Rojas, T. (2003). Construction of a systemic quality model for evaluating a software product. *Software Quality Journal, 11*, 219–242. doi:10.1023/A:1025166710988

Ounaies, H. Z., Jamoussi, Y., & Ben Ghezala, H. H. (2009). Evaluation framework based on fuzzy measured method in adaptive learning system. *Themes in Science and Technology Education, 1*(1), 49–58.

Oussena, S., & Barn, B. (2009). *The Pspex project: Creating a curriculum management domain map.* Retrieved 29-07-2009 from http://www.elearning.ac.uk/features/pspex

Paes, C., & Moreira, F. (2008). Aprendizagem com dispositivos móveis: aspectos técnicos e pedagógicos a serem considerados num sistema de educação. In *Proceedings of the V Conferência Internacional de Tecnologias de Informação e Comunicação na Educação.* IEEE.

Parsons, D., & Ryu, H. (2007). Software architectures for mobile learning. In Parsons, D., & Ryu, H. (Eds.), *Mobile Learning Technologies and Applications.* Wellington, New Zealand: Massey University.

Parsons, D., Ryu, H., & Cranshaw, M. (2007). A design requirements framework for mobile learning environments. *Journal of Computers, 2*(4). doi:10.4304/jcp.2.4.1-8

Parupalli, R. (2009). Dynamic content adaptation to mobile devices. In *Proceedings of the 3rd National Seminar on e-Learning and e-Learning Technologies.* IEEE.

Passani, L. (2010). *Introducing WALL: A library to multi-serve applications on the wireless.* Retrieved from http://wurfl.sourceforge.net/java/tutorial.php

Passani, L. (2012). *Wireless universal resource file (WURFL).* Retrieved from http://wurfl.sourceforge.net/

Paterson, I., & Saint-Andre, P. (2010). *XEP-0206: XMPP over BOSH.* Retrieved April 14, 2011, from http://bit.ly/xep0206

Pawlowski, J. M., & Adelsberger, H. H. (2002). Electronic business and education. In *Handbook on Information Technologies for Education and Training* (pp. 653–672). Berlin, Germany: Springer-Verlag.

Peldschus, F., & Zavadskas, E. K. (2005). Fuzzy matrix games multi-criteria model for decision-making in engineering. *Informatica, 16*(1), 107–120.

Pfleeger, S. L., Fenton, N., & Page, S. (1994). Evaluating software engineering standards. *Computer, 27*(9), 71–79. doi:10.1109/2.312041

Pietriga, E., Vion-Dury, J., & Quint, V. (2001). VXT: A visual approach to XML transformations. In *Proceedings of the 2001 ACM Symposium on Document Engineering.* ACM Press.

PKWARE. (2007). ZIP file format specification, version: 6.3.2, revised: September 28. *PKWARE Inc.* Retrieved April 30, 2011, from http://www.pkware.com/documents/casestudies/APPNOTE.TXT

PLANETS. (2009). *PLANETS: Tools and services for digital preservation. PLANETS Product Sheet.* New York, NY: PLANETS.

Plugin, J. G. (2011). *jQuery grid plugin - Grid plugin.* Retrieved from http://www.trirand.com/blog/

Poitner, M. (2008). Mobile security becomes reality. *The Mobile Security Card.* Retrieved April 14, 2011, from http://www.ctst.com/CTST08/pdf/Poitner.pdf

Pokorny, J. (2002). XML data warehouse: Modelling and querying. In *Proceedings of the Baltic Conference, BalticDB&IS 2002,* (Vol. 1, pp. 267-280). BalticDB&IS.

Porto, U. (2011). *Open repository and thematic repository - Repositorio.up.pt.* Retrieved from http://repositorio.up.pt/repos.html

Prud'hommeaux, E., & Seaborn, A. (2008). *SPARQL query language for RDF.* Retrieved from http://www.w3.org/TR/rdfsparqlquery/

Queirós, R., & Leal, J. P. (2009). Defining programming problems as learning objects. In *Proceedings of ICCEIT.* Venice, Italy: ICCEIT.

Queirós, R., & Leal, J. P. (2009). *Schem@Doc: A web-based XML schema visualize.* Paper presented at Inforum - Simpósio de Informática - 7th edition of XML: Aplicações e Tecnologias Associadas. Lisboa, Portugal.

Queirós, R., & Leal, J. P. (2012). Using the common cartridge profile to enhance learning content interoperability. In *Proceedings of ECEL - 10th European Conference on e-Learning.* Brighton, UK: ECEL.

Queirós, R., & Pinto, M. (2010). ESEIG mobile: An m-learning approach in a superior school. In *Proceedings of the Enterprise Information Systems International Conference,* (vol. 110, pp. 355-363). Viana do Castelo, Portugal. IEEE.

Rabin, J., & McCathieNevile, C. (2008). *Mobile web best practices 1.0 – Basic guidelines.* Retrieved from http://www.w3.org/TR/mobile-bp/#ddc

Rahman, A. U., David, G., & Ribeiro, C. (2010). Model migration approach for database preservation. In *Proceedings of the Role of Digital Libraries in a Time of Global Change, 12th International Conference on Asia-Pacific Digital Libraries, ICADL 2010,* (pp. 81-90). Gold Coast, Australia: Springer.

Ramalho, J. C. Ferreira. M., Faria, L., & Castro, R. (2007). Relational database preservation through XML modelling. In *Proceedings of Extreme Markup Languages 2007.* IEEE.

Ramalho, J., & Henriques, P. (2002). *XML and XSL - Da teoria à prática.* Lisbon, Portugal: FCA Editora Informática.

Recordon, D., & Reed, D. (2006). OpenID 2.0: A platform for user-centric identity management. In *Proceedings of the Second ACM Workshop on Digital Identity Management,* (pp. 11-16). ACM Press.

Resource Description Framework. (2010). *Website.* Retrieved 2011, from http://www.w3.org/RDF/

Rice, R. (2007). *DISC-UK DataShare: Data sharing continuum.* Retrieved November, 2011, from http://www.disc-uk.org/docs/data_sharing_continuum.pdf

Rogers, E. M. (1995). *Diffusion of innovations.* New York, NY: The Free Press.

Roussos, G., Peterson, D., & Patel, U. (2003). Mobile identity management: An enacted view. *International Journal of Electronic Commerce, 8*(1), 81–100.

Saaty, T. L. (1990). How to make a decision: The analytic hierarchy process. *European Journal of Operational Research, 48*(1), 9–26. doi:10.1016/0377-2217(90)90057-I

Saaty, T. L. (2008). Relative measurement and its generalization in decision making: Why pairwise comparisons are central in mathematics for the measurement of intangible factors – The analytic hierarchy/network process. *Review of the Royal Spanish Academy of Sciences, Series A. Mathematics, 102*(2), 251–318.

Saint-Andre, P. (Ed.). (2004). *Extensible messaging and presence protocol (XMPP): Core.* RFC 3920. Retrieved from http://www.ietf.int

Saint-André, P., Smith, K., & Tronçon, R. (2009). *Definitive guide series.* New York, NY: O'Reilly.

Santoso, H., Hawa, S., & Abdul-Mehdia, Z. (2010). *Ontology extraction from relational database: Concept hierarchy as background knowledge.* London, UK: Elsevier. doi:10.1016/j.knosys.2010.11.003

Schmidt, A., Waas, F., Kersten, M., Carey, M. J., Mano-lescu, I., & Busse, R. (2002). XMark - An XML benchmark project. In *Proceedings of the 28th VLDB Conference.* Hong Kong, China: VLDB.

Semantic Web. (2010). *Website.* Retrieved 2011, from http://www.w3.org/standards/semanticweb/

Services. (2004). *Data sharing - Frequently asked questions.* Retrieved December, 2011, from http://grants.nih.gov/grants/policy/data_sharing/data_sharing_faqs.htm - 898

Services. (2011). *Australian national data service website.* Retrieved November 20, 2011, from http://ands.org.au

Seung-Won, N. (2005). Design and implementation of resource sharing system for creation of multiple instructions in mobile internet environment. *Advances in Intelligent and Soft Computing, 29,* 797–807. doi:10.1007/3-540-32391-0_84

SFA. (2008). *SIARD format description. Technical Report.* Berne, Switzerland: Federal Department of Home Affairs.

Shaffner, B. (2001). *Managing hierarchical data: A look at XML repositories.* Retrieved from http://www.techrepublic.com/article/managing-hierarchical-data-a-look-at-xml-repositories/1045074

Sinclair, P. (2010). *The digital divide: Assessing organizations' preparations for digital preservation.* PLANETS White Paper. New York, NY: PLANETS.

Sivilevicius, H., Zavadskas, E. K., & Turskis, Z. (2008). Quality attributes and complex assessment methodology of the asphalt mixing plant. *Baltic Journal of Road and Bridge Engineering, 3*(3), 161–166. doi:10.3846/1822-427X.2008.3.161-166

Sloep, P. B. (2004). Learning objects: The answer to the knowledge economy's predicament? In Jochems, W., Koper, R., & Merriënboer, J. V. (Eds.), *Integrated E-Learning.* London, UK: Routledge/Falmer.

Song, G., & Zhang, K. (2004). Visual XML schemas based on reserved graph grammars. In *Proceedings of the International Conference on Information Technology: Coding and Computing (ITCC 2004),* (Vol. 1). ITCC.

Song, D., & Bruza, P. (2003). Towards context sensitive information inference. *Journal of the American Society for Information Science and Technology, 54,* 321–334. doi:10.1002/asi.10213

Sørensen, C., & Snis, U. (2001). Innovation through knowledge codification. *Journal of Information Technology, 16*(2), 83–97. doi:10.1080/026839600110054771

Sperberg-McQueen, C. M., & Burnard, L. (1994). *A gentle introduction to SGML.* Oxford, UK: Thibodeau, K. (2002). Overview of technological approaches to digital preservation and challenges in coming years. In *the State of Digital Preservation: An International Perspective. Documentation Abstracts, Inc.* New York, NY: Institutes for Information Science.

Spinks, R., Topol, B., Seekamp, C., & Ims, S. (2001). Document clipping with annotation. *IBM DeveloperWorks.* Retrieved from http://www.ibm.com/developerworks/ibm/library/ibmclip/

Stallings, W. (1996). IPv6: The new internet protocol. *IEEE International Communications Magazine, 34,* 96–108. doi:10.1109/35.526895

Stanford Center for Biomedical Informatics Research. (2011). *Website.* Retrieved from http://protege.stanford.edu/

Storm, J., & Börner, D. (2009). *Online desirability kit.* Retrieved 08-02-2010, from http://desirabilitykit.appspot.com/

Sun Microsystems. (2009). *The XML performance team: XML processing performance in Java and. NET.* Retrieved February 22, 2012, from http://java.sun.com/performance/reference/whitepapers/XML_Test-1_0.pdf

Teeuw, W. B., & Van den Berg, H. (1997). *On the quality of conceptual models.* Paper presented at the ER 1997 Workshop on Behavioral Models and Design Transformations: Issues and Opportunities in Conceptual Modeling. Los Angeles, CA.

Thibodeau, K. (2002). *Overview of technological approaches to digital preservation and challenges in coming years.* Paper presented at the State of Digital Preservation: An International Perspective. Washington, DC.

Thomas, H. (2009). *SIARD suite manual.* Berne, Switzerland: Federal Department of Home Affairs.

Tonge, A., & Morgan, P. (2007). *SPECTRa - Submission, preservation and exposure of chemistry teaching and research data.* Cambridge, UK: Cambridge University.

Tracy, K. (2008). Identity management systems. *IEEE Potentials, 27,* 34–37. doi:10.1109/MPOT.2008.929295

Trinkunas, J., & Vasilecas, O. (2007). Building ontologies from relational databases using reverse engineering methods. In *Proceedings of the International Conference on Computer Systems and Technologies – CompSysTech 2007.* ACM Press.

Tulchinsky, V. G., Yushchenko, A. K., & Yushchenko, R. A. (2008). Graph queries for data integration using xml. *Cybernetics and Systems Analysis, 44*(2), 292–303. doi:10.1007/s10559-008-0029-2

Turskis, Z., Zavadskas, E. K., & Peldschus, F. (2009). Multi-criteria optimization system for decision making in construction design and management. *Inzinerine Ekonomika – Engineering Economics, 1,* 7–17.

Turskis, Z. (2008). Multi-attribute contractors ranking method by applying ordering of feasible alternatives of solutions in terms of preferability technique. *Technological and Economic Development of Economy, 14*(2), 224–239. doi:10.3846/1392-8619.2008.14.224-239

Unwin, L., Felstead, A., Fuller, A., Bishop, D., Lee, T., & Jewson, N. (2007). Looking inside the Russian doll: The interconnections between context, learning and pedagogy in the workplace. *Pedagogy, Culture & Society, 15*(3), 333–348. doi:10.1080/14681360701602232

Van Assche, F. (2007). *Linking learning resources to curricula by using competencies.* Paper presented at the First International Workshop on Learning Object Discovery & Exchange (LODE 2007). Retrieved from http://ceur-ws.org/Vol-311/paper11.pdf

Van Lamsweerde, A. (2000). Formal specification: A roadmap. In A. Finkelstein (Ed.), *The Future of Software Engineering: 22nd International Conference on Software Engineering.* ACM Press. eXchanging Course-Related Information. (2006). *Website.* Retrieved from http://www.xcri.co.uk/schemas/xcri_r1.0.xsd

Vranec, M., & Mlýnková, I. (2009). FlexBench: A flexible XML query benchmark. In *Proceedings of DASFAA,* (pp. 421-435). DASFAA.

W3C Incubator Group. (2009). *A survey of current approaches for mapping of relational databases to RDF.* Retrieved from http://www.w3.org

W3C International Community. (2011). *Website.* Retrieved from http://www.w3.org/

Wiley, D. A. (2000). Connecting learning objects to instructional design theory: A definition, a metaphor, and a taxonomy. *Utah State University.* Retrieved from http://www.reusability.org/read/

Williams, S. (2000). *The associative model of data.* New York, NY: Lazy Software.

Wilson, A. (2007). *Significant properties report.* InSPECT Work Package 2.2, Draft/Version 2.

Wireless Application Protocol Forum, Ltd. (2012). *User agent profile (UAProf).* Retrieved from http://www.openmobilealliance.org/tech/affiliates/wap/wap-248-uaprof-20011020-a.pdf

World Wide Web Consortium. (2003). *XML: Extensible markup language.* Retrieved from http://www.w3.org/XML/

Wyles, R., et al. (2006). *Technical evaluation of selected open source repository solutions.* Retrieved from http://www.eprints.org/community/blog/index.php?/archives/118-Technical-Evaluation-of-selected-Open-Source-Repository-Solutions.html

Xu, J., & Li, W. (2007). Using relational database to build OWL ontology from XML data sources. In *Proceedings of the International Conference on Computational Intelligence and Security Workshops.* Washington, DC: IEEE Computer Society.

Yao, B. B., & Ozsu, M. T. (2003). *XBench - A family of benchmarks for XML DBMSs.* Retrieved from http://se.uwaterloo.ca/ ddbms/projects/xbench/

Zarri, G. P. (2006). RDF and OWL. In *Encyclopedia of Knowledge Management.* Academic Press. doi:10.4018/978-1-59140-573-3.ch101

Zavadskas, E. K., & Antucheviciene, J. (2007). Multiple criteria evaluation of rural building's regeneration alternatives. *Building and Environment, 42*(1), 436–451. doi:10.1016/j.buildenv.2005.08.001

Zavadskas, E. K., Kaklauskas, A., Peldschus, F., & Turskis, Z. (2007). Multi-attribute assessment of road design solutions by using the COPRAS method. *The Baltic Journal of Road and Bridge Engineering*, 2(4), 195–203.

Zavadskas, E. K., & Turskis, Z. (2008). A new logarithmic normalization method in games theory. *Informatica*, 19(2), 303–314.

Zavadskas, E. K., & Turskis, Z. (2010). A new additive ratio assessment (ARAS) method in multicriteria decision-making. *Technological and Economic Development of Economy*, 16(2), 159–172. doi:10.3846/tede.2010.10

Zavadskas, E. K., Turskis, Z., Tamosaitiene, J., & Marina, V. (2008). Multicriteria selection of project managers by applying grey criteria. *Technological and Economic Development of Economy*, 14(4), 462–477. doi:10.3846/1392-8619.2008.14.462-477

Zavadskas, E. K., Zakarevicius, A., & Antucheviciene, J. (2006). Evaluation of ranking accuracy in multicriteria decisions. *Informatica*, 17(4), 601–618.

Zeleny, M. (1982). *Multiple criteria decision making*. New York, NY: McGraw-Hill.

Zhang, W., Kunz, T., & Hansen, K. M. (2007). Product line enabled intelligent mobile middleware. In *Proceedings of the 12th IEEE International Conference on Engineering of Complex Computer Systems*, (pp. 148-157). Auckland, New Zealand: IEEE Press.

Zhang, S., Wang, J. T. L., & Herbert, K. G. (2002). XML query by example. *International Journal of Computational Intelligence and Applications*, 2(3), 329–337. doi:10.1142/S1469026802000671

Zierau, E., & Wijk, C. (2008). *The PLANETS approach to migration tools*. Bern, Switzerland: Society for Imaging Science and Tech.

Zloof, M. M. (1975). Query-by-example: The invocation and definition of tables and forms. In *Proceedings of the 1st International Conference on Very Large Data Bases*, (pp. 1-24). ACM Press.

About the Contributors

José Carlos Ramalho graduated in 1991 as a Systems and Informatics Engineer. Since his graduation, he has worked as a freelancer software developer and as a network technician for Apple. During this time, he also taught several courses about computer programming for several public institutions. In 1991, he joined the Department of Informatics as an Assistant and started his MSc work. He has worked as a teacher since 1991 until the present. He also has been a researcher of Algoritmi's Research Center until 2004. In 2004, he moved from Algoritmi to the newly created CCTC Research Center. He finished his PhD in 2000 under the subject "Structured Documents Semantics." From 1996 until the present, he has been researching in structured documents area (currently, he is coordinating several projects in digital archives and libraries field). He was responsible for the creation of the conference series called XATA (starting in 2003 until now). He has written two books and many articles presented in international and national conferences. During 2008, together with two former post-graduation students, he launched KEEP Solutions, a spin-off software company focusing on information archiving, information management, information access, and information deployment.

Alberto Simões is a PhD in Natural Language Processing affiliated with the Polytechnic Institute of Cávado and Ave (Portugal), and works as a Researcher at the Computer Science and Technology Center of the University of Minho. His research interests focus on parallel corpora alignment, probabilistic translation dictionaries, and bilingual terminology extraction. Some of his major publications are NATools—a statistical word aligner workbench in Procesamiento del Lenguaje Natural 31 (2003), Makefile::Parallel dependency specification language. In Anne-Marie Kermarrec, Luc Bougé, and Thierry Priol, editors, Euro-Parl 2007, volume 4641 and Portuguese-English word alignment: some experiments. In LREC 2008 – The 6th edition of the Language and Resources Evaluation Conference, Marrakech (2008).

Ricardo Queirós is an Assistant Professor at the School of Industrial Studies and Management (ESEIG) in Vila do Conde, which is responsible for courses in the area of ICT and Programming Languages. He is a Ph.D. student of the Doctoral Program in Computer Sciences in the Faculty of Sciences of the University of Porto (FCUP). His scientific activity is related with e-learning standards and interoperability, languages for XML, architectural integration with focus on the development of e-learning systems. He is an Associate Member of the Center for Research in Advanced Computing Systems (CRACS)—an INESC-Porto Associated Laboratory—and a founding member of KMILT (Knowledge Management, Interactive, and Learning Technologies) research group.

* * *

Carlos Filipe Pereira Aldeias was born in Vila do Conde and raised in Póvoa de Varzim, Portugal. He took the Masters program in Informatics and Computing Engineering from the Faculty of Engineering, University of Porto (FEUP). He contributed to the DBPreserve project (funded by Portuguese FCT), where he researched on preservation of databases and data warehouses. He is currently a Researcher at Information and Computer Graphic Systems Unit of INESC TEC (formerly INESC PORTO). His research interests include information systems, databases, information management, Web technologies, and computer graphics.

Alexandre B. Augusto is a MSc student in Engineering of Networks and Informatics Systems at the Department of Computer Science of the Faculty of Science of the University of Porto, Portugal. He is currently a Researcher in the field of identity and access management and a member of CRACS team, a partner of INESC TEC Porto, where he is responsible for research authentication, authorization, and data aggregation methods related to identity and access management based on user centricity. He also has a special interest in mobile devices and computer security with a special focus on privacy, anonymity, and cryptography.

Adriana J. Berlanga is Assistant Professor at the Centre for Learning Sciences and Technologies of the Open University of The Netherlands. Her research is focused on how Technology-Enhanced Learning can foster lifelong learning, exploring topics such as learning networks, novel tools for e-learning, standards and specifications, peer-support, Social Web, and online learner identities.

Manuel E. Correia got his MSc in Foundations of Advanced Information Processing Technologies from the Imperial College of London in 1992 and his PhD in Computer Science from Oporto University in 2001. He is currently a Lecturer at the Department of Computer Science of the Faculty of Science of Oporto University and a Researcher in the field of computer security at the CRACS group of INESC TEC Porto, where he is responsible for research projects related to anomaly detection and identity management and the security aspects of several industry contracts. He is also consultant for some Portuguese public agencies (health and education) in computer security.

Daniela Carneiro da Cruz received in October 2011 a Ph.D. degree in Computer Science at University of Minho, under the MAPi doctoral program. She teaches different courses in the area of Compilers and Formal Development of Languages Processors and Programming Languages and Paradigms (Procedural, Logic, and OO). As a researcher of gEPL, Daniela is working on the application of semantic-based slicing techniques to programs with contracts. She has also been involved in different research projects, such as CROSS—an infrastructure for Certification and Re-engineering of Open Source Software; Hermes—Learning and Populating Ontologies from Textual Sources (bilateral Brasil-Portugal joint research project); Quixote Problem Domain Models to interrelate Operational and Behavioral views in software systems (bilateral Argentina-Portugal joint research project); PCDSL—Program Comprehension for Domain Specific Languages (bilateral Slovenia-Portugal joint research project); and PCVIA (Program Comprehension by Visual Inspection and Animation).

Gabriel de Sousa Torcato David (born in Lisboa, 1958) got a Ph.D. in Informatics, Artificial Intelligence branch, at Universidade Nova de Lisboa, 1994. He is currently Associate Professor at the Informatics Engineering Department, Engineering Faculty of the University of Porto (FEUP), where he integrates the FEUP Scientific Board and the Scientific Committees of the Information Science Bachelor and Master Programs. He is also the Director of the MAP-i Doctoral Program in Computer Science. He has led the development team of SIGARRA, the U.PORTO Academic Information System, from 1996 to 2010. He has been a Researcher at INESC Porto since 1985. His main research interests are in information systems, databases, and information management. He has been the leader of projects (funded by Portuguese FCT) MetaMedia on multimedia archives and DBPreserve on preservation of databases.

Flavio Miguel Xavier Ferreira graduated in Systems Engineering and Computer Science from the University of Minho (Braga, Portugal) in 2007. He devoted himself, soon after, as a continuation of his internship, to the development of the (virtual) Museum of Emigration. Then, Flavio attended between October 2009 and June 2010 a PhD in the Institut Telecom SudParis (CNRS lab Samovar) in a partnership with the University of Minho (Lab CCTC), with the theme the personalized information retrieval in structured documents associated with semantic descriptions. After that date, he dedicated himself to being a freelancer.

Daniela Morais Fonte graduated in Computer Science and System Engineering (Lic. Em Engenharia Informática) at University of Minho (UM), Braga, Portugal. From September 2009 to September 2010, she received a grant for young researchers from CCTC (a FCT-funded research laboratory at UM on Computing Science and Technologies). During that period, she joined gEPL team and worked on a project aimed at the application of the Query-by-Example paradigm to XML document collections; as proof of concept, she developed a tool called GuessXQ. Under that context, two conference papers were published. She is currently getting a M.Sc. degree in Informatics (MEI at UM) doing two specializations, one in Language Engineering and another in Intelligent Systems. In that context, she developed a tool, Quimera—an evolution of traditional automatic Grading Systems that also gave rise to a new conference paper.

Ricardo André Pereira Freitas graduated in 2002 in Electrical and Computer Engineering at the Lusíada University of Vila Nova de Famalicão. He was soon invited to collaborate with the Department of Informatics at the same university in Computer Systems Development. Since then, he also provides training in various courses of professional and technological specialization in the field of informatics and information systems, as well as lecturing in the Faculty of Economics and Business Sciences at the same university. In addition, he is a member of Lusíada Researcher Centre for Research and Development in Industrial Engineering and Management (CLEGI). In 2008, he completed his MSc work at the School of Engineering, University of Minho, where he gave evidence in defense of the thesis titled "Digital Preservation of Relational Databases." He participated in national and international conferences with scientific papers related to the subject of databases and its digital preservation issues, which are related to his Doctoral Program (MAP-i) in which he is currently working.

Alda Lopes Gancarski graduated in Informatis and Systems Engineer, at the CCTC Laboratory of University of Minho (UM), Braga, Portugal, in March 1996. From September 1997 to September 1999, she was Lecturer at the Productions and Systems Department of UM. In March 1999, she got a MSc in Informatics at the Informatics Department of UM. In October 1999, she started her PhD thesis at the Informatics Laboratory of the University Pierre et Marie Curie Paris 6 (Laboratoire d'Informatique de Paris 6, LIP6), Paris, France. She got her PhD in January 2005. She did a Post-doc at CCTC and LIP6 from April 2005 to September 2006. Since October 2006, she is Associate Professor at Institut Telecom, developing her research at the CNRS UMR Samovar laboratory.

Pedro Rangel Henriques got a degree in Electrotechnical/Electronics Engineering at FEUP (Porto University), and finished a Ph.D. thesis in "Formal Languages and Attribute Grammars" at University of Minho. In 1981, he joined the Computer Science Department of University of Minho, where he is a Teacher/Researcher. Since 1995, he is the Coordinator of the Language Processing Group at CCTC (Computer Science and Technologies Center). He teaches many different courses under the broader area of programming: Programming Languages and Paradigms; Compilers, Grammar Engineering, and Software Analysis and Transformation; etc. Pedro Rangel Henriques has supervised Ph.D. (11) and M.Sc. (13) theses, and more than 50 graduating trainingships/projects, in the areas of: language processing (textual and visual), and structured document processing; code analysis, program visualization/animation and program comprehension; knowledge discovery from databases, data-mining; and data-cleaning. He is co-author of the *XML & XSL: Da Teoria a Prática* book, published by FCA in 2002; and has published 3 chapters in books, and 20 journal papers.

José Janssen is Assistant Professor at the Centre for Learning Sciences and Technologies (CELSTEC) of the Open University of The Netherlands with expertise in the field of lifelong learning, e-learning, and learning technology standards. She holds a PhD in Learning Sciences and Technologies. Her research interests include documentation and recommendation of formal, non-formal, and informal learning paths, e-Portfolio, and usability.

E. J. R. (Rob) Koper, Open Universiteit Nederland, is the Dean of the Centre for Learning Sciences and Technologies (CELSTEC), the research and innovation institute of the Open University of The Netherlands. The Centre has a history of about 30 years and gained worldwide recognition as one of the top research institutes in the field. See celstec.org for more information. Rob Koper has published more than 200 scientific journal articles and books in the intersection of ICT and Learning Sciences.

Eugenijus Kurilovas is Research Scientist in Vilnius University Institute of Mathematics and Informatics, Associate Professor in Vilnius Gediminas Technical University, and the Head of International Networks Department of the Centre for Information Technologies in Education of the Ministry of Education and Science of Lithuania. He is a member of Editorial Boards and Programme Committees of 20 international journals and conferences on e-learning. He is/was the leader of work packages and Lithuanian team in 12 large-scale EU-funded R&D projects. He has published over 60 scientific papers (abstracted / referenced in Thomson ISI Web of Science, Scopus, IEEE, Springer, ERIC, etc.), 4 books chapters, and 2 monographs on e-learning.

José Paulo Leal is Assistant Professor at the Department of Computer Science of the Faculty of Sciences of the University of Porto (FCUP) and Associate Researcher of the Center for Research in Advanced Computing Systems (CRACS). His main research interests are eLearning system implementation, structured document processing, and software engineering. He has a special interest in automatic exercise evaluation, in particular in the evaluation of programming exercises, and in Web adaptability. He has participated in several research projects in his main research areas, including technology transfer projects with industrial partners. He has over 60 publications in conference proceedings, journals, and book chapters.

João Correia Lopes holds a PhD in Computing Science from Glasgow University. He is an Assistant Professor at the Department of Informatics Engineering, University of Porto, a Researcher at INESC-Porto and teaches undergraduate and graduate courses in Databases, Software Engineering, and Web Technologies. His research interests include structured and semi-structured data management, distributed information systems, service oriented architectures, and orthogonal persistent languages.

Mário Pinto is an Associate Professor in Informatics Department, at the Management and Industrial Studies School, of the Polytechnic Institute of Oporto. PhD in Informatics from Portucalense University in 2008, MSc in Electrical and Computer Engineering in 2000 from Faculty of Engineering, University of Porto, and Diploma Degree in Applied Informatics in 1989 from Portucalense University. He is a founding member of KMILT (Knowledge Management, Interactive, and Learning Technologies) research group, researcher at Portucalense University, and member of ISPIM. His main research interests are related with learning management systems, knowledge management systems, and support decision systems.

Maria Cristina de Carvalho Alves Ribeiro holds a PhD in Informatics from Universidade Nova de Lisboa. She is an Assistant Professor at the Department of Informatics Engineering, University of Porto, a Researcher at INESC-Porto, and teaches undergraduate and graduate courses in Information Retrieval, Markup Languages, and Knowledge Representation. Her research interests include information retrieval, multimedia databases, and digital repositories.

João Rocha da Silva has a MsC in Informatics Engineering from Faculty of Engineering of the University of Porto. After some experience in the consulting business, he is currently a PhD student of the Doctoral Programme in Informatics Engineering and Researcher at FEUP. His main research topics include information retrieval, Semantic Web technology, and data preservation.

Index